MW01096421

ENDORSEMENTS

"As entrepreneurs, we're always seeking an advantage—new mindsets and strategies to achieve bigger goals faster and more easily. In *Quantum Accountability*, Dr. Kevin Kremer and Kelley Kremer, M.Ed. provide a powerful synthesis of science and time-tested personal growth principles. By tapping into the paradoxical truths of quantum physics, the Kremers reveal how we can break through our self-imposed limitations and recognize possibilities and opportunities. Their insights allow us to take individual responsibility for our reality to achieve our greatest goals. This book blends intellectual concepts with practical wisdom. The real-world examples and exercises make the abstract tangible and *Quantum Accountability* an indispensable tool for any entrepreneur seeking to exponentially uplevel their results. In my over 40 years of experience coaching visionary entrepreneurs, I've seen firsthand that mindset is the ultimate key to achieving freedom and success. *Quantum Accountability* provides a powerful framework for mastering your mindset. I highly recommend this book to any entrepreneur ready to make the quantum leap."

DAN SULLIVAN,
Co-Founder & President, Strategic Coach®

"In this groundbreaking work, Dr. Kevin Kremer and Kelley Kremer, M.Ed. blend principles insights from   quantum physics with profound personal growth insights. *Quantum Accountability* will shatter your preconceptions about accountability and reality itself. It is your guide to making your unconscious conscious. With clarity and wisdom, Dr. Kevin Kremer and Kelley Kremer, M.Ed. reveal how the strange paradoxes of quantum mechanics are not just esoteric science - they contain powerful metaphors for taking radical responsibility for our lives. You'll learn to overcome limited beliefs, shatter self-sabotaging patterns, and realign yourself with the unified field of infinite possibilities. Blending science and spirituality like never before, this book is a quantum leap for anyone seeking to manifest their deepest desires and live their greatest life. Highly recommended for anyone ready to dismantle their self-imposed prisons and unleash their limitless potential. *Quantum Accountability* is a real-world guide to personal mastery."

GINO WICKMAN
Author of Traction & Shine, Creator of EOS®

"In a world where enduring principles often seem overshadowed by fleeting success, Dr. Kevin Kremer's *Quantum Accountability* stands as a beacon of timeless wisdom. This transformative guide offers more than just strategies for professional and personal growth; it provides a blueprint for a mindset rooted in accountability that unlocks true abundance. Dr. Kremer's insights demonstrate that real prosperity flows from a deep understanding of our potential and the disciplined application of our unique gifts. By embracing the principles laid out in this book, readers will not only navigate the challenges of their journey but will also inspire and lead others with a mindset focused on growth, gratitude, and giving. I recommend you don't just read it, you study it. You might even consider this to be a reference book to refer back to often. I wholeheartedly recommend this book to anyone committed to living a life of purpose and significance. Read it, ponder it, apply it, and return to it often. You will be a better leader in your home, in your community, and in your workplace. Dr. Kremer's work echoes the essence of what we refer to as an Arrows Out™ mindset, encouraging us to think of others first and to use our gifts to enrich the lives of those around us. Prepare to be inspired and transformed as you embark on this journey of *Quantum Accountability*."

LEE BROWER

Founder of Empowered Wealth

Author, Speaker, and Coach

Champion of Enduring Wealth and the Th'River Mindset

"What if I told you that you already possess the power to shape reality itself and manifest any dream you can envision? In their groundbreaking book entitled *Quantum Accountability*, Dr.

Kevin Kremer and Kelley Kremer (M.Ed.) demonstrate that this is not just a metaphor—it's the literal truth according to our most advanced scientific understanding.

By masterfully interweaving the mind-bending principles of quantum physics with transformative personal growth insights, the authors provide a revolutionary new framework for achieving total self-mastery. You'll discover that the universe is an endlessly abundant field of infinite possibilities, and you have the ability to collapse any possibility into your reality through focused energy and intention. This book is a powerful call to shatter the illusion of your limited self and realign your consciousness with the unified field of potential. Through an array of practical exercises and inspiring stories, the authors give you the tools you need to dismantle self-sabotaging beliefs, overcome fears and doubts, and step into your ultimate power as a conscious creator. *Quantum Accountability* offers a mind-expanding journey that will awaken you to your true nature as an infinite vibrational being. If you're ready to transcend your perceived constraints and live an extraordinary life of abundance, joy, and freedom, this book is an essential guide. Highly recommended!"

ARUN K. GARG, DMD
Professor, Author, Entrepreneur, Surgeon, Inventor

"Dr Kevin Kremer has always walked his talk. He has been a friend, colleague, business partner and collaborator with Fortune for over a decade. Kevin has built and lead a multi-million dollar dental group that has made a major contribution to his community. This book accentuates what it takes to build a quality organization built on a foundation of leadership, quality communication, and culture, as well as sharing his psychology of success. Congrats my friend."

BERNIE STOLTZ
Chairman of the Board
Fortune Management

"We underestimate the importance of accountability in our life. Every successful person I admire demonstrates a mindset of accountability. In *Quantum Accountability*, Dr. Kremer shows us how to create and own our mindset, & as a result, reach levels of success that we've never seen before."

CHAD WILLARDSON
Founder of Pacific Capital and Platinum Elevated
5x Bestselling Author

"Quantum Accountability is the quintessential book of a business owner's journey to an entrepreneurial mindset."

MARK MURPHY
Critical Thinker and Key Business Strategist
CEO at Northeast Private Client Group

"Quantum Accountability is a transformative book that redefines responsibility and performance in both personal and professional spheres. By integrating quantum principles, the author provides a fresh perspective that aligns perfectly with my 'Just Add a Zero' philosophy, which emphasizes exponential thinking and growth. As an entrepreneur dedicated to identifying invisible opportunities and driving enterprise value, I find the insights in this book both enlightening and actionable. The strategies for fostering accountability, sync with my methods, such as 'Remove the FILM' and '100X Collaborations'. *Quantum Accountability* is a vital

resource for leaders committed to pushing boundaries and achieving exponential growth. Its practical advice and real-world examples make it an invaluable resource for inspiring teams, cultivating trust, and creating lasting change."

CHAD T. JENKINS,
Author of Just Add a Zero

"Achieving your goals requires not only identifying what you truly want but building the right mindset to acquire it. In *Quantum Accountability*, Dr. Kevin Kremer dives deep into both, giving you the tools to both craft and capture your dreams."

DR. BRYAN LASKIN
Bestselling Author, *The Patient First Manifesto and Dental Disorder*

"*Quantum Accountability* is the go-to compendium for personal accountability development. Start here!"

ANGELA QUAIL
Principal Consultant
The Table Group

"In *Quantum Accountability*, Dr. Kevin Kremer and Kelley Kremer present a groundbreaking approach to personal and professional growth by merging the principles of quantum thinking with practical accountability strategies. This book is a must-read for anyone looking to transform their mindset and achieve extraordinary results. Drawing from their experience in the dental industry and beyond, the Kremers provide compelling case studies and actionable insights that are universally applicable across all fields. Their unique perspective on the unseen quantum level of our thoughts and beliefs offers a powerful framework for understanding how our mindset shapes our reality. *Quantum Accountability* is a practical guide filled with techniques to help you harness the power of your mindset, take ownership of your actions, and create a life of abundance and fulfillment. The Kremers' wisdom and expertise shine through every page, making this book an invaluable resource for leaders, entrepreneurs, and anyone committed to personal excellence. I highly recommend *Quantum Accountability* to anyone ready to embrace a new level of accountability and unlock their true potential. This book will inspire you to take control of your destiny and achieve the success you've always envisioned."

NICK SONNENBERG
Founder and CEO of Leverage
WSJ Bestselling Author of *Come Up for Air*

"*Quantum Accountability* by Dr. Kevin Kremer dives deep into the interconnectedness of attitudes, beliefs, and success, revealing how they impact every aspect of our lives. This enlightening book not only provides replicable patterns for achievement but also underscores the transformative power of mindset ownership. By emphasizing the pivotal role of accountability and a positive outlook, readers are equipped to navigate life's challenges with resilience and determination. Just as in dental practices where precision and attention to detail are paramount, this book underscores the importance of cultivating a mindset that fosters success in every endeavor. It's a must-read for those ready to unlock their potential and achieve personal and professional fulfillment."

DR. SEAN MOHTASHAMI
Best Selling Author of *There's No Standing Still*
Founder of 4M Institute
CEO of 4M Dental Implant Centers

QUANTUM
ACCOUNTABILITY

QUANTUM
ACCOUNTABILITY

THE PROVEN PLAYBOOK TO MASTER YOUR MINDSET, UNLOCK EXTRAORDINARY SUCCESS, AND TRANSFORM YOUR LIFE AND BUSINESS

DR. KEVIN KREMER
KELLEY KREMER, M.ED.

STRONGPrint
PUBLISHING

Requests for permission to make copies of any part of the work should be emailed to the following address: kevin@kremerleadership.com.

This publication is not intended to be a source of expertise or advice. The advice and strategies contained herein may not be suitable for your situation. The information contained should not be used as a substitute for the advice of an accredited professional in your jurisdiction. The publisher and the author make no guarantee of results obtained by using this book. Neither the publisher nor the author shall be liable for any loss of profit or other damages.

Published and distributed by STRONGPrint Publishing

Colorado, USA

Library of Congress Control Number: 2024912898

Quantum Accountability: The Proven Playbook to Master Your Mindset, Unlock Extraordinary Success, and Transform your Life and Business
978-1-962074-14-8 - Hardcover
978-1-962074-15-5 - Paperback
978-1-962074-16-2 - eBook

DEDICATION

To our children, whose curiosity and zest for life inspire us daily;

To our parents, whose love and wisdom guide us;

To our mentors, whose insights shape our path;

And to our readers, may this book ignite your journey of growth and accountability.

CONTENTS

FOREWORD

It is with great pleasure and admiration that I introduce you to *Quantum Accountability* by Dr. Kevin Kremer and Kelley Kremer, M.Ed. This book is a profound exploration of how our mindset, deeply rooted in the unseen quantum level, can be harnessed to achieve extraordinary results in both our personal and professional lives.

In my decades of experience working with some of the most successful entrepreneurs and business leaders, I have come to understand that the most significant breakthroughs often come from within. The Kremers have masterfully captured this essence, presenting a compelling case for the transformative power of mindset and accountability.

Quantum Accountability is not just another self-help book; it is a blueprint for a new way of thinking. By delving into the principles of quantum mechanics and applying them to our daily lives, the Kremers offer a unique perspective on how we can take control of our destiny. They provide practical techniques and real-world examples that demonstrate how a shift in mindset can lead to profound changes in our reality.

One of the most striking aspects of this book is its universality. While Dr. Kevin Kremer draws from his extensive experience in the dental industry, the concepts and strategies presented here are applicable to anyone, regardless of their field or background. Whether you are an entrepreneur, a professional, or someone seeking personal growth, the lessons in *Quantum Accountability* will resonate with you.

The Kremers emphasize the importance of taking ownership of our thoughts, beliefs, and actions. They remind us that our current reality is a reflection of our mindset up to this point and that by embracing accountability at a profound, unseen quantum level, we can shape our future. This message is both empowering and inspiring, encouraging readers to take initiative and responsibly manage the gifts and resources entrusted to them.

As you embark on this journey through *Quantum Accountability*, I encourage you to approach it with an open mind and a willingness to embrace change. The insights and strategies presented in this book have the potential to transform your life, helping you navigate the complexities of modern existence with clarity and purpose.

Dr. Kevin Kremer and Kelley Kremer, M.Ed. have provided us with a valuable tool for personal and professional growth. Their wisdom, combined with their practical approach, makes "Quantum Accountability" a must-read for anyone looking to achieve greater fulfillment and success.

I am confident that this book will leave a lasting impact on you, just as it has on me. Embrace the adventure, harness the power of your mindset, and watch as your greatest story unfolds.

With admiration and respect,

JAY ABRAHAM

Marketing Strategist, Business Consultant, and Author

INTRODUCTION

Are you living the dream, or has your reality shifted off course? Life's journey is filled with unexpected twists and turns. Even the most driven among us can hit a wall, feeling lost in the wilderness of our own narratives. But it's in the heart of these uncharted territories where the real magic unfolds. When equipped with an effective mindset, every obstacle can transform into a launchpad, catapulting you towards growth and victory.

Embrace the adventure, for your greatest story is written in the stars you have yet to chart.

As both a professional and an entrepreneur, becoming adept at navigating the tightrope of professional advancement while juggling the diverse demands of your business can be a challenge. From the intricacies of financial management to the pursuit of customer delight, this is no small undertaking. As you chart your course through competitive business terrain, your sights are set on crafting an abundant life with fulfillment for both you and those you hold dear.

Congratulations to you for embarking on this path. As admirable as your endeavor is, though, you probably feel overwhelmed and confused at times. Despite how hard you have searched thus far, that yellow brick road leading you on a clear path to the wisdom you seek may not have been as visible as you had hoped. However, if you can become comfortable harnessing the power of the discomfort you are feeling, it can fuel your transformation. You can set forth on a quest to restore equilibrium and empower your life and business. Your mind is a fertile ground for lofty aspirations that is teeming with potential; though it may feel unclear right now, the path you are on may stretch further than you ever imagined.

You have undoubtedly faced obstacles along your path and will continue to face many more. In moments of slow progress, it's natural to measure your strides against those of your contemporaries or to yearn for meaningful connections that currently seem just beyond reach. The shadow of societal benchmarks may loom over you, or you may feel compelled by your own relentless drive for more. The quest for professional accolades and personal contentment is akin to steering through the confluence of two mighty rivers, each vying for dominance, as you strive to keep the waters of work and life flowing in unison without succumbing to the pull of their divergent tides.

No matter the challenges you face, your aspiration is to reach greater heights. Even so, the path forward may still seem unclear. Desiring innovation, leadership, and success in your field, you feel there is a gap between your ambitions and current achievements. The overwhelming chaos, pressure, and uncertainty of balancing roles and priorities can be intense, leaving little room to savor life. If you find yourself unsure of your direction amidst the busyness, rest assured that there are steps to navigate through the chaos towards a more peaceful and abundant professional and personal life.

Others have discovered the path before.
And success leaves clues.

In all honesty, I came close to giving up on my path and abandoning dental school. Before diving into the challenges of entrepreneurship and the rigors of dentistry, I grappled with the prospect of a career in which patients dreaded their visits. Growing up as a dentist's son, I understood that dental appointments were often seen as a necessity rather than a choice. I questioned how to find fulfillment and purpose in such an environment. Reflecting on my journey, the pivotal moment that transformed every aspect of my life was not a visible shift like a new routine or material possession; it was an internal quantum leap.

What was this quantum leap that transformed my path to success? I took ownership of my mindset and committed to continuous growth and development across all facets of my life. This subtle yet profound change made all the difference.

A powerful mindset is the key to navigating life's challenges and transforming chaos into clarity. Understanding the origins of this chaos and consciously shaping your ideal reality are crucial steps in bringing that reality to fruition. Success in your career, your business, your relationships, and your overall life satisfaction all begin with the mindset you cultivate. This book emphasizes that you hold the reins of your destiny; your current reality is a reflection of your thoughts and beliefs up to this point in your life. Taking accountability for your mindset, beliefs, and actions sets the stage for abundance and fulfillment in every aspect of your life.

If you want to succeed in your career, it starts in your mind.
If you want to build a thriving business, it starts in your mind.
If you want to enjoy deeper, more fulfilling relationships, it starts in your mind.
If you want to enjoy a life of abundance, it starts in your mind.

Embracing this truth requires a level of accountability that operates at a profound, unseen quantum level that echoes wisdom passed down through generations regarding the transformative power of mindset and belief systems. In the book of Matthew, this concept of accountability is taught via a parable that illustrates the stark contrast between the character's mindsets and how it influenced their beliefs, actions, and results:

MATTHEW 25:14-30: THE PARABLE OF THE BAGS OF GOLD

"Again, it will be like a man going on a journey, who called his servants and entrusted his wealth to them. To one he gave five bags of gold, to another two bags, and to another one bag, each according to his ability. Then he went on his journey. The man who had received five bags of gold went at once and put his money to work and gained five bags more. So also, the one with two bags of gold gained two more. But the man who had received one bag went off, dug a hole in the ground and hid his master's money.

"After a long time the master of those servants returned and settled accounts with them. The man who had received five bags of gold brought the other five. 'Master,' he said, 'you entrusted me with five bags of gold. See, I have gained five more.'

"His master replied, 'Well done, good and faithful servant! You have been faithful with a few things; I will put you in charge of many things. Come and share your master's happiness!'

"The man with two bags of gold also came. 'Master,' he said, 'you entrusted me with two bags of gold; see, I have gained two more.'

"His master replied, 'Well done, good and faithful servant! You have been faithful with a few things; I will put you in charge of many things. Come and share your master's happiness!'

"Then the man who had received one bag of gold came. 'Master,' he said, 'I knew that you are a hard man, harvesting where you have not sown and gathering where you have not scattered seed. So I was afraid and went out and hid your gold in the ground. See, here is what belongs to you.'

"His master replied, 'You wicked, lazy servant! So you knew that I harvest where I have not sown and gather where I have not scattered seed? Well then, you should have put my money on deposit with the bankers, so that when I returned I would have received it back with interest.

"'So take the bag of gold from him and give it to the one who has ten bags. For whoever has will be given more, and they will have an abundance. Whoever does not have, even what they have will be taken from them. And throw that worthless servant outside, into the darkness, where there will be weeping and gnashing of teeth.'"

This story reminds us of the transformative power of our mindset. We are accountable for our actions. By taking initiative and responsibly managing gifts that have been entrusted to us, we will encounter growth and reward. However, if we fail to act and aren't responsible for the resources at our disposal, then we will encounter loss and regret.

As you commit to living according to this principle of accountability as outlined in Christ's parable, you will begin a natural sequence that will ultimately lead to a life of abundance. This sequence is best described in what my wife and I have come to call the Quantum Awareness Model.

THE QUANTUM AWARENESS MODEL

The process of the Quantum Awareness Model starts with awareness, progresses to accountability, which then ignites action. This transformative sequence leads to abundance as you take ownership of your decisions, paving the path to prosperity and success across all facets of your life. The diagram below illustrates this model. We employ it throughout this book to help you understand these concepts.

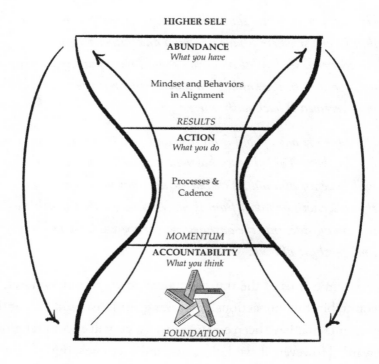

There are three stages in this Quantum Awareness Model: Accountability, Action, and Abundance. The pages that follow will be a deep dive into the first principle of Accountability. You will see applications of Action and Abundance throughout the book, but all in the context of how they result from and, in turn, influence your personal accountability.

By focusing on the first component, we will provide a solid foundation that you can build upon to improve your life exponentially. Future books will take a deeper dive into the topics of action and abundance.

Amidst life's uncertainties and challenges, assuming responsibility for your mindset, choices, and outcomes acts as a powerful catalyst, shaping the trajectory of your journey. This book explores this profound concept, what we have come to identify as the principle of Quantum Accountability—taking responsibility for your thoughts, beliefs, feelings. virtues, and attitudes and how they govern what you do in your physical reality.

As you study the words on these pages, this book will guide you on a path of self-discovery, empowerment, and growth. You will gain invaluable insights into the ways accountability can elevate your business, strengthen your relationships with loved ones and colleagues, and ultimately lead you to success and abundance. By embracing accountability as a fundamental pillar of personal development, you will unleash your potential, surmount obstacles, and craft a purposeful, resilient, and fulfilling life. On your journey to success, accountability is the compass, a pivotal tool that can enable you to chart your course toward a brighter and more fulfilling future.

WHAT TO EXPECT

This book is a valuable resource for business owners to share with their teams and family members, fostering a collaborative journey towards embracing quantum principles. By integrating these concepts into your work environment, you can enhance service quality, organizational efficiency, relationships, and overall satisfaction. Collaborating with your team to study, understand, and apply what you learn from this book will reinforce principles through knowledge sharing and verbal expression, facilitating a deeper understanding. Consider engaging in a guided 12-week book club (available on kevinkremer.com) with your team or family members using this book to explore and apply Quantum Accountability principles.

Both the website and the book offer resources and activities to support your integration of these principles into both personal and professional spheres, guiding you to define your ideal life and work environment, set goals, make informed choices, enhance self-discipline, maintain focus, and hold yourself accountable for results. Both serve as tools for self-assessment and course correction, empowering you to align your mindset with your desired outcomes and transform your life trajectory.

Embracing a commitment to succeed will unlock the full potential of this book, guiding you to discover how others have turned the impossible into the possible. As you delve into its pages, dedicate yourself to applying the principles of Quantum Accountability, crafting a personalized roadmap for your journey. This book offers the blueprint; your task is to blend your unique experiences with these guidelines and assess the outcomes. Sometimes, despite following the recipe closely, the result may not meet your expectations. This isn't failure; it's a step towards refining your approach and discovering a version of yourself that aligns with your aspirations. If at first you don't succeed, reassess and adjust. Persistence is key—continue refining and experimenting until you achieve the success you envision. Remember, perseverance transforms possibility into reality.

THE OPPORTUNITY COST OF INACTION

If you're hesitating at the brink of change, consider the opportunity cost of remaining stagnant. While your life may currently reside in the realm of the good and adequate, those modest confines can never begin to capture the breathtaking horizons of the exceptional, the transcendent, the extraordinary that lies waiting to be unlocked within you. Extraordinary achievements hinge on realizing your full potential—a potential that your current skill set has only begun to tap into. The true cost lies in the unrealized possibilities of what you could become.

Don't let the comfort zone be your life's greatest trap; it's beyond these familiar boundaries that growth and opportunity await. Venture out, for it's on the limb where the ripest fruits can be found.

This book is your guide through the uncertainties, a testament to the transformative power of accountability in crafting the life you aspire to lead. Quantum Accountability is more than a concept; it's a journey of self-discovery, empowerment, and growth that unlocks your potential and paves the way to a life of purpose, resilience, and fulfillment—the extraordinary life you've always imagined. And it begins with a single step: embracing Quantum Accountability.

SECTION 1

EMBARKING ON A POWERFUL JOURNEY WITHIN

Within each of us lies an extraordinary power—the power to shape your reality through taking accountability for the very thoughts, beliefs, and attitudes that govern your inner world. This first section invites you to embark on a transformative journey of self-discovery, where you will unlock the secrets to harnessing this innate power and aligning with your deepest aspirations.

Your mindset is the foundation upon which our experiences are built. It is a tapestry woven from the threads of your thoughts, beliefs, feelings, virtues, and attitudes. These elements are not abstractions; they are the driving forces that propel you towards your goals or hold you back from realizing your full potential. By cultivating an awareness of these internal dynamics, and then taking accountability for them, you gain the ability to consciously direct your life towards the outcomes you truly desire.

Thoughts are the seeds from which your realities bloom. They shape your perceptions, influence your decisions, and ultimately manifest as the circumstances you encounter. Beliefs act as the fertile soil, providing the nourishment and support for your thoughts to take root and flourish. Feelings, on the other hand, are the vibrant petals that add color and depth to your experiences, guiding you towards what truly resonates with your authentic selves. Virtues serve as the sturdy stems, upholding your values and principles, while attitudes are the fragrant essence that permeates every aspect of your being, attracting or repelling the opportunities that align with your mindset.

As you dive into this section, you will embark on a profound exploration of these interconnected elements, uncovering the power they hold over your life's trajectory. Master the art of aligning your thoughts, beliefs, feelings, virtues, and attitudes. Unlock a world of limitless possibilities. Let your dreams become tangible realities, and unleash your true potential.

CHAPTER 1

EMBRACING QUANTUM UNDERSTANDING AND PERSONAL ACCOUNTABILITY

"Embrace the quantum nature of accountability, where every thought and action you take ripples through the fabric of your reality, unveiling your power and shaping the infinite possibilities of your journey."

– KEVIN KREMER

You have likely heard the word "quantum" in reference to quantum physics, quantum mechanics, or even a quantum leap. But what exactly does quantum mean? The word itself is derived from the Latin word "quantus," meaning "how much", and is often used to explain the smallest quantity something can have. For example, in quantum mechanics, the word describes the behavior of matter and energy at the smallest scales, at or below the scale or atoms.

The principles of quantum theory were developed in the early 20th century and revolutionized scientific knowledge. When scientists turned their focus to behaviors and energy on both the atomic and subatomic levels, they focused on the seemingly invisible and were able to develop groundbreaking technologies that have challenged and expanded our understanding of the nature of reality.

Similarly, when you turn your attention to what is happening at the smallest levels within you (the quantum level), you will be able to develop and grow in equally groundbreaking ways. The concept of using the word "quantum" to describe how our minds function stems from the intersection of quantum physics and consciousness studies. Some hypotheses propose that quantum-mechanical phenomena, such as entanglement and superposition, may play a role in the brain's function and aspects of consciousness. This idea suggests that the brain's operations could involve non-localized quantum effects at smaller scales than cells, influencing cognitive processes.

Just like in the cosmos, despite significant advancements in scientific knowledge, there are vast expanses of unknowns that still shroud our understanding of both the universe and the human mind. Despite these uncertainties and the limits to our knowledge, the beauty of the understanding we do have is in its capacity to increase our awareness and inspire our curiosity about the boundless mysteries that shape our perceptions of both the cosmos and our minds.

We have taken the liberty to mold these fascinating but ever-evolving scientific concepts to the truths we have learned through study and experience as business owners, professionals, teachers, parents, life coaches, and most importantly, human beings. In doing so, we connect the scientific truths about the quantum forces shaping our lives to the principles of accountability that lead to a truly abundant life.

Thus, for the purposes of this book, "quantum" refers to things and forces that are occurring on a level which is unseen; things that are happening on an energetic level that you are not always aware of in your physical reality, but have a powerful impact on that reality.

Western Society tends to place most of its focus on visible matter, and less on the energy that cannot be seen. Everything is energy—from all matter that makes up the physical world to the contemplations in your head. Every thought, creative spark, or idea all begins as energy. Everything starts on a quantum level before it manifests in the physical world. Entrepreneurs, inventors, and engineers harness the power of their minds and then manifest this energy into reality via action, creating products, building roads, or providing services. Authors imagine ideas on a quantum level and then convey the intricacies of their minds in stories and novels. Your job, whatever your profession or life pursuit may be, is to transfer your energy from the quantum level, which cannot be seen, to the physical world, which can be seen.

If you operate your life merely from the physical level, you may feel chaotic, stressed or overwhelmed. Order begins on the quantum level, remember the Quantum Awareness Model displaying the hierarchy. You cannot reach the expansive abundance you are seeking if you do not first master the mindset that controls and guides your actions. Focusing on the quantum will bring you the success that manifests in your present, physical reality.

The more you become aware of and are accountable for your quantum reality, the greater control and enjoyment you will experience in your physical reality. The key to harnessing the power of your physical reality—your existence, who you are in this world—is Quantum Accountability. Accountability is ownership. It is being completely responsible for who you are: your physical self, your mental self, and the things that you attract into your reality.

Quantum Accountability means taking responsibility for your thoughts, beliefs, feelings. virtues, and attitudes and how they govern what you do in your physical reality. Your mindset acts as a sieve, filtering experiences to form your perspective and guiding actions and who you become. In the coming chapters, we will embark on a transformative journey that cuts deep into the heart of Quantum Accountability. We will explore what it is and why it is of paramount importance for you. We'll unravel the intricate web of connections between accountability, mindset, and success in life. When you take accountability for your mindset, your world changes.

This book is divided into four sections. In Section One, we will examine the foundational principles of Quantum Accountability, analyzing the upward trajectory that forms the foundation of the Quantum Awareness Model via thoughts, beliefs, virtues, feelings, and attitudes. Once we have mastered the principles of accountability, the final three sections will address accountability to yourself, accountability to others, and accountability to your purpose.

Accountability is an omnipresent yet often overlooked factor in business and life. When ingrained in your being and embraced, accountability shapes every decision, action, and consequently, your entire trajectory and overall experience on this Earth. Accountability is the willingness to accept responsibility for your actions.

On a societal level, have you seen a shift? A shift from 'if you work hard, you will get rewarded' to a lack of accountability that 'you deserve to get rewarded just because?' Rather than 'I create a level of abundance based on the value I provide to society', many have shifted to believe

'I am entitled to certain luxuries just because I am alive.' Many people are becoming less and less accountable for their actions. Has your experience been that many young people are less accountable in their work? Is 'Quiet Quitting' affecting you and or your business enterprises? Is 'Quiet Quitting' something you may have noticed in your personal relationships?

You do not have to continue down this path. You can reclaim your accountability and reverse the shift, if not on a societal level, at least on a personal level. The effect will ripple out and impact the lives you touch. So, let's begin the deep dive right here and now.

THE POWER OF EMBRACING IMPERFECTION

Accountability is not about being perfect. It is about taking accountability for our imperfections. There is a difference. Greek Mythology provides many stories which serve as examples of characters failing to take accountability for their imperfections. One such myth is that of Sisyphus, a cunning and manipulative king who was punished for his trickery by the gods of Olympus. They sentenced him to roll a boulder up a hill, only for it to roll back down each time he reached the top. This eternal punishment serves as a cautionary tale about the consequences of pride, manipulation, and the necessity of being accountable for your thinking and behaviors.

Taking accountability for our imperfections is not an easy road. It is built into our human nature to avoid feeling negative emotions such as shame or regret. But if we fail to take accountability for our mindset and imperfections, we will become like Sisyphus, constantly pushing the boulder up the hill, never making progress and never obtaining relief from our burdens.

Another story from Greek Mythology that illustrates this concept is about Narcissus. This story illustrates how we can sometimes become mesmerized with ourselves, blind to our weaknesses because we only focus on our strengths. Narcissus was a beautiful youth who became infatuated with his own reflection in a pool of water, unable to tear himself away from his own image. Despite warnings and advice from others, Narcissus was consumed by his self-absorption and vanity, leading to his downfall. This myth serves as a cautionary tale about the consequences of excessive optimism and the refusal to acknowledge your weaknesses, highlighting the destructive nature of being consumed by your own thinking and failing to take accountability for your imperfections.

Let's face it, we all make mistakes; we are all perfectly imperfect. However, our minds tell us that mistakes are wrong, bad, and sometimes even unacceptable. Admitting a mistake somehow means we are not enough. Admitting a mistake somehow means we are imperfect. This admittance creates negative feelings. We do more to avoid pain than we do to seek pleasure. So, more often than not, we do not take accountability for our mistakes. Instead, we either ignore the mistake or validate our actions. By doing this, we reject accountability, thereby shutting the door to any room for improvement.

The power we hold is in embracing our imperfections. Let's be honest, admitting our errors is difficult, but it shows personal strength. Even with our imperfections, we are worthy. Change in our mindset as we embrace our imperfection and face it head on coincides with subtle shifts on the quantum level. Shifts towards greater success and abundance. When we can alter our mindset to see our mistakes and imperfections as opportunities for growth, we are taking control of our life on the quantum level.

Again, accountability is not about being perfect. It is about being honest with yourself and others and being willing to learn and grow from your mistakes. It's not the mistakes we make in life but what we do after we make them that makes all the difference. The power lies in the opportunity awarded by imperfection.

When new team members join our dental office, I am often reminded of the importance of this principle. In my dental office, we perform complex procedures that require multiple steps that take time to understand. New team members who haven't acclimated to the ins and outs sometimes cannot foresee what instruments will be needed in infrequent circumstances. I want team members who take accountability and react to these situations with the attitude of, "Yes, I will get you the instrument right now, and in the future I know to have that instrument on hand." I do not want team members whose reaction reflects, "Oh, well no one told me you may need that instrument. It's not my fault." Life is not a perfect science. How we learn, grow, and respond to our mistakes or inadequacies makes a difference. You only grow when you acknowledge the room for improvement.

Have you had a similar situation in your business or personal life? Have you had the opportunity to take accountability? Whether you are facing such a moment now or are confronted by one in the future, remember that the power of imperfection lies in the opportunity for improvement.

Dr. Wayne Dyer, a world-renowned self-help author and inspirational speaker, echoes this idea. He teaches us that accountability is an opportunity for growth and self-improvement. It is a chance to become a better person, a better leader, and a better partner. It is an opportunity to create a better work environment and better relationships. Dr. Dyer instructs us that when you accept total responsibility for everything in your life, you empower yourself to change anything. What most people don't realize is that accepting total responsibility for everything in life is a choice—a choice that leads you to creating the life you want.

Author Michael Singer also highlights the transformative potential of embracing accountability as a conduit for both personal and spiritual growth. In his book, The Untethered Soul, he teaches of the discipline of maintaining an open heart and mind, even in moments of imperfection, to tap into a profound source of inner peace and fulfillment. Singer suggests that by becoming aware of subtle, quantum-level forces that shape our mindset, we can unlock a deeper understanding of ourselves and our place in the universe.

Our invitation to you is to embrace your imperfections so that you can maintain this open heart and achieve the full level of accountability required to unleash its transformative power in your life.

ACCOUNTABILITY ANCHORS:

After each chapter, we will list accountability anchors. The concept of an anchor when applied to personal accountability serves as a powerful metaphor. Just as a physical anchor prevents a ship from drifting away due to currents or winds, these accountability anchors serve to anchor your attention to what we deem the most important concepts in the chapter. Amidst life's challenges and distractions, it is far too easy to lose sight of what's most important. These anchors will keep your mind from drifting as we navigate all the principles tied to Quantum Accountability.

ACCOUNTABILITY ANCHORS:

1. Quantum refers to things and forces that are occurring on a level which is unseen.

2. Accountability is ownership.

3. Quantum Accountability means taking ownership for things and forces that are occurring on a level which is unseen: your thoughts, beliefs, feelings. virtues, and attitudes and how they govern what you do.

CHAPTER 2

CULTIVATING A MINDSET FOR SUCCESS

"Whatever the mind can conceive and believe, it can achieve."

– NAPOLEON HILL

The power of your mindset cannot be overstated. It is through the intricate tapestry of your thoughts and beliefs that you sculpt the reality you experience, steering you towards the fulfillment of your deepest aspirations. This chapter highlights the foundational principle that your mental landscape is the fertile ground from which your actions sprout, ultimately determining what you reap in your garden of life—annoying weeds or beautiful flowers. By nurturing a mindset rooted in accountability, you unlock the power to perceive all circumstances in your life as opportunities for growth and abundance. This is the power to perceive that your life is happening for you, not to you.

The story of the Chinese farmer, often associated with Taoist and Buddhist philosophies, teaches this same powerful lesson by emphasizing the importance of embracing the flow of life and the limitations of our own human judgment. It encourages us to view the circumstances in our lives with a sense of curiosity. Could this circumstance mean something different than the meaning I gave to it? Could this circumstance be viewed as an opportunity for growth and abundance? Could this circumstance be influenced by factors beyond my perception?

The story goes something like this: Once there was a Chinese farmer who worked his poor farm together with his son and their horse. When the horse ran off one day, neighbors gathered to sympathize with the old man over his bad luck. He shrugged his shoulders and calmly said, "Bad luck? Good luck? Who knows?"

A week later, the horse returned with a herd of wild horses from the hills and this time the neighbors congratulated the farmer on his good luck. His reply was, "Good luck? Bad luck? Who knows?"

Then, when the farmer's son attempted to tame one of the wild horses, he fell off its back and broke his leg. Everyone thought this was very bad luck. Not the farmer, whose only reaction was, "Bad luck? Good luck? Who knows?"

Some weeks later, the army marched into the village and conscripted every able-bodied youth they found there. When they saw the farmer's son with his broken leg, they let him off. Now was that good luck? Bad luck? Who knows?

The moral of the story is that life's events are interconnected in complex ways, and the full implications of any single event cannot be judged in isolation. It teaches the importance of maintaining a perspective of curiosity and not jumping to conclusions about the inherent goodness or badness of occurrences. Most importantly, it illustrates that we each have a choice. We decide how our mind interprets and gives meaning to circumstances. The true nature of events in your life are defined by your mindset.

But what exactly is a mindset? To unravel this, let's first explore the nature of the mind itself. Though often associated with the three-pound organ in your skull—your brain—the mind is a far more elusive, non-physical entity. Reliant on sensory inputs to perceive the external world, the mind exists in a realm devoid of sound, taste, smell, or physical sensation, experiencing reality solely through these filtered senses.

Consider this, when an event unfolds on the other side of the world, how do you learn about it? You cannot see or hear it directly; instead, you must rely on news sources to investigate and relay information. Yet, this information is inherently filtered, never providing the full, unvarnished truth. Similarly, the data entering your mind is not a perfect representation of reality, as it too undergoes a process of filtration and interpretation.

This is where mindsets come into play—they serve as the final filters, shaping how we perceive and make sense of the world around us. Just as news sources don't deliver 100% accurate information 100% of the time, the mind doesn't receive a complete, unadulterated truth. It is this interplay between sensory input, information processing, and the mindset that ultimately defines our experience of reality.

Despite years of study, experts agree we are only beginning to understand our mind and the role our mindsets play in diffusing information. As new light emerges about the mind and how we control and influence it, there is much that we can take and apply to improve our lives, especially at the quantum level. Let's take some time to look at differing views of neuroscientists and psychologists to help us understand how we think our fascinating minds function. Let's begin with an oldie but a goodie, Dr. Sigmund Freud.

HISTORICAL PERSPECTIVE

Almost a century ago, the Austrian psychologist Sigmund Freud introduced the psychological concept that the mind can be seen as having three distinct but important parts. This was a breakthrough in thinking, as before Dr. Freud, the mind was thought to be one single entity. Each of the three distinct parts function independently yet work together to reach common goals. It can be said that each of the three parts "have a mind of their own." Dr. Sigmund Freud termed these three parts: the id, the ego and the superego.

THE ID

The id is the unconscious part of the mind that contains our primitive urges and desires. It drives our self-preservation instincts and fuels our desire for things like food, shelter, and mates, which are essential for survival and reproduction. If the mind is an iceberg, then the Id is the portion of your mind that resides below the surface.

THE SUPEREGO

The superego, on the other hand, represents our internalized moral and societal values. The superego is our moral conscience that has developed throughout our lives based on our upbringing, social influences, and experiences. In the Iceberg Model, the Superego is the visible ice above the surface.

THE EGO

In Freud's view, the ego acts as the mediator between the id and the superego. It is neither the villain nor the hero. It gives us the perspective of self-awareness. Against the backdrop of reality, the ego balances the id's desires with the superego's moral standards to achieve results that are both realistic and socially appropriate.

Freud described the ego as the mind's executive, responsible for decision-making, reality testing, and problem-solving. The ego is like the CEO of the mind. We like to call this the CEgO of the mind. It helps us navigate the demands of the external world and the internal conflicts within the mind to maintain a sense of equilibrium.

In his 1933 book New Introductory Lectures on Psychoanalysis, Freud compared the relationship of the id and the ego to a horse and rider. The horse represents the id, a powerful force of energy that propels forward momentum, while the rider represents the ego, the conscious guide steering the id's power toward a specific destination.[1]

But what does this have to do with mindset? The ego's ability to successfully navigate the intricacies of life depends on what you feed it. It is not the ego itself that leads to ideal outcomes but how you take accountability for it. If you take accountability for your ego and give it the care and attention it needs, then as the mediator between your unconscious and conscious self, the ego will be empowered to

---

1   Freud, *New Introductory Lectures on Psychoanalysis*, Norton & Co, 1933.

help you rather than hinder you along your path. It requires consistent assessment, care, and understanding.

MINDSET THEORY

Sigmund Freud's enduring legacy lies in his recognition that the mind is a multifaceted entity, with the most powerful aspects hidden beneath the surface, like an iceberg's submerged bulk. The Id, Freud's term for this subconscious realm, generates impulses, desires, and aversions that covertly influence our thinking and decision-making. Quantum Accountability empowers us to become aware of these unseen, governing forces within the mind, transforming us into the CEgO—the Chief Executive Officer—of our own mental landscape.

Consider the times you've looked back on past decisions, wondering, "What was I thinking?" More often than not, it was the Id's unacknowledged influence, lurking beneath the conscious level, that shaped those choices, rather than your own deliberate reasoning. Quantum Accountability illuminates these hidden drivers, granting us the self-knowledge to navigate our minds with intention and clarity.

Another way we can look at the mind is via Mindset Theory, attributed to the psychologist Carol Dweck. In her research, Dweck noticed that some children avoided challenges while others actively sought them. These observations later led Dweck and colleague Mary Bandura to study whether one's approach to challenges depends on how one interprets the meaning of failure. What she found is that mindset comes down to a belief about growth. Either ability is static and permanent, what she termed a fixed mindset, or one can develop over time with effort, what she termed a growth mindset. This view was instrumental in understanding the advantages and weaknesses of differing mindsets and helped to categorize peoples' outlooks on their lives. The implications from Dweck's research had profound effects, especially in education.

THE MINDSET CONTINUUM

To better grasp the varieties of mindset one can have, we developed the Mindset Continuum. This tool illustrates the transition from negativity to positivity. By recognizing mindsets as a fluid spectrum, we can cultivate the awareness needed to anchor ourselves in the most constructive and empowering states of mind. As we navigate the ebb and flow of daily life, facing an array of experiences, our mindsets shift and adapt, serving as critical lenses to focus our perception in a world brimming with sensory abundance. In this way, our mindsets help us to make sense of our complicated world.

Scientists have used many different terms to explain mindsets: fixed, pessimistic, victim, scarcity, optimistic, growth. So, we will use the same terms.

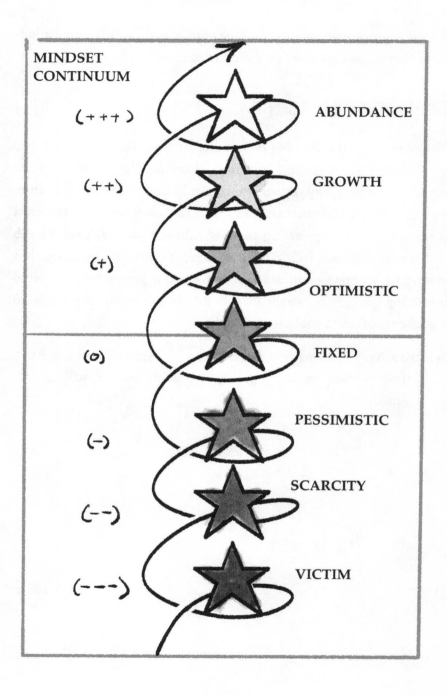

1. THE FIXED MINDSET

The continuum begins with the fixed mindset at the Zero or Neutral point, because by definition, it is fixed or stationary. It is neither good nor bad. It just is. A fixed mindset seeks constant validation from others or measures one's self-worth based on external achievements, material possessions, or social status. It also often lets the ego drive the body.

A fixed mindset is where someone believes their abilities, characteristics, and personality are present at birth. They either have "it" or they don't. Their mindset doesn't change. Their mindset is not malleable. People with a fixed mindset have a lot of rules and conditions that make them feel comfortable with what they can and cannot do. Someone with a fixed mindset might say there's no point in trying.

"I can't learn this." " I was never good at math." " I'm too old to start again." Or, " I'm not someone who goes to the gym." Those beliefs are rigid and allow no room for growth, change, or opportunity.

When the ego operates within a fixed mindset, a person may be more prone to deflect blame onto others or refuse to admit mistakes to protect their self-image. They might prioritize their ego's need to appear faultless over being accountable for their actions. In extreme cases, they engage in self-aggrandizement, self-promotion, or self-centered behaviors.

One of the challenges associated with the ego is its tendency to create a narrative or story about ourselves based on our past experiences, beliefs, and perceptions. This egoic self-concept can become rigid and limiting, defining who we think we are and what we are capable of. It can also lead to identification with roles, labels, and social constructs, such as job titles, social status, or cultural identities, further reinforcing the egoic sense of self.

People with a fixed mindset often report that they are frustrated, angry, or depressed and that somehow other people have it better than them. The truth is that some people do have it better than others. However this isn't because they won the lottery, it is because they have a more effective mindset. The great thing about mindsets is that they are just a collection of rules and conditions based upon beliefs that can be changed. Even someone with a fixed mindset can begin to change their thinking and, therefore, also their mindset.

2. THE PESSIMISTIC MINDSET

A pessimistic mindset is characterized by a tendency to focus on the worst aspects of situations, consistently expecting negative outcomes and often doubting that positive results are achievable. Pessimists may view life through a "glass is half empty" lens, emphasizing obstacles and potential failures over opportunities and successes. This outlook can lead to a range of negative effects on both mental and physical health, including increased anxiety, poor overall work performance, low self-esteem, and even physical health ailments like sleep difficulties, heart disease, and hypertension.

Although it may seem that this pessimistic mindset is never a good one to employ, despite its drawbacks, a certain level of pessimism, known as "defensive pessimism," can have its benefits. This involves thinking about and preparing for potential negative outcomes, which can help manage expectations and engage in preventative behaviors to mitigate risks. For example, pessimists might be more diligent about their health due to concerns about potential illnesses, leading to healthier lifestyle choices, and therefore happier lives.

However, excessive pessimism can be detrimental, affecting one's quality of life, relationships, career, and overall well-being. It's important to find a balance between pessimism and optimism (the fifth mindset we will discuss), aiming for a realistic outlook that acknowledges potential challenges without being overwhelmed by negativity. For this reason, It is a -1 on the Mindset Continuum.

3. SCARCITY MINDSET

A scarcity mindset is a -2 on the continuum. It is a way of thinking that focuses on limitations and insufficiency, particularly regarding resources such as time, money, or other assets. Individuals with a scarcity mindset often feel that there is never enough to go around, and they become preoccupied with what they lack rather than what they have. This mindset can lead to a range of negative behaviors and emotions, such as anxiety, jealousy, and short-term decision-making, as well as a decrease in cognitive functions like problem-solving and impulse control.

The scarcity mindset can be triggered by various factors, including financial difficulties, societal pressures, or personal experiences of deprivation, especially during childhood. It can manifest in behaviors like procrastination, overscheduling, fear of loss, and reluctance to share or collaborate due to the belief that one's gain is another's loss. The Scarcity Mindset breeds an outlook of the world that can be categorized as the opposite of collaboration. Life is a competition and there's not enough to go around for everyone.

4. THE VICTIM MINDSET

You have likely encountered someone with a victim mindset. A victim mindset is characterized by a belief that external forces, circumstances, or other people control one's life and outcomes. Individuals with a victim mindset tend to attribute their difficulties and failures to factors beyond their control, often feeling powerless and helpless. They may avoid taking responsibility for their actions and decisions and may constantly seek sympathy or external validation. This mindset can hinder personal growth and development, as individuals may not take proactive steps to change their circumstances or overcome challenges.

These are people whose lives are one series of drama after another, and it's never their fault. As soon as they come into the room, they are there to share their latest drama, fiasco, and tale of woe. Their stories are full of excuses. Everything is unfair. And everyone else gets better job opportunities, bonuses, and perks than they do. This is a victim mentality, or what I like to call the 'poor me' mindset.

When you first meet this person, you'll likely listen with concern and compassion, but eventually, you'll get annoyed with the constant blaming of others for their own decisions and failings. Someone with the victim mentality feels disadvantaged because of someone else's problems, considerations, or issues.

Sometimes, these people might like it when they get attention or people feel sorry for them due to their misfortunes. They might get some strange excitement from showing off an injury and creating a whole story about this latest problem. They also refuse to accept responsibility for their problems and have no desire to change. At some level, being the victim works for them.

Someone with a victim mentality can cause much damage to a family, a relationship, or a work group. The constant complaining can damage morale, irritate and annoy people in the group, and ruin the team's overall happiness. They can damage productivity by causing or making mistakes that create delays that could have been prevented, and then they blame others, further damaging the morale of the group.

Lastly, they damage relationships and break trust. As their behavior swings from victim to victimizer, they break their partner's trust in the group. One minute they play the victim to seek attention, and then the next minute they blame someone else or hurt someone who was trying to help them in the first place. The overall response is that you will no longer be able to trust them or expect them to take responsibility for an outcome.

The easiest way to identify the signs of the victim mentality is to listen to how they talk and what they talk about. Their conversations tend to be centered around their problems with the expectation that others will feel sorry for them. They frequently create 'woe is me' stories to validate their lack of success in life and they frequently blame others when things go wrong. They reject the chance to join in with fun activities and often complain that other people have received preferential treatment. It is tough to set clear goals and boundaries with people who are not accountable and have adopted a victim mindset.

Urging everyone in your company or family to be personally accountable for their outcomes and choices and take responsibility for their actions is vital to avoiding the destructive power of the victim mindset. The endless drama and excuses of individuals with a victim mindset must be dealt with swiftly and effectively to protect the group. And if the person continues to miss deadlines and blame others, or their behavior becomes too damaging, it may be time to cut ties.

The Victim Mindset is the lowest on the continuum at -3. We all have tendencies for all mindsets and can go into any one of these at different moments (just think of how you react when someone cuts in front of you in line). It is important to limit the Victim Mindset as much as possible, and move out of that mindset quickly when you recognize you are in it. People who choose to live at this level, have unfortunately built a life validating this mindset, and it can be difficult to see change. If you cannot help a person who is a victim, you will find yourself spending very little time with them.

5. THE OPTIMISTIC MINDSET

An optimistic mindset (+1) is characterized by an attitude of hope and the expectation that good things are going to happen. Optimists tend to attribute positive events to internal causes and view negative events as external. Optimists are more likely to view hardships as learning experiences or temporary setbacks, and they maintain the belief that "tomorrow will probably be better." They believe in their ability to influence positive outcomes and see setbacks as expected obstacles on their road to success. This mindset is linked to several benefits, including increased resiliency, lower stress levels, better physical health, and a generally higher quality of life.

However, it's important to balance optimism with a dose of realism. Being overly optimistic without acknowledging the risks can lead to impractical expectations and decisions. A balanced approach that combines optimism with a realistic assessment of situations is often the most beneficial for achieving goals and maintaining well-being in our chaotic world.

6. THE GROWTH MINDSET

A growth mindset, +2 on the Continuum, views challenges and failures as opportunities for learning and growth rather than threats to one's ego or self-worth. The ego supported by a growth mindset allows us to be open to feedback, criticism, and self-improvement and willing to make necessary changes and adjustments to achieve our goals and aspirations.

Someone with a growth mindset might believe they were born with unlimited potential and opportunities; all they have to do is go out and get them. Another belief in the growth mindset is that there's more than one outcome, and failure is just an outcome I didn't want, so I will keep trying again until I get the desired result.

Another hallmark belief in a growth mindset is continual improvement. We can always get better at something if we keep trying, keep learning, keep asking, keep reading, and keep watching. The list of possibilities for improvement is endless. Overall, individuals with a growth mindset have an overriding belief that if they apply themselves, things will improve.

If you talk to a successful person in their field, you will encounter someone with a growth mindset. Those with a fixed mindset might think this person was born with some special gift or had a family opportunity they didn't have. Yes, some people have more opportunities than others. Still, the reality is that those with a growth mindset take advantage of the opportunities they have and seek out even more opportunities. Conversely, those with less effective mindsets have the tendency to turn away from opportunities, or they believe things are too good to be true or beyond their reach, and stop dead in their tracks.

The reality is that every day we see people succeed. Ordinary people with ordinary skills create extraordinary lives and extraordinary outcomes. They have jobs, careers, or creative pursuits that most of us can't imagine. And it all begins in the imagination. Successful people have a mindset that allows them to imagine a different future for themselves, their company, their family, and their lives. Then they use ideas from their imaginations and develop a strategic plan.

Growth Mindset people believe in themselves. They have a level of confidence that they will succeed. They see setbacks as opportunities and believe they are in control of their destiny.

7. THE ABUNDANCE MINDSET

The pinnacle of the Mindset Continuum (+3) is the Abundance Mindset. This is where we want to get, and where we want to stay. This is our goal in the human experience. This mindset is displayed by taking full ownership, responsibility, and accountability for your thoughts, beliefs, virtues, attitude, and feelings. This is what is meant by Quantum Accountability. It is the premiere mindset that is the most effective and efficient in getting you to your goal to a life of Abundance.

Having an abundance mindset means that you are creating the ideal reality for yourself. It means you are living a level 10 out of 10 version of your life on the Circle of Abundance, which we will discuss later in this book. You have a strong, vibrant, healthy mindset where you are constantly operating at a level 10 of abundance. You are living in level 10 relationships. You have financial abundance to the point that you are free of monetary constraints. You have freedom of time to choose how you spend your time. This level of abundance means you monitor and maintain your health to ensure that you are thriving for the stage in life that you are in.

You have realized that who you are, what you do, and what you have are in alignment, and you are living your purpose. Your purpose-driven life has created a level of joy and bliss so you feel fulfillment. In the Abundance Mindset you have a deep spiritual connection, and you are living your ultimate version of your highest self here on earth. This is the ideal goal for all humanity.

THE MINDSET STAR

Mindset is the lens through which we view our journey of growth and challenges; it's not just about reaching the destination but about being accountable for every step we take on the way there. In the remaining chapters of Section One, we will further explore how to develop a Mindset of Abundance through a visual we call the Mindset Star.

Drawing on the profound insights of neuroscientists and psychologists, we delve into the complexities of the mind, building upon the robust foundations laid by these intellectual titans. We aim to extend their pioneering work, exploring new frontiers in our understanding of the human psyche. We'd like to introduce you to a metaphor we call the Mindset Star which will aid us in gaining a better understanding of how the mind works. We will use the following chapters to define each of the points on the star, discuss how they share information and affect each other, and finally, how each plays an integral role in creating your mindset.

Imagine drawing a five-pointed star without raising your pen from the paper. Begin at an arbitrary point and draw a line. Then draw another line and continue the process until all five interconnected lines have been drawn. Without raising your pen, trace the five lines. Now trace over them again. Like an infinity symbol, the star can continue forever, in a constant state of flow.

The five points represent the five components of your mindset; all interconnected but also able to stand on their own. We will use this Mindset Star to help us understand how the five points: thoughts, beliefs, virtues, feelings, and attitudes affect our life experiences.

CHANGING YOUR MINDSET

Anyone can shift from a mindset that is not serving them to a more effective one. Transforming an unproductive mindset into one that propels you forward is within anyone's reach—it simply requires mindfulness and commitment. Picture the ease of adjusting a toaster's lever: with just a gentle nudge, you can achieve the golden, irresistible crunch of perfectly toasted bread. This metaphor is backed by compelling research in neuroplasticity, which offers concrete proof that while the adult brain may have established circuits, it remains impressively adaptable. Embrace the potential for change, and watch as new, more effective thought patterns emerge, as malleable as the brain itself.

Neuroplasticity unveils the brain's remarkable capacity to evolve and adapt at any stage of life, shattering the old myth that its malleability ceases after childhood. Just as the most rewarding achievements demand persistence and effort, reshaping your brain's pathways is a journey of transformation. With each repetition, your neural connections strengthen, akin to the way muscles fortify with exercise. Conversely, neglecting mental exercise can lead to atrophy, much like unused muscles can weaken. If you don't use it, you lose it. You can harness the power of neuroplasticity by actively engaging your brain in different circumstances requiring different neural pathways to be created.

Each time you repeat a thought, you reinforce specific neural pathways, just like when you complete a set of bicep curls in the gym. If you have a new thought, you create new neural pathways, just like new muscle cells gained from completing a new exercise in the gym. If you do this enough, these tiny adjustments change how your brain functions. The same goes with your mindset.

We talked earlier about identifying your type of mindset. This is as easy as taking a piece of paper and thinking about your beliefs when you experience a drastic change in your life. If it's a good change, do you believe it resulted from luck or hard work, and if it's a bad change, did it just happen by chance or do you take accountability for it? This is the first step in understanding your mindset.

It is important to note that your mindset isn't stagnant. It changes over time with life experiences and circumstances. It can also change on the same day. Imagine you are having an awful day at work; your top manager gives her two-week notice, your credit card payment for office supplies didn't get posted, and your Indeed post for more help has yielded a 0% ROI. If asked, you may label your mindset as Pessimistic. There are several issues that are capitalizing your thought patterns and all are negative. It's hard to see the sun through the clouds.

However, like we've said, your mindset isn't stagnant. Now imagine you return home and find a delicious dinner awaiting. You are surrounded by family and friends who energize your soul to the core. You feel love and connection. What is your mindset now? Possibly, Optimistic? This is the power of Quantum Accountability.

If you discover that your mindset falls below the optimal level on the spectrum, leaning towards a fixed perspective, consider elevating it by either transforming your thoughts—a topic we'll delve into in an upcoming chapter—or by altering your environment. Employing either or both of these approaches can significantly aid in shifting your mindset towards a more positive and growth-oriented direction.

Your view of the world is intricately tied to the boundaries of your comfort zone. This means your thoughts, choices, and perceptions are shaped by what feels familiar, not necessarily what is pleasant or beneficial. "Comfortable" here signifies the realm of the known, a space where predictability, even of the negative kind, offers a peculiar sense of security. As we delve deeper into the realm of thoughts in Chapter 3, we'll explore how Negative Thought Patterns can tether us to this deceptive comfort, and how stepping beyond can transform our perspective on life.

Setbacks in life are unavoidable, and how we handle them largely depends on our mindset's adaptability. Those with either Negative or Fixed Mindsets often find it harder to cope with change, whether good or bad. In times of success, they may become complacent, attributing achievements to talent or luck, and may resist further improvement, hindering their own growth. On the other hand, individuals with a Growth or Abundance Mindset view positive changes as chances to learn and evolve. They attribute success to hard work and persistence, making them more resilient and open to adapting in challenging times, paving the way for ongoing personal and professional development and a fulfilling life.

ACCOUNTABILITY ANCHORS:

1. Your mindset is composed of your thoughts, beliefs, feelings, virtues, and attitudes.

2. Mindsets are malleable.

3. Understanding The Mindset Continuum and operating at a level of abundance is the key to an abundant life.

4. Effective Mindsets lead to success in all aspects of your life.

CHAPTER 3

NEGOTIATING THE TAPESTRY OF YOUR THOUGHTS

The happiness of your life depends upon the quality of your thoughts.

— MARCUS AURELIUS

Your mindset shapes how you perceive the world, while your thoughts add color to your existence, weaving the rich tapestry that is your life. The reality you live in is a masterpiece crafted by your thoughts, which hold the power to materialize into concrete outcomes—what we whimsically term 'the K to the G,' where thoughts (what we thinK) transform into reality (turn into thinGs).

Take a moment to observe your surroundings; every object and experience began as a mere thought, from the ink on the pages of a book to the plastic of your e-reader's keypad. Even the office you work in first existed as an idea, which then unfolded into a blueprint, and ultimately, into the tangible space around you.

Napoleon Hill, a pioneer of self-help literature and author of the book *Think and Grow Rich*, had a core philosophy that one's thoughts have a significant influence on one's life. His saying "Thoughts become things" encapsulates this belief. He proposed that we shape our reality with our thoughts and beliefs and that mental attitudes can attract real-world outcomes.

Many understand that our thoughts impact our health—negative thoughts induce stress, weakening the immune system and potentially leading to illness, while positive thoughts foster calm and cellular healing, enhancing physical well-being. Moreover, our mental state profoundly influences pain perception, with our thoughts and emotions capable of intensifying or diminishing the pain we feel.

Thoughts are powerful architects that can sculpt our destiny. They hold the capacity to mold our reality, echoing the principle that our essence is shaped by our inner reflections. Yet, it's crucial to understand that thoughts are merely the surface expressions of our deeper consciousness. Beyond this, there's an unseen quantum realm influencing our reality, reminding us that we transcend our thoughts and minds. Our brains and minds are adaptable, and so are our thoughts.

Consider this, have your tastes ever dramatically changed over time? Perhaps a food you once detested as a child, like sushi, wine, or dark chocolate, has become a favorite. Recall dismissing fish as "yucky" at ten, only to find yourself savoring sushi with wine as an adult. What shifted? It wasn't just your mind, but your thoughts evolving with you.

Your mind is malleable, and so are your thoughts, which serve as your mind's messengers. Your ongoing internal monologue that narrates your life daily—these are your thoughts. While they can be constructive, they can also lead to stress or negativity. Often, we're not even conscious of our thoughts until we feel a physical reaction, like a sudden increase in heart rate. In the hustle of life, we're frequently too preoccupied with external events to notice our internal dialogue. You might not realize you're troubled until someone close to you points it out, prompting you to recognize a shift in your thought patterns or the impact of a single negative thought. Remember, words have power, especially the ones we tell ourselves.

Picture yourself on the cusp of a career breakthrough, sitting outside the CEO's office, poised for the final round of interviews for a dream job. You've aced the previous stages, standing as one of the top two contenders. Armed with thorough research about the company, dressed impeccably, and brimming with confidence, you're ready to tackle any question. Yet, unexpectedly, a nagging doubt creeps in, "What if they discovered something unfavorable in a reference check?"

Or, imagine being out with friends, spotting someone attractive across the bar. The eye contact extends, your heart races, and palms sweat. Suddenly, an intrusive thought surfaces, "Does my breath smell?" Over time, we learn that such fleeting doubts don't define us. Gaining confidence means learning to sideline these thoughts, especially when we're about to take bold steps towards our desires.

Why do these thoughts pop into your head at these inopportune times? Thoughts, like comments, either bring us closer to our goals or move us farther away. Your conscious mind—with clear-set goals—certainly would not choose to think these thoughts at these particular moments in time. Here's the deal, you are not your thoughts.

Your thoughts are mere electrical impulses and nothing more. We know from Dr. Freud that there is a part of our mind that we do not control, what he termed the Id. It's the Id that is acting on our behalf. It's acting in order to protect us, if you can believe it. Our brains still have many similarities to our ancient ancestors who had to be constantly on the lookout for predators. To this day, our brains still act in the same way. We can be thankful that they protected us from lurking dangers outside the cave, but nowadays the dangers are in different forms and less frequent, yet our brains remain the same.

This may be news to you as you may have never thought about this reality before. You may have thought that what you choose to think is completely up to you, just as you choose the next Streaming Video Drama Series on Netflix. Many of us go through life thinking that we are in complete control of our thoughts.

Still not 100% convinced? Let's do a little mini-experiment. Don't think of a polar bear. Did it work? How'd you do? Were you able to not think of the white, fluffy, cold-weather loving animal? I would guess that even though you are an educated, intelligent individual, you were unsuccessful at this easy task. To test the experiment's reliability, try it again…think about anything other than an apple. Successful this time? Could be red, green, or even yellow, Macintosh, Red Delicious or Granny Smith. You most likely were not successful in this second endeavor either. Why is it that we seem to lack control over our own minds?

You are not alone, in 1863 the Russian novelist, Fyodor Dosotevsky gave his readers the same polar bear challenge. He proved the point that we are not always 100% in control of the thoughts in our head, even when we try to be. This mere realization is the beginning of self-awareness. Congratulations, you are now more self-aware than you were a couple of pages ago.

In 1987, Dan Wegner began researching and publishing studies on what he calls Ironic Process Theory (IPT), which examines why we think the things we do. We appear to be consistently in a game of tug-of-war with one end representing us as the thinker and the other representing our thoughts.

WHO IS IN CHARGE?

Most of the time we aren't even considering or consciously aware that thoughts are coming and going in and out of our conscious perception. But other times, we seem to struggle with the power and energy these thoughts bring into our existence. And sometimes, by trying not to think about something, that something becomes paramount and king of the hill on the mountain of thoughts in our head. At times, we as the thinker are winning the battle. Other times, our thoughts are completely in control of the game. We react with emotional and sometimes behavioral effects. Does anyone remember when we agreed to be a part of this tug-of-war? And will it ever end?

Ironic process theory (IPT) may shed some light on the struggle we have with debilitating, negative thoughts at inopportune times. IPT is a psychological phenomenon[2] suggesting that when individuals

---

2 Wegner, Daniel M. (1994). "Ironic processes of mental control". *Psychological Review*. **101** (1): 34–52. doi:10.1037/0033-295x.101.1.34. PMID 8121959

intentionally try to avoid thinking a certain thought or feeling a certain emotion, a paradoxical effect is produced.

In our real lives this process can occur with external distractions as well, such as catchy Slogans like: "Just Do It" or "America runs on Dunkin." These phrases can interrupt thought processes and cause distraction. We will explore this idea even more in Chapter 11 where we'll explore the concept of Focus.

Even worse than mind clutter from advertisements, thoughts can also lead to negative thinking, which causes negative emotions and feelings. Our minds spontaneously go to thoughts we don't want to think about; the death of a parent (real occurrence or possible future), or that fight with a spouse. Why do these and other negative thoughts based upon traumatic memories or dramatic possibilities pop into our heads and hinder our thinking?

Negative thoughts, despite their discomfort, can serve various purposes, and understanding these functions can be key to managing and responding to them effectively and, therefore, increasing our self-awareness. Here are some potential purposes of negative thoughts:

- **Survival Instinct:** From an evolutionary perspective, the human mind has evolved to prioritize potential threats. Negative thoughts can be a part of this survival instinct, helping individuals identify and respond to dangers in their environment.
- **Problem-Solving:** Negative thoughts may prompt problem-solving and strategic thinking. When faced with challenges or obstacles, the mind often engages in critical analysis and planning, which can involve negative considerations.

Noticing your thinking is like having a backstage pass to the chaotic concert that is your mind. It's that moment when you realize you're both the main act and the frantic person trying to find their seat.

NEGATIVE THOUGHT PATTERNS

Negative thought patterns often have a more profound impact than positive thought patterns, a trait rooted in our evolutionary past. Consider the early humans, whose survival hinged on constant vigilance against threats. Imagine being a hunter-gatherer; a single ignored rustle behind a boulder could mean a fatal bear encounter. This hardwired caution has shaped our brains to prioritize potential dangers, fostering a pessimistic mindset designed to keep us safe. While this instinct has been crucial for survival, it also presents modern challenges by predisposing us to negative thinking, which can create barriers in our contemporary lives.

Negative thought patterns—whether they are based on fact or reality—are also known as cognitive distortions or thought distortions. Just take a look at some of these thoughts we allow to take over our mind and consider which ones you are prone to believing.

- I'm not lucky; I never win anything.
- I got an F on my English paper. I'm no good at school, so I should quit.
- My date was late. They probably took one look at me and left.
- My client didn't call, so they probably chose someone else because I'm not good enough.

Thought distortions can craft a damaging and false perception of reality, leading to undesirable outcomes if we base our decisions on such skewed views. These distortions are misleading because they don't reflect the actual state of affairs. The ego aims to make decisions grounded in reality, but it relies on the information provided to it. Feeding it with erroneous thoughts shapes a distorted reality it perceives as true.

Fortunately, our thoughts are pliable, allowing us to reshape or dismiss those that are detrimental or incorrect. As we explore the concept of manifesting our reality through our thoughts, it's crucial to be aware of these cognitive missteps. While everyone occasionally succumbs to thought distortions, repeatedly indulging in them can alter neural pathways, potentially leading to anxiety, depression, strained relationships, and other life challenges. A significant warning sign is finding yourself in a negative mood, besieged by pessimistic thoughts and feelings.

Research indicates that thought distortions often arise as a means to cope with challenging or traumatic experiences. The intensity and duration of these experiences can increase our reliance on such negative thought patterns for coping. Take black-and-white thinking, for instance, where individuals see situations in absolute terms, leading to beliefs of inevitable success or failure, or viewing people as wholly good or evil. This rigid mindset can stifle creative problem-solving and is characteristic of a fixed mindset.

Overgeneralization is another pervasive cognitive distortion, where one draws broad conclusions from a single event. For example, if a presentation doesn't go well, you might prematurely label yourself as a poor public speaker, based on this one instance. This sweeping judgment can prevent you from recognizing your potential for growth and improvement in public speaking, trapping you in a cycle of negative self-perception.

THE POWER OF JOURNALING TO BREAK NEGATIVE THOUGHT PATTERNS

Looking through old journal entries is an excellent way to examine your negative thought patterns. The writing process allows you to take your thoughts out of the quantum and put them in front of your physical eyes to examine and understand more deeply. Reviewing what you've written can illustrate how your thoughts may have changed and shine light on the influence of feelings. Past entries can serve as a treasure chest containing 'the way you used to think.' This can lead to examining, improving, and learning how your mind works. It is also an excellent record of progress and improvement—or a signal for when it might be a good time to enlist the aid of a therapist, coach, or mentor.

Whether you use a pen to paper or a digital device, most thought leaders agree that journal writing has significant power and benefits. From problem-solving to goal setting to insight healing, growth, and change, the simple pen and paper in a quiet environment can create staggering improvements.

When you express yourself on paper, you stimulate certain parts of your brain that contribute to improved learning. Learning becomes easier when you write things down. If you are working on moving from a fixed to a growth mindset or changing your limiting beliefs or thought distortions, a good way is to write that change down to yourself on paper to aid in memory recall.

Writing in a journal can help you benefit from your journaling practice. Many research studies compare college students who take notes by hand versus a laptop, and the students who wrote by hand remembered lectures better. This may be because our brains have developed over thousands of years; hand-written notes are a return to cave paintings while digital devices are a relatively new occurrence.

Writing by hand can have similar benefits to meditation. Alpha journaling is a technique I learned from Jose Silva of the Silva Method. It helps me focus on improving areas of my life—emotional, physical, and psychological—through meditation and visualization.

Alpha journaling is when you enter an 'alpha level' of mind, a state of relaxed and focused concentration (typically through meditation) and then journal your thoughts, feelings, and ideas. The goal is to tap into your subconscious mind, gaining clarity, insights, or creative ideas that may not be as easily accessible in your normal state of consciousness.

If you don't want to or cannot use the Silva Method with your morning obligations, here is a quick way to start a ten-minute-a-day journaling practice. Date your entry and start with one of the simple prompts either during your evening reflection or first thing in the morning:

- What were my three biggest wins yesterday/ today?
- What are my biggest obstacles?
- What are some potential solutions?
- What are some next action steps?
- What are my three WMIs (what's most important) that I intend to accomplish today?

The three WMI's (What's Most Important) concept is a productivity strategy that involves identifying and prioritizing the most important tasks or goals to focus on during a specific period, typically a day or weekend. After deciding on your most important goals, rank them based on need, urgency, and importance. Limiting and ranking help you avoid confusion and feeling overwhelmed, and make sure you give your attention to the most critical ones.

Here are some additional writing prompts to offload your mind:

- I'm worried about…
- I'm having a problem with…
- What am I going to do about…
- What's bothering me is…
- I am unhappy about…

Daily writing may not work for you. You can still benefit from journaling even if you can only write in a journal occasionally. Studies show that writing once or twice weekly is enough to create a journaling habit. And if you find journaling too time-consuming, you'll likely benefit from a less stressful approach than doing this daily.

CONQUERING NEGATIVE SELF-TALK

Once you have identified your negative thought patterns, you will be empowered to eliminate them and replace them with healthy, positive thoughts and beliefs. Accepting your feelings is the starting point because you can't change what you can't identify. Self-talk refers to the dialogue you have with yourself, either out loud or internally. It often reflects your thoughts, beliefs, and feelings and can be both conscious and unconscious, as well as both positive and negative.

1. Positive Self-Talk: This is when your inner dialogue is supportive and affirmative. Positive self-talk can boost your confidence, mood, and overall outlook on life. Examples include statements like "I can do this," "I'm good enough," or "I'm capable of achieving my goals."

2. Negative Self-Talk: This is when your inner dialogue is critical or demeaning. Negative self-talk can cause stress, decrease your self-esteem, and negatively impact your overall mental well-being. Examples include statements like "I'm not good enough," "I always mess up," or "I can't do this."

Self-talk plays a significant role in your perception of yourself and the world around you. It's closely linked to your mental health and overall well-being. If your self-talk is negative, criticizing, or time-traveling (ruminating about the past or predicting doom and gloom in the future), it's time for a self-talk reset. A self-talk reset is when you jot down the five or six prevailing thoughts in your mind and then write the opposite. The simple addition of a negation word like "no" or "not" in the track running in your monkey mind is often enough to stop that thought from running away with you.

Here's an example: *I'm going to fail. I never should've tried this. What was I thinking?* With a simple switch, these negative thoughts can become, *I'm going to succeed. I will find a way. I'm glad I tried this. I could do it, and I will.* With the simple adjustment, you just used self-talk to get in the right mood to decide. Positive self-talk doesn't just create an attitude and mindset; it helps you keep going to finish your work.

You can elevate your journey to conquer negative self-talk with the transformative power of positive affirmations. Positive affirmations transform your mindset by crafting empowering statements and repeating them with conviction throughout your day. Imagine replacing the doubt-laden question, "Am I capable?" with the unwavering affirmation, "I am capable." Such affirmations act as beacons, guiding you through the fog of uncertainty and reinforcing your path to success. By changing your self-talk, you can change your feelings.

When negative self-talk clouds your vision, actively seek rays of inspiration. Dive into a book that sparks your imagination, lose yourself in films that lift your spirits, or immerse yourself in podcasts that fuel your ambition. These are not mere distractions but tools to silence your inner critic and amplify your voice of positivity, reshaping your feelings and mindset for the better.

Our uniqueness as humans—and as entrepreneurs—lies in our extraordinary capacity to observe, analyze, and transform our thought patterns. Individual thoughts provide glimpses into our current attitude, yet collectively, they weave the fabric of our belief systems. Embrace the profound human ability to shift your thinking, to construct a new set of beliefs that not only challenge the status quo but propel you towards achieving the extraordinary. This is the essence of growth and abundance, enabling you to manifest realities beyond your most ambitious dreams.

EFFECTIVE VS. INEFFECTIVE THINKING

Cultivating your thoughts is akin to nurturing a garden; it requires time, patience, and consistent effort to flourish. Recognize that the mind you've cultivated over the years will need careful rewiring. To embrace Quantum Accountability, take charge of your thoughts by becoming acutely aware of them. Assess each thought critically, as you would scrutinize items on a grocery shelf, asking yourself whether it serves your purpose or leads you astray.

As you hone this awareness, you might discover a preponderance of ineffective or unproductive thoughts. Scientists estimate that individuals think up to 70,000 thoughts per day, and a staggering 90% of these thoughts fall into the category of "ineffective or unproductive". This is akin to sifting through an inbox flooded with 70,000 emails, most of which are spam. Wouldn't you install a spam filter for such an inbox? Similarly, it's prudent to establish a mental filter, a guardian at the gates of your consciousness, to sift through and neutralize those ineffective thoughts. This vigilant self-awareness is the cornerstone of Quantum Accountability, setting the stage for a transformative mental journey.

Effective thinking is the cornerstone of innovation, problem-solving, and personal growth. It involves the deliberate and strategic use of your cognitive abilities to analyze situations, make decisions, and generate solutions. By cultivating effective thinking, you can transcend conventional boundaries, uncover novel insights, and approach challenges with a fresh perspective. This mode of thought is crucial not only for achieving personal and professional goals but also for navigating the complexities of modern life. It empowers you to critically evaluate information, discern truth from falsehood, and make choices that align with your virtues and aspirations. In essence, effective thinking is the engine that drives progress, enabling you to transform obstacles into opportunities and dreams into realities.

Are you ready to embark on the transformative journey from the murky waters of ineffective thinking to the clear skies of effective thought? Are you convinced about the benefits of shifting to effective thinking? Put it to the test with a straightforward exercise. Use a pen and paper to track your thoughts, recording them at the end of each day. Maintain this practice for a week and then review what you've written. You'll likely notice recurring patterns in your thoughts, with many of the same ideas repeating daily and weekly. Original thoughts tend to be rare, but this exercise can help you identify and cultivate them more frequently.

Once you have several days of data, take a blank piece of paper and divide it into three columns. Label the first column effective and the third column ineffective. Label the second column as thoughts that are either background noise or inconclusive. Now, take each thought and put it into one of the three columns. For example, the thought, "Remember to do the laundry tonight," could be either effective or ineffective depending on its timing. For me, it would be an effective reminder if the thought popped into my mind while I am creating my To-Do List for the day, but ineffective if it came in the middle of my sales presentation.

You may start to notice that these thoughts create feelings. We will explore this idea in depth in Chapter 5. If you are stuck on the categorization of a thought, say it out loud to yourself and notice how it makes you feel. If it's a 'good' feeling then it's effective, if it's a bad feeling, then it's ineffective. It's as simple as that. Please note, however, that sometimes effective thoughts can produce bad feelings. In this way, they urge us to act on something. Maybe you have been procrastinating on a report due next week? Or you need to research an anniversary trip for your wife? But to keep it simple, we want more good feelings and less bad feelings.

Now, look at your thoughts in the third column. Are there any thoughts in the third column that you could adjust a bit or drastically so that they can become effective? Pick just one and try it. Here's an example:

Ineffective thought: "I really screwed up today."

Change to: "That did not go how I had planned. What's the lesson?"

This is how you cultivate new thoughts. As we've discussed, thoughts come in patterns and these patterns become habits. If you want to have a plentiful garden, then you must have habits that cultivate it. Just like a garden, you must develop habits to cultivate your thoughts. So now that you've changed one of your thoughts into a new thought, let's make it a belief or pattern in your mind.

WHAT ARE YOU FEEDING YOUR MIND?

The adage "you are what you eat" extends beyond diet to encompass the stewardship of our physical bodies through our choices in nutrition, activity, and exposure. Our bodies are, in essence, the result of our actions and decisions. The composition of our diet—proteins, fats, sugars, artificial additives, fiber, and vitamins—dictates our physical well-being. Every decision, from selecting groceries to choosing between physical activity and sedentary leisure, shapes our health.

Similarly, the nourishment we provide our minds—through thoughts, beliefs, feelings, virtues, and attitudes—plays a critical role in our mental health and vitality. Just as the physical sustenance we consume affects our bodily health, the quality of our mental "diet" influences our psychological state. The unseen elements that feed our minds ultimately define our being. Thus, it's worth reflecting on what we're feeding our minds and the impact of these choices on our life's quality.

A person with a steady diet of television, news, and social media has a view of themselves and the world that is largely shaped by what they consume and the sources that created it. We know as conscious consumers that these sources only sell if it's negative, dramatic, sensational, and holds your attention. Studies have proven that if an advertisement can make you feel bad about yourself and then promise that the product will fix it for you, the likelihood of you buying that product increases dramatically.

This criterion is also valid for many streaming shows and services. Suppose we compare our entertainment choices to our health choices. In that case, many of us consume a steady diet of mental junk food that creates an environment of fear, comparison, isolation, loneliness, addiction, distraction, and unrealistic expectations for the mind. We call this **Mental Obesity**.

How often have you watched a disturbing horror film that hooked you from the beginning to the ending credits? Then you took your dog for a walk, expecting the serial killer to jump out from behind the bushes or crawl in a neighbor's window to kidnap their sleeping child? These modern-day ghost stories are rooted in reality, but only the smallest number of people will ever experience such a situation. Even so, your mind can struggle to know the difference. If you are constantly feeding it a diet of fear and violence, your mind will begin to interact with the world according to that projected reality (rather than reality itself).

This is a simple example that illustrates a principle that not only applies to the media you consume but also to the thoughts that you think and the people you surround yourself with who influence your attitudes and beliefs. If you have been feeding your mind an unhealthy diet, your understanding of reality and your ego's ability to mediate based on that reality will be compromised.

To return your mind to a healthier state, you will need a better diet. And just as someone who wants to lose weight needs the combination of diet and exercise to get rid of unwanted fat, those who want to shed their **Mental Obesity** will need a combination of consuming a healthy mental diet and exercising their mind to reverse the consequences of the years of unhealthy choices. Quite simply, you are accountable for what sensory inputs come into your mind that determine your mindset. And because you are accountable, you can consciously choose what input you are exposed to. You choose what you listen to, what you watch, and who you spend your time with.

ANCIENT WISDOM

There is a Native American legend often attributed to the Cherokee tribe, though its exact origins are not definitively known. It is commonly known as "The Tale of Two Wolves" or "Which Wolf Do You Feed?" The legend goes something like this: An old Cherokee is teaching his grandson about life. "A fight is going on inside me," he said to the boy. "It is a terrible fight, and it is between two wolves. One is evil. He is anger, envy, sorrow, regret, greed, arrogance, self-pity, guilt, resentment, inferiority, lies, false pride, superiority, and ego."

He continued, "The other is good. He is joy, peace, love, hope, serenity, humility, kindness, benevolence, empathy, generosity, truth, compassion, and faith. The same fight is going on inside you, and inside every other person, too."

The grandson thought about it for a minute and then asked his grandfather, "Which wolf will win?"

The old Cherokee simply replied, "The one you feed."

This story serves as a metaphor for the internal struggle between competing thoughts within each person. It emphasizes the power of accountability and the importance of awareness and nurturing the qualities that lead to personal growth, happiness, and peace.

ACCOUNTABILITY ANCHORS:

1. Thoughts are mere electrical impulses in your brain.
2. Thoughts become things.
3. Thoughts reoccur in thought patterns.
4. Thoughts can be divided into either Effective or Ineffective Patterns.
5. Thoughts and thought patterns are malleable.
6. What we put into our mind directly impacts our mental health and vitality.
7. Embarking on a Powerful Journey Within

CHAPTER 4

HOW YOUR WORLD IS SHAPED THROUGH BELIEFS

"It is through our beliefs that we can either awaken ourselves towards future success or limit ourselves to remain in our current mindset."

– KEVIN & KELLEY KREMER

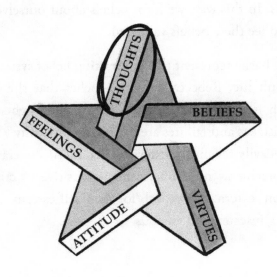

The second point on the Mindset Star is labeled beliefs. You were not born with your present beliefs. Your current beliefs weren't your birthright; they were etched into your psyche through life's myriad experiences. Consider how beliefs, especially self-beliefs, take root. Imagine being a child again, facing the intimidating roar of a parent's reprimand, "Use your head! What's wrong with you?" Confused and hurt, you ponder, "Why is he so angry?"

As a child, your survival hinges on the safety of your parents, making it unthinkable to doubt their judgment. Instinctively, you turn the blame inward, reasoning, "If my father is upset, it must be my fault. I must be inadequate." This becomes your truth, a painful interpretation of a distressing moment. With each subsequent outburst, the belief that "I am unworthy, I am not enough" is further cemented, all within the confines of your own mind.

This is the silent, invisible process of belief formation at work, shaping our self-image. As we grow, we unwittingly seek out confirmation for these beliefs, perpetuating a cycle that colors our perception of ourselves and our capabilities. All of this happens at the quantum level, only in our own heads. In this way, we form beliefs about ourselves, and then we continue to see these beliefs validated.

Rebecca and Charlie represent two contrasting belief systems and their impact on adult life. Rebecca harbors a belief that she is not good enough, which is reflected in her self-defeating thoughts: "I am not important. Mistakes and failures are bad. I am unworthy." Her sense of self-worth is heavily reliant on external validation; she craves frequent positive reinforcement from others and is sensitive to criticism. This dependency on external approval for her self-esteem likely leaves Rebecca feeling insecure and anxious.

On the other hand, Charlie embodies a belief in his inherent worth, leading to empowering thoughts like "I am important. Failures are learning opportunities. I am worthy." He finds affirmation within himself and values constructive feedback as a means for improvement. Charlie's internal source of worth and his view of effort and resilience as the keys to success likely contribute to a more positive emotional state.

Given these dynamics, Charlie is likely to experience greater happiness, more fulfilling relationships, and a more successful career. He is also more inclined to feel comfortable expressing his true self in the world. In contrast, Rebecca's reliance on external validation may hinder her happiness, relationships, career, and self-expression.

This comparison illustrates how deeply ingrained childhood beliefs can shape our adult lives. It underscores the importance of recognizing and reassessing the meanings we've attached to past experiences. The thoughts and beliefs we formed in our youth can significantly influence our current well-being and life trajectory.

Beliefs evolve from fleeting thoughts into deep-seated convictions— ideas that we hold as absolute truths. They are the product of thoughts that have been consistently reinforced by our life experiences, whether through education, family, culture, or social interactions. Beliefs wield significant influence over our mindset, carrying more weight than transient thoughts due to their repeated nature, which amplifies their impact within the quantum field of energy.

These beliefs often cluster together, forming intricate belief patterns within the mind. Gaining insight into these patterns is crucial for evaluating their soundness. You may discover that some of your most entrenched beliefs are based on outdated assumptions and interpretations. Despite this, we cling to these beliefs because they provide a sense of comfort and predictability in an otherwise unpredictable world. However, it's often more beneficial to critically assess these belief patterns and consider adopting what we term a Most Valuable Paradigm—an updated, more effective set of beliefs that better serves our current understanding and aspirations.

MOST VALUABLE PARADIGMS

In life, our discoveries often mirror those of an experienced player in a worldwide treasure hunt, as we typically uncover exactly what we seek. This 'Where's Waldo' method of discovery is not just a metaphor but is rooted in our biology. The Reticular Activating System (RAS) in our brain plays a key role in this process. It acts as a filter for incoming data, selectively seeking out evidence that confirms our pre-existing thoughts, feelings, and beliefs, thus reinforcing them in a continuous feedback loop. Over time, these reinforced cognitive and emotional patterns form paradigms—comprehensive frameworks that encompass our thought processes, emotions, and convictions.

By examining and questioning the validity of our current paradigms, we open the door to developing More Valuable Paradigms. These are refined belief systems that more effectively serve our needs and aspirations. They are the building blocks of mindsets that drive better decision-making and lead to more positive outcomes. Embracing this process of evaluation and renewal is the essence of Quantum Accountability, where we take charge of our mental and emotional narratives to shape a more fulfilling interaction with the world.

THE POWER OF I AM

Joel Osteen, in his 2016 book The Power of I Am: Two Words That Will Change Your Life Today, focuses on the transformative power of positive self-affirmation. He emphasizes the concept that what we attach to the words "I am" can shape our lives in significant ways. The phrase "I am" is not only a powerful phrase but is also essentially a declaration of who we are and who we aspire to be. When we say things like "I am blessed," "I am strong," or "I am successful," we are not just making a statement; we are invoking a vision of our future selves, and our lives tend to move in the direction of that vision.

For example, consider a student who is preparing for a challenging exam. If she consistently tells herself, "I am capable, I am intelligent, and I am prepared," she is not only boosting her confidence but also encouraging a mindset that can help her perform at her best. She begins to see herself as capable, intelligent, and prepared, which can guide her actions and decisions. In contrast, if that same student were to constantly say, "I am not smart enough, I am unprepared," she is likely to feel defeated even before taking the exam. Her self-doubt may prevent her from studying effectively or may cause anxiety that inhibits her performance.

In 2007, after studying philosophers, stoics, and personal empowerment mentors, I came to the realization of the profound impact of those two simple words, I am. This culminated in the belief that what we think, we then say to ourselves repeatedly. These patterns become what we believe and this molds our mindset. I founded a company called, "I am…". The company developed powerful, bold statements such as, I am strength, I am love, I am abundance, I am health. We created custom logo wristbands, stickers, and apparel with the 'I am' phrases.

This idea of 'I am' aligns with Carol Dweck's mindset theory, particularly the concept of a growth mindset. When people cultivate a growth mindset, they tend to embrace challenges, persist in the face of setbacks, and see effort as the pathway to mastery. Using "I am" statements can be a powerful way to reinforce this type of effective mindset.

Beliefs have a powerful impact on your reality because they are a crucial aspect of your mindset. Your beliefs shape how you view yourself, others, and the world. Those beliefs are, in turn, affected and created by your experiences, relationships, education, and culture. What you read, the places you go, the groups you are a part of, and your family and friends, also influence your beliefs. What they believe can quickly become what you believe.

From a career perspective, beliefs influence where you go to school, and which profession you decide upon. Thus, it is easy to understand why beliefs are the foundation upon which your life is built. In short, beliefs are the driving force behind who you are, what you do, and how you do it, constantly shaping and reshaping your reality.

As Dr. Wayne Dyer often emphasized, your beliefs are not just a passive part of your life, they are active and constantly shaping your reality. When you hold limiting beliefs, such as "I'm not good enough," "I can't achieve my goals," or "I'll never be successful," they can prevent you from reaching your full potential and living the life you truly desire. On the other hand, when we adopt empowering beliefs, such as "I am worthy," "I can achieve my goals," and "I am destined for success," you open yourself up to new possibilities and opportunities.

On the professional front, limiting beliefs such as, "I can't figure this out" or "I'll never be successful," stop you from trying, making it almost impossible to succeed. To practice your profession, you need more than just classroom instruction and hands-on training, you need a belief that you are capable. When you have empowering beliefs, such as "I can do it" and "I will figure it out," you give yourself new possibilities and opportunities for a better outcome.

You can begin to examine your belief system by asking yourself how you feel about a subject, question, or issue, and then listening to your answer away from other people or influences. As an example, let's examine your beliefs surrounding success. What you think is success or failure depends on the framework you've constructed. Take Joe, for instance, who has a goal for his yearly income to be $150,000. He currently makes $85,000. At the end of the following year, Joe makes $145,000. Is Joe a failure or a success? He was successful and almost doubled his income, but he failed to make his goal by $5,000. How Joe chooses to evaluate his success is up to him. It might be helpful to take a look every once in a while at the beliefs you hold and determine their validity at this point in your life. Also examine your paradigms.

Are your beliefs still serving you? Are your paradigms still serving you? Beliefs should aid you in your quests.

You might find that you still hold onto beliefs that are no longer valid, meaning they aren't helping you reach your goals. In fact, they may even be impeding your progress. Sometimes, beliefs take root from experiences you had as a child. Most of our belief systems are in fact, rooted in our childhood. They were created at a time and place by a person who you might not even recognize if you passed them on the street. You have changed tremendously since childhood. Yet, you still cling to those beliefs. Why? Because they are familiar. And as we've discussed, we find comfort in familiarity.

Beliefs can be elusive in their roots, like weeds. Scan the garden of your mindset. You will find flowers but you will also find weeds. Weeds are normal. Although your caregivers had good intentions, sometimes they passed along beliefs that may limit you. These are weeds. One area where these weeds often show up is in an individual's relationship to money. " Filthy Rich", or "Money Doesn't Grow on Trees" are two such examples of a scarcity mindset towards money. How many times as a child did you hear this or a similar ideology identifying the rich as bad and the poor as good? It most likely started as an interesting thought, the first point on the Mindset Star, then after a while it might have become ingrained on the second point of the Mindset Star, a Belief, without you noticing it. It became one of your truths that your mindset used to filter the world. The points on the mindset star are funny like that, they can morph without your awareness.

If you do have beliefs which are limiting, it is important to change those beliefs in order to attain new goals and aspirations. In evaluating your beliefs you might discover that certain beliefs serve you in your desire to reach certain goals in life, while others may be limiting you on your path to your ideal life. These are referred to as self-limiting beliefs.

SELF-LIMITING BELIEFS

It's no secret that our beliefs can limit us. These beliefs, though, may be in your subconscious and might be poisoning your progress without you even being aware. They lurk in the shadows of your mind.

Remember, as discussed in Chapter 2 regarding the Mindset Continuum, the types of mindsets that reside underneath Fixed Mindsets on the spectrum are often the result of self-limiting beliefs of varying degrees. All mindsets are based upon beliefs that have both issues and advantages. For example, a Pessimistic Mindset could plausibly be built upon the belief, "This business idea/ relationship will never work." No person in their right mind would invest time and assets into a union with someone with this self-limiting. However, the belief "I am not very smart, I have to work smarter than everyone else," could motivate someone to an advantageous habit. Similarly, the Optimistic Mindset built upon the belief, "It will all work out perfectly each and every time," might cause chaos in your mind if you experience a tragedy. But, its advantage is that it sets you up for success in difficult situations as it boosts confidence and self-esteem. Point being, beliefs can build various types of mindsets. What is essential is to understand how your beliefs are impacting your future success.

It may seem silly to understand because why would you even try if you believe you can't achieve a goal? If you are aware, you wouldn't, but most people aren't aware. For example, a limiting belief I had when I graduated from dental school was in regards to where I would choose to practice and establish my career. Having spent time in Santa Barbara, my wife and I enjoyed the community and the tranquility of the area. I had a self-limiting belief that Santa Barbara was overpopulated with dentists, and that I would have little chance of success there. We decided not to try. As I changed my mindset and shifted my belief systems over the following decade, I came to realize that I could succeed in any area of my choosing, if I have the right mindset and take the right actions towards success. To clarify, being in the right industry in the right place at the right time will have a significant impact on your level of success; however, with the right mindset and ambition, we can succeed in the place of our choosing. Have you had that same experience? Have you ever had the belief that you couldn't succeed? Was this 100% true or could it have been a limiting belief?

If you navigate life with a compass of limiting beliefs, you create self-fulfilling prophecies that are ingrained deeper and deeper in your imperfect belief system. It takes a lot of work to identify the beliefs that hold you back. But if the proof is in the pudding, or the crème brûlée, isn't it worth the risk of trying? Hey, life is meant to be lived. Life is meant to be a challenge, life is meant to be fruitful. As we've said before, go out on that limb because that is the only place you'll find the fruit.

The first step in finding the fruit is to begin to understand the belief and where it came from. Your views are shaped by your language, religion, culture, family, and friends, as well as other sources. You create thoughts about what you see, feel, hear, and experience based on your current circumstances, future expectations, and prior experiences. You make sense of the world around you, mold the information into beliefs, and use these beliefs to predict future outcomes in the things that you attempt to do.

Remember, your beliefs function as facts, meaning they are so heart-felt that you are most likely unaware of their true validity. And then, you make choices that reinforce your beliefs. But, you aren't even aware of where these beliefs came from in the first place. Neuroscientists call this confirmation bias. You could choose to call it ego, and Dr. Sigmund Freud would agree. You are feeding your Freudian ego with a misconstrued interpretation of reality. Put enough of these misconstrued beliefs together, and you've created an operating system or a map of the world that isn't the one that is going to get you to your destination.

Just like computers operate on binary codes of 1's and 0's, every person has a mental operating system, though far more nuanced and complex. Instead of simple binaries, our minds process a spectrum of inputs, akin to receiving 20,000 emails every second. While managing such a volume is daunting—we struggle with just a hundred daily emails—this system is nature's design for rapid decision-making, often bypassing conscious thought. However, this mental operating system has its constraints; it can restrict us, particularly when saddled with outdated or self-limiting beliefs. To function optimally in a constantly evolving world, it's crucial that our belief systems adapt and evolve as well.

We have a team member who was convinced she was not good at math. We watched her handle complicated transactions with money in her head. When we complimented her on her excellent math skills, she looked confused. She hadn't ever equated money with math. She most likely developed this belief sometime in her childhood and never took the time or energy to assess its validity. She never took the time to look at what was happening in the quantum realm of her mind. This was an example of a limiting belief that most likely held her back and was an impediment to her success.

So, now you know, beliefs can have a profound impact on your actions and shape your worldview. They act as the lenses through which you perceive the world, influencing your thoughts, feelings, and behaviors.

When you come upon a belief system that doesn't serve you or your road to success, it's time to change.

In the following narrative, we'll explore how a belief held by an individual—the belief that "people don't like me"—can be transformed through a simple but powerful change in behavior and perspective.

THE BELIEF: "PEOPLE DON'T LIKE ME"

Imagine an individual, let's call him Max, who carries the belief that people don't like him. This belief, deeply ingrained, has led to a self-fulfilling prophecy. Max's thoughts, feelings, attitudes, choices, and behaviors are all influenced by this self-limiting belief. He avoids social interactions, keeps to himself, and perceives every interaction with others as negative or hostile. This belief not only affects his personal life but also impacts his professional relationships. He is in a dead-career and has no real meaningful friends or a significant other.

THE CATALYST: A TRANSFORMATIVE ARTICLE

One day, Max comes across an article that catches his attention. The article discusses the idea that how you show up in the world can influence your reality. It suggests a simple experiment: say hi and smile at everyone you meet. This small behavioral change can have a ripple effect on how others respond and, consequently, on his attitude toward the world.

TAKING ACTION: SAYING HI AND SMILING

Intrigued by the article, Max decides to give it a try. He makes a conscious effort to greet people with a friendly "hello" and a warm smile, even to strangers. Initially, it feels uncomfortable. However, Max persists, recognizing that change requires effort and stepping out of his comfort zone.

THE TRANSFORMATION BEGINS: CHANGING INTERACTIONS

As Max starts saying hi and smiling more often, something remarkable begins to happen. People respond positively to these small gestures of friendliness. Co-workers return smiles, neighbors engage in conversation, and even strangers seem more approachable. The world that once felt unfriendly and unwelcoming starts to look different.

THE SHIFT IN WORLDVIEW: A NEW PERSPECTIVE EMERGES

Over time, Max's interactions and experiences shift his perspective. He realizes that his belief that "people don't like me" was, in many ways, a self-imposed limitation. By changing his behavior and opening up to positive interactions, he has allowed a different reality to emerge.

A POSITIVE FEEDBACK LOOP: REINFORCING NEW BELIEFS

As Max experiences more positive interactions and begins to see the world in a more positive light, his belief system undergoes a profound transformation. He starts to believe that people can be friendly and welcoming. This newfound belief further reinforces his positive actions and interactions, creating a self-reinforcing cycle. This is another example of what Psychologists term Confirmation Bias, but this time it is from a negative side of the continuum.

THE RIPPLE EFFECT: IMPACT ON RELATIONSHIPS AND SUCCESS

The impact of this transformation extends beyond Max's personal interactions. In the workplace, he becomes more approachable and collaborative, leading to improved professional relationships and opportunities. In his personal life, his social circle expands, and he develops deeper connections with others.

APPLY IT

Be the subject in your own experiment by invoking two different scenarios. The next time you go to the grocery store, smile and focus on being friendly and engaging with the world around you. Hold the belief, "I am an out-going person in a warm, friendly world." See what happens.

The next time you go to the same store, keep quiet, don't make eye contact, and ignore anyone who strikes up a conversation. Hold the belief "I am an introvert in a dangerous, cold world." See what happens. These two vastly different circumstances will result in two vastly different realities of the same world.

This is just one example of how beliefs affect your reality. This is why it is important to examine beliefs because, as you learn and grow, you will often find thoughts no longer serve you. If you were raised in a strict household, you might have learned not to speak up, which kept you safe and out of trouble with your parents. However, that belief of staying silent in your new job will work against you. Coworkers might find you cold and not able to contribute, and your employer might take your silence for disinterest.

Examples such as these illustrate why it is essential to sit down and look at beliefs from time to time. Become aware of beliefs that are no longer helpful, which are holding you back, so that you can live the best possible life. This is the work of Quantum Accountability, taking responsibility for what is going on under the surface and actively working to change.

This is particularly important to do after a significant life event such as a career change, a divorce, a death, or a move. When you experience periods of high emotion, you can create limiting beliefs to protect yourself both emotionally and physically. For example, if a business associate decides to dissolve a partnership, you might think: "I am not able to work efficiently with others. I shouldn't pursue other business partnerships."

The power of our beliefs to shape our reality cannot be overstated. By consciously choosing to engage with the world through different lenses, we can directly observe how our perceptions influence our experiences. This self-experimentation serves as a vivid reminder of the importance of regularly evaluating and updating our beliefs to align with who we are and who we aspire to be.

As we navigate life's inevitable changes and challenges, embracing this process of reflection and adaptation allows us to overcome self-imposed limitations and move forward with greater confidence, openness, and resilience. By taking charge of our beliefs, we empower ourselves to create a more fulfilling and positive life, demonstrating the transformative potential of Quantum Accountability in action.

Fundamentally, your reality is shaped by your beliefs and actions. These elements interact to form the experiences and outcomes you encounter on a daily basis. The experiments you conduct in your daily life, whether consciously or unconsciously, demonstrate the profound impact your mindset has on your experience of the world. By choosing to adopt a belief, you set the stage for how you interact with your environment and, in turn, how it responds to you. The beliefs you hold act as a lens through which you perceive your surroundings and your actions. It is through the deliberate examination and transformation of your beliefs, especially after life-altering events, that you can reshape your world, fostering a reality that reflects your true aspirations and potential. By embracing this dynamic interplay of belief and action in the quantum realm, you can unlock the power to sculpt a life that resonates with your deepest desires, ensuring that you are not merely a product of your past but an architect of your future.

As we navigate through life's transitions and challenges, it becomes imperative to reassess and recalibrate our belief systems, especially those that are self-limiting. These beliefs, often formed during periods of vulnerability, can significantly hinder our progress and fulfillment. By identifying and actively challenging these restrictive thoughts, we empower ourselves to shed unnecessary burdens and embrace a more efficient, productive mindset. This process of introspection and adjustment is not just about discarding outdated beliefs but also about fostering new, supportive ones that align with our current aspirations and circumstances. Ultimately, the journey to overcoming self-limiting beliefs is a continuous one, requiring vigilance and commitment to personal growth and resilience.

LIMITING VERSUS EMPOWERING BELIEFS

As we have discussed, limiting beliefs hinder progress and lead to self-sabotage. Limiting beliefs often stem from a mindset that falls below the Fixed Mindset on the Mindset Continuum. Limiting Beliefs can significantly impact all areas of your life by sabotaging your mindset. They are an energy drain from a quantum standpoint as they hinder self-esteem and lessen our abundance in life. Limiting beliefs sometimes result from subconscious thoughts and thought patterns. Here is some of the damage Limiting Beliefs can cause:

- **Tainting Life Experiences** - If you believe roller coasters are dangerous, you may be missing out on thrilling experiences.
- **Reduced Efficiency** - If you believe that college isn't financially feasible, but you dream of earning your MBA, this may lead you to wasting time and money on courses that aren't on the direct path to your graduate-level degree goal.
- **Unintentional Harm** - Limiting beliefs can be contagious. Being around Debbie-Downer who openly shares your Limiting Beliefs perpetuates the cycle of self-imposed constraints.
- **Self-Esteem and Mindset** - The belief you are not good enough leads to anxiety, added stress, low self-esteem, and a defeatist attitude. We will continue this discussion of attitudes in Chapter 7.
- **Communication and Performance** - If you believe public speaking is scary, your career may be impacted, especially if your success depends upon presenting opportunities to potential clients, for example.

EXAMPLES OF EMPOWERING BELIEFS

It is beneficial to become aware of and recognize the difference between self-limiting and empowering beliefs. This seems easy, but remember, you have had your beliefs for as long as you can remember, and most of them reside in your unconscious mind, at the Quantum level.

Contrary to what Debbie-Downer believes, the good news is it is just as easy to have a Limiting Belief as it is an Empowering Belief. Both require the same amount of mental energy on a quantum level. Empowering Beliefs influence behaviors by boosting confidence, motivation, and performance. Here are a few examples of Empowering Beliefs that you can adopt:

- I am someone who tries new things.
- I am persistent.
- I am excited for what is ahead.
- I am responsible for the life I create.
- I am stronger than I think I am.
- I am a powerful creation.
- I am someone who is always learning new skills.
- I am open to taking risks.
- I am someone who improves myself daily.
- It's always possible to begin again.
- I can.
- I will find a way. I will succeed.

DAILY RITUALS TO CREATE EMPOWERING BELIEFS

One of the most potent things about personal beliefs is that we have the ability to change them. We are not stuck with the beliefs we have been taught or have adopted throughout our lives. We can let go of limiting beliefs and replace them with empowering ones. This is not always an easy process, and it may take time and effort, but it is possible.

First, surround yourself with Empowering Beliefs. Read the list of Empowering Beliefs above and choose a few that speak to you. The energy on a quantum level will then manifest itself into physiological reactions. Print out these beliefs and display them around your house, office, car—anywhere you'll see and read them repeatedly. Remember, the brain will automatically read anything it comes into contact with, so even if you aren't consciously reading the statements, your brain is!

Another way to change our personal beliefs is through the power of affirmations. Affirmations are positive statements that we repeat to ourselves regularly. Science tells us that we should repeat these affirmations at least three times a day. They can be used to reinforce new beliefs or to counteract limiting beliefs. For example, if we want to adopt the belief that "I am worthy," we can repeat the affirmation "I am worthy" to ourselves in the rearview mirror before we head off to work. Affirmations are a great way to start the day.

You could also do visualization. Visualization involves creating a mental image of what we want to achieve and then focusing on that image as if it were already real. If you want to adopt the belief, "I can achieve my goals," you can visualize yourself reaching your goals and focus on how you feel in that moment. It's all about the feeling, as the feeling you get when you visualize is what solidifies the connection between belief and action, all on the quantum level.

Celebrating progress is another effective method for changing limiting beliefs to empowering beliefs. Small wins celebrated lead to BIG victories. When you take time to recognize success, you positively reinforce the connection between your beliefs and your actions. This is called classical conditioning, and on the quantum level, it reflects the same principle as Pavlov's dog salivating. It will motivate your mind for future success.

And finally, surrounding yourself with positive and supportive people can also help change personal beliefs. If we surround ourselves with people who believe in and support us, we are more likely to adopt similar empowering beliefs. Proximity is powerful. At the end of the day, you are accountable for your beliefs.

ACCOUNTABILITY ANCHORS:

1. Every belief you have is learned through experience.
2. Beliefs can limit us.
3. Beliefs can empower us.
4. Beliefs should be examined consistently and changed if needed.
5. Most Valuable Paradigms effectively create mindsets, influence choices, and therefore positively shape outcomes.

CHAPTER 5

FEELINGS-ASSIGNING MEANING TO YOUR EMOTIONS

"Our feelings are our most genuine paths to knowledge."

– AUDRE LORDE

"When you do things from your soul, you feel a river moving in you, a joy."

– RUMI

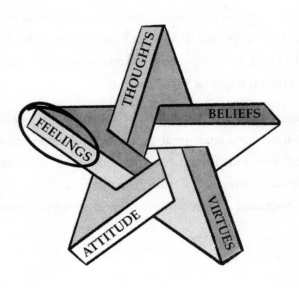

Emotions and feelings play a crucial role in understanding ourselves and the world around us. Emotions are not just reactions to our experiences but are also profound sources of insight and wisdom. This perspective values emotional intelligence by recognizing that the meaning we give to our emotions can guide us to deeper truths about our personal realities, relationships, and life's circumstances.

Emotions are often the first response to situations and people. They can alert us to what matters most to us, signaling our values, fears, desires, and boundaries. Our feelings represent our response to the attitudes and actions of others. When we have feelings of comfort and security, we feel open. When we have feelings of discomfort, we resist.

Embracing emotions as valid and valuable tools for navigating life, rather than dismissing them as irrational or secondary to logic, we can reflect on our emotional experiences. Emotional awareness is a pathway to self-knowledge and wisdom, both in how we respond to others and how others respond to us.

The distinction between emotions and feelings is an important one to understand. Emotions are the physiological experiences or states of awareness that arise subconsciously in response to a significant event or stimulus. They originate in various brain regions like the amygdala and are considered instinctual and unconscious reactions - the body's immediate, visceral response to a situation.

Feelings, on the other hand, are the conscious awareness and interpretation of those emotional experiences. When the brain assigns meaning and conscious thought to the underlying emotion, the result is the experience of a feeling. Emotions come first, before the conscious experience of feelings. The emotion triggers a physiological response, which is then processed and given meaning by the higher cognitive functions of the brain, resulting in the felt sense of the feeling.

Emotions are more basic, universal, and tied to survival instincts, like the 6 basic emotions identified by Paul Ekman (happiness, sadness, fear, disgust, anger, surprise). Feelings, however, are more complex, nuanced, and shaped by individual experiences, culture, and beliefs. Happiness, joy, and contentment are examples of positive, pleasant feelings that often arise from experiences of closeness, safety, and sensory pleasure. Words like love, relief, amusement, and pride can be used to further describe these uplifting emotional states. In contrast, sadness is a more somber feeling that may stem from loss, rejection, or disappointment. Individuals experiencing sadness may use words like lonely, heartbroken, gloomy, hopeless, or miserable to convey their emotional state. Anger is an intense feeling that can compel someone to fight back or protect themselves. Feelings of irritation, rage, resentment, or indignation fall under the category of anger. Fear and anxiety are feelings one can experience to perceived threats or uncertainty. Words like terror, panic, alarm, and worry are used to articulate these uneasy, apprehensive feelings. Disgust, on the other hand, is a feeling of revulsion, contempt, or strong dislike, often directed at something deemed unpleasant or offensive. Feelings like confusion, doubt, and indifference represent more neutral or ambiguous states, where someone may feel uncertain, disinterested, or unsure of how to interpret their internal experience.

While emotions are involuntary and instinctual, feelings can be more actively regulated and managed through practices like emotional intelligence. which we will discuss in chapter 15 and self-awareness. Understanding this distinction between the physiological experience of emotions and the conscious awareness of feelings can greatly enhance your understanding and ability to navigate this human experience and live a fulfilling life.

EMOTIONS BECOME FEELINGS

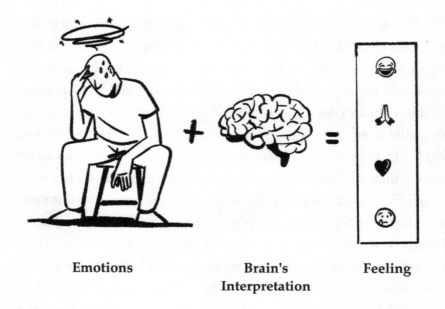

| Emotions | Brain's Interpretation | Feeling |

The fable of "The North Wind and the Sun," is attributed to the famous storyteller, Aesop. It illustrates the power of the comfortable feelings of gentleness and persuasion over the uncomfortable feeling of force. In the fable, the North Wind and the Sun argue over who is the strongest. They see a traveler walking on the road and decide to settle their dispute by seeing who can make the traveler remove his cloak. The North Wind blows as hard as he can, but the traveler only wraps his cloak tighter to keep warm against the cold wind. Then, the Sun gently shines its warm rays, and as the day grows warmer, the traveler feels comfortable and willingly removes his cloak.

The moral of the story is that kindness and gentle persuasion are more effective than force. This fable teaches us about feelings in response to the attitudes and actions of others. Our approach can influence others' emotions, feelings, and behaviors. Creating feelings of comfort and security in others can lead to openness and change, whereas instilling feelings of attack and adversity can cause resistance.

People don't remember what you do or say. People remember how you make them feel. Feelings come from thoughts and thoughts come from feelings. It's a bi-directional relationship. If you want to change your feelings, change your thoughts or your interpretation of those thoughts. And this brings us to the next point on the Mindset Star, Feelings.

Feelings are an essential part of what makes us human. Your unconscious thoughts are reflected in your body as emotions. Emotions are physiological responses to your mind that create a feedback loop between your thoughts and your physiological reactions. Your brain then interprets the reasoning behind your bodily sensations and creates a label to name the feeling. All of this happens on the quantum level without your awareness.

Your brain uses sensory input clues: sights, sounds, tastes, smells, touch from your environment as well as intuition, and scans itself for past memories or future expectations in order to label what it is you are feeling. These feelings can manifest in various ways:

- **Anxiety**: lump in your throat, trembling, butterflies in your stomach, sweating, shortness of breath, feeling weak in the knees
- **Anger**: Hot or flushed face, fists of rage, clenched jaw, shaking, trembling, increased heart rate
- **Joy**: lightness in your step, butterflies in your stomach, fast breathing
- **Sadness**: heartache, heaviness or tightness in your chest, fatigue, crying, quivering upper lip
- **Shame**: lowered eye-gaze, sunken body posture, failure to look others in the eyes

- **Fear**: Dizziness, weakness in legs, goosebumps, fast breathing and heart rate, sweaty palms

A small family-owned business was thrown into disarray when their dedicated office assistant, Sarah, abruptly quit without notice. Mr. Smith, the owner, relied on Sarah for everything from scheduling appointments to managing paperwork. It was a busy Wednesday morning when she stormed into his office and dropped the letter of resignation on his desk. Mr. Smith read the letter and he began to feel nauseous. His heart rate increased to 90 beats a minute and he began to sweat intensely. Mr. Smith remembered the last time this had happened two years ago with Mary, and it took him weeks to find a replacement who also didn't work out. His mind then wandered to his Friday afternoon appointment with Mr. Johnson. Mr. Johnson was taken with Sarah, would he lose this important client as soon as he found out that Sarah was leaving? He wondered if she was enticed by his competitor and if she would share everything he had taught her with that dastardly man.

Mr. Smith's emotional reactions included nausea, increased heart rate, and increased sweating. His brain then interpreted his emotional response by looking for sensory clues, obviously the letter of resignation, past experiences, and future possibilities. Taking all this information into consideration, Mr. Smith could then label his feelings: possibly, fear, regret, anxiety and stress. This is what is known as the mind-body connection. It starts on the quantum level and then manifests in outward signals.

HOW TO CONNECT EMOTIONS AND BODY SENSATIONS

When you go about your day, you may start to become aware of how your body is reacting to certain circumstances and or people. You may even notice that these circumstances or people create certain feelings. Learn to pause and interrupt by taking a moment to reflect when noticing an emotional response. Take a few deep breaths and know that these are normal bodily reactions. Next, explore your emotional response by conducting a body scan to identify tension or discomfort, starting from your head down to your toes. Observe which parts of your body are most affected and which are less affected. Next, label the emotional response. What exactly are you feeling? Focus on your body's reactions. For example, reframing your thoughts from "I am stressed" to "I feel butterflies in my stomach" helps in understanding reactions accurately.

Our mind-body connection takes what's happening at the quantum level in our minds and broadcasts it via our bodily responses. It's the outward signs of inward happenings. The cardiovascular, musculoskeletal, neuroendocrine, and autonomic nervous system can all be affected. For instance, an increase in adrenaline and cortisol levels can be triggered by thoughts. Entering a haunted house causes increased heart rate and breathing, sweaty palms, and increased alertness. You are on the lookout for Dracula as he may lunge at you from the dark shadows at any moment. After the bodily response, your brain then intercepts the incoming sensory information, scans for past memories or possible future expectations and then may label your response as fear. Fear is the feeling.

Here is a list of common feelings which can vary in both intensity and duration

1. **Enjoyment:** happiness, love, relief, contentment, amusement, joy, pride, excitement, peace, satisfaction.
2. **Sadness:** lonely, heartbroken, gloomy, disappointed, hopeless, grieved, unhappy, lost, troubled, resigned, miserable.

3. **Anger:** dislike, revulsion, loathing, disapproving, offended, horrified, uncomfortable, nauseated, disturbed, withdrawn, aversion.
4. **Fear:** anxiety that looks like anger at first, racing heart. dry mouth, pale skin.
5. **Happiness:** light feeling in chest, energetic overall, flushed skin.
6. **Disgust:** dislike, revulsion, loathing, disapproving, offended, horrified.

In conclusion, the profound interplay between our emotions and bodily sensations underscores the essential nature of the mind-body connection. This dynamic relationship highlights how our mental states can significantly influence physical responses, and vice versa. By becoming more attuned to the signals our bodies send in response to emotional stimuli, we can gain deeper insights into our overall health and well-being. This awareness not only helps us manage stress and emotional challenges more effectively but also empowers us to live more harmoniously within our bodies. Recognizing and respecting this connection is crucial for fostering a balanced and healthy life, where mind and body work together seamlessly to enhance our human experience.

THE FEELINGS PLAYGROUND

We choose to feel. We unconsciously pick only three to four feelings. Of all the feelings we could choose to experience in life's playground, we limit ourselves. These three or four feelings create your feelings' addiction. Face it, you receive a pleasurable feeling by choosing to feel the same feelings. It's a cycle and it's a trade-off, you'd rather know what you're going to feel than leave it up to the fates. On the quantum level, you fear you could feel much worse than you do right now. You have a tendency to like familiarity.

This is what we call the **Feelings Playground**. Your three or four chosen feelings are the swings, slides, and tetherballs of the playground. This is where you feel safe to play. Of all the equipment to try out on the playground, your addiction encourages you to use the same equipment by positively reinforcing your choices. Occasionally, we will venture over to the Monkey Bars, and we experience a new feeling. This is the toe-tip test in the pool of life. How does it feel? Warm, like you want to dive in and stay awhile? Or cold and uninviting like you'll pass? We try out the new feelings, but on some level it doesn't seem familiar, so we head back over to the slide where we feel safe.

We move towards circumstances, people, and conditions in life that make us feel safe. We like the slide because we know what to expect each and every time. We may even remain in circumstances that produce uncomfortable feelings, like abusive relationships. We often choose toxic familiarity over untoxic unfamiliarity in our lives for this very reason. This idea is closely related to the psychological theory of hedonic adaptation, which proposes that people tend to return to a relatively stable level of happiness despite major positive or negative changes in their life circumstances. On a quantum level we are attracted to safety and familiarity, so unless we take accountability and action to change that energy pattern, we will remain in the addiction.

A better strategy is to determine which feelings you like and which you don't like. Know that, at first, any new feelings will be uncomfortable and that your mind will try to get you to fall back into the addiction. But when you take accountability and learn to actively seek out bigger and better feelings, you can begin to move towards the feelings you want to feel more of.

To move towards the feelings we want, it's essential to actively be aware of our circumstances and thoughts. There are several strategies for achieving this goal. First, identify and reduce triggers by recognizing situations or thoughts that initiate negative feelings and work on strategies to reduce their impact. This might involve changing your environment, avoiding certain stressors, or reframing your thoughts from them. Tune into physical symptoms by paying attention to how your body responds to different feelings. Physical awareness can be a cue to recognize and address your feelings early on.

Engage in positive self-talk by challenging negative thought patterns and replacing them with positive affirmations. This can help shift your mindset at the quantum level. Practice mindfulness by being present in the moment and accepting your thoughts and feelings without judgment. Techniques like meditation, deep breathing, and journaling can enhance mindfulness and help you become more aware and accepting of your emotions. Develop emotional intelligence by working on understanding and managing your feelings, as well as recognizing and responding to the emotions and feelings of others. This can improve relationships and your ability to navigate emotional situations. Cultivate gratitude by focusing on the positive aspects of your life and expressing gratitude for them. Keeping a gratitude journal or sharing what you're thankful for with others can boost your mood and overall well-being. Connect with others by building and maintaining supportive relationships. Sharing your feelings with trusted friends or family members can provide comfort, perspective, and a sense of connection.

Seek professional help if needed. If you find it challenging to manage your feelings, or if they're significantly impacting your life, consider seeking support from a mental health professional. Therapies like Cognitive Behavioral Therapy (CBT) and Dialectical Behavior Therapy (DBT) can be effective in teaching regulation skills. Prioritize self-care by taking time for activities that relax and rejuvenate you. This could include hobbies, spending time in nature, or simply taking a few moments to breathe and relax each day.

And last but not least, exercise regularly. Science proves that physical activity can significantly impact your mood and emotional well-being. Find an activity you enjoy and make it a regular part of your routine.

By implementing these strategies, you are taking accountability for your feelings. You can actively work towards experiencing more positive feelings and improving your overall mindset in the quantum realm.

We put out into the world what we feel. Gracious people grace people. Angry people anger people. Hurt people hurt people. What are the feelings you want to feel and experience in the world?

In life, you yearn for a feeling. It's not the promotion or the sports car, the attractive partner or the luxurious life you truly crave, it's the feeling you think you'll experience when you get the promotion, the sports car, the attractive partner, or the luxury.

Emotions can either enhance or impair your cognitive capacities, with positive feelings boosting creativity, focus, and social aptitude, while negative or "uncomfortable" emotions hinder performance and well-being. However, it's important to recognize that feelings themselves are neither inherently good nor bad, they are simply messengers that communicate the state of your internal landscape.

Research indicates that how we perceive and respond to these uncomfortable feelings can significantly impact our overall health and happiness. Rather than suppressing or ignoring them, the healthier approach is to acknowledge these signals and learn from them. By accepting and identifying your emotions, you can gain valuable insights into your internal quantum state, using these physical sensations as diagnostic tools to better understand yourself.

Embracing this perspective empowers you to harness the power of your emotions, leveraging positive feelings to enhance cognitive performance, while using uncomfortable emotions as opportunities for growth and self-discovery. By attuning to the wisdom of your inner world, you can navigate life's ebbs and flows with greater clarity, resilience, and fulfillment.

NEGATIVITY BIAS

The Negativity Bias, a well-documented phenomenon, explains why negative feelings often register more intensely than positive feelings. This tendency of the brain to prioritize and respond more strongly to negative events or emotions has its roots in our evolutionary past.

Certain brain regions, such as the right inferior frontal/insular cortex and the amygdala, exhibit heightened activity when processing negative stimuli compared to positive ones. From a social perspective, this makes sense, emotions like grief and pain were perceived as more threatening, prompting a greater focus on addressing these uncomfortable feelings over positive ones like happiness. After all, our ancestors were constantly on the lookout for potential dangers, like predators or hazardous environments. This survival instinct hardwired the brain to register negative signals more acutely, as they signaled the need for immediate action to ensure safety.

While this Negativity Bias serves an important purpose in our evolutionary history, it can also lead to an imbalance in how we process and respond to the full spectrum of human emotions in the modern world. Understanding the neurological and social roots of this bias can help us cultivate a more balanced perspective, allowing us to navigate both positive and negative feelings with greater awareness and resilience.

AN ENTREPRENEUR'S JOURNEY AND FEELINGS

The entrepreneurial journey is a rollercoaster of feelings, impacting founders at every age and stage. This emotional landscape can test your commitment and resilience, as entrepreneurs typically navigate four distinct phases:

1. **The Busy Phase:** Entrepreneurs often start with a sense of exhilaration and anticipation, tackling your to-do lists with enthusiasm.
2. **The Second Thoughts Phase:** As the initial momentum wanes, self-doubt and a dimming of your entrepreneurial flame can set in.
3. **The Self-Doubt Phase:** Feelings of loneliness and being overcommitted characterize this stage, accompanied by anxiety, frustration, and even burnout.
4. **The Been There, Done That Phase:** The journey culminates in either a triumphant mindset of "I Came, I Saw, I Conquered" or a rueful mindset of "What the Hell was I Thinking?" —or perhaps a mix of both.

This entrepreneurial marathon (not a sprint) underscores the profound emotional toll that can influence decision-making, motivation, and overall well-being. Research emphasizes the importance of understanding and managing these feelings. Entrepreneurial passion can fuel innovation while feelings like joy and fear affect risk tolerance.

Navigating the emotional rollercoaster of entrepreneurship requires resilience, self-awareness, and a willingness to embrace the full spectrum of human experiences. By acknowledging and addressing these emotional challenges, entrepreneurs can harness the power of their feelings to drive their ventures forward with greater clarity, purpose, and fortitude.

ACCOUNTABILITY ANCHORS:

1. Your brain processes sensory inputs—sights, sounds, tastes, smells, and touch—along with intuition, to identify your feelings based on past memories and future expectations.
2. We tend to only feel 3-4 feelings.
3. In life, you yearn for a feeling.
4. We put out into the world what we feel.
5. Negative feelings are often felt more intensely than positive feelings due to a phenomenon known as the Negativity Bias.

CHAPTER 6

EMBRACING YOUR VIRTUES FOR A FULFILLING LIFE

Be more concerned with your character than your reputation, because your character is what you really are, while your reputation is merely what others think you are.

– JOHN WOODEN

Your character is determined by the virtues you hold near and dear to your heart. John Wooden, the famous 'Wizard of Westwood', was arguably known as much for his motivational words and wisdom off the court as he was for his ability to win championships on it. He preached the virtues of simplicity, patience, and character building; and his pyramid of success has been used in board rooms and locker rooms alike. He inspired former players, including Kareem Abdul-Jabbar and Bill Walton, but his motivational words reached beyond the stands, too, influencing the lives of many more. Copies of the Pyramid of Success hang in our office and in our garage as a reminder to stay true to our virtues.

Virtues—derived from the Latin word, "virtus"—encompasses the qualities of moral excellence, social grace, and intellectual prowess. Virtues are traits of excellence and are considered the building blocks of humanity. Virtues aid us in choosing actions that uphold moral standards and in doing what is right, even in challenging situations. They motivate us to choose the right action at the right time in the right manner.

Philosophers like Aristotle and Kant researched and wrote on virtues extensively. Aristotle looked at virtues as "excellences at being human" and identified intellectual virtues like knowledge and wisdom. Kant emphasized that true virtue lies in behaving according to moral principles rather than mere benevolence or sympathy. Virtues help us to make ethical decisions and live a life aligned with high moral standards. Virtues represent qualities that embody moral excellence, social grace, and intellectual acumen. Aligning your behaviors with your virtues is called being virtuous. When you are in alignment, you will experience fulfillment, inner peace, and a sense of purpose in life.

Virtues exist whether we recognize them or not—they are part of our mindset. When we make choices or decisions that align with our virtues, we feel at ease. However, if our choices conflict with our virtues, we experience discomfort or even a sense of chaos. Have you ever found yourself influenced by a group or someone important to you whose values differed from your own? In such situations, you likely felt an unsettling feeling, as your actions did not reflect your true virtues.

This experience is common—we've all encountered moments where we've compromised our principles to appease others—but these instances leave us with an uncomfortable internal discord, as our behaviors do not match our core beliefs. Recognizing this dynamic is the first step towards cultivating greater self-awareness and integrity in our decision-making. By staying attuned to the virtues that guide us, we can make choices that foster a sense of alignment and authenticity, rather than dissonance.

Knowing your virtues empowers you to make wiser choices in your relationships, friendships, and work environments, ensuring alignment with your core values. Accountability is about understanding who you are, what you value, and then aligning yourself accordingly. When you are clear on your principles, you can use them as a guiding compass to make better decisions about how, where, when, and with whom you share your life. These values can inform the type of job or career path you pursue, whether to start your own business or seek alternative employment. Being accountable means recognizing your values and then choosing to work, live, love, and play in an environment that reflects your authentic self.

By cultivating this self-awareness and integrity, you can create a life that is truly in harmony with your deepest beliefs and aspirations. Aligning your choices, relationships, and professional pursuits with your virtues fosters a profound sense of fulfillment, as you navigate the world as your genuine, unapologetic self.

While virtues are generally stable throughout our lifetime, they can evolve as we encounter new life experiences. Falling in love, having a child, or adopting a pet may shift our priorities from success to family, for instance. Regardless of whether our virtues remain constant or change, the first step is to identify them so we can consciously align our lives accordingly.

THE BIRTH OF BENJAMIN FRANKLIN'S 13 VIRTUES

Benjamin Franklin, one of America's Founding Fathers, was a dedicated practitioner of self-improvement. He developed a personal code of conduct comprising thirteen virtues, which he diligently followed to enhance his character and lead a more virtuous life. Franklin's practice of defining, executing, tracking, and reflecting upon his virtues played a pivotal role in his ability to align his actions with his ideals.

This example underscores the importance of self-awareness and intentionality when it comes to our values. By taking the time to identify our current virtues, we can then make conscious choices to ensure our lives are in harmony with these guiding principles, even as they may shift over time. This alignment between our ideals and our actions is the essence of living with integrity and purpose.

A QUEST FOR MORAL EXCELLENCE

In his autobiography, Benjamin Franklin outlined his journey toward moral excellence and personal growth. Recognizing the essential role of virtue in achieving success and happiness, he decided to focus on cultivating thirteen specific virtues, cycling through them one per week.

DEFINING VIRTUES AND ESTABLISHING A PLAN

Franklin meticulously defined each virtue to ensure a clear understanding of his aspirations. For instance, he defined "temperance" as "Eat not to dullness, drink not to elevation." He then created a chart with the virtues listed and a column for each day of the week, adding a short description next to each to serve as a daily reminder.

TRACKING PROGRESS: THE SCORECARD

One of the most ingenious aspects of Franklin's approach was his use of a scorecard. Each evening, he would reflect on his actions and mark his progress for each virtue, giving himself a checkmark for a successful day and a cross for a shortcoming. This immediate feedback fostered accountability and provided a visual representation of his commitment to self-improvement.

DISCIPLINE AND REFLECTION: THE KEYS TO MASTERY

Franklin's practice demanded discipline and self-control. By consistently reviewing his scorecard, he honed his ability to align his actions with his ideals, recognizing patterns and making necessary adjustments through daily reflection.

THE RIPPLE EFFECT: IMPACT ON CHARACTER AND SUCCESS

As Franklin persisted in his virtue practice, he found that it not only improved his character but also contributed to his success in various aspects of life. His commitment to frugality and industry, for instance, fueled his entrepreneurial and inventive achievements.

THE LEGACY OF FRANKLIN'S VIRTUE PRACTICE

Benjamin Franklin's dedication to aligning his actions with his ideals serves as an enduring inspiration for personal growth and moral excellence. His life and approach continue to remind us that the path to self-improvement begins with a commitment to conscious and continuous effort.

ARISTOTLE'S 12 VIRTUES

Aristotle is one of the best-known Greek philosophers and one of the greatest contributors to philosophical thought in all of history. In his work, he named morality and intellect as the main categories of virtues—categories he further broke down into what he judged were the 12 most important virtues. He emphasized the need to exercise each of the virtues in moderation to avoid deficiencies and excesses. His list of virtues includes:

- Courage – including valor and bravery
- Temperance – restraint and controlling one's self
- Liberality – generosity to others
- Magnificence – spending great sums for honor's sake
- Pride – ambition, worthy of great things
- Magnanimity – healthy belief in one's own value
- Good Temper – keeping a level head, patient
- Friendliness – sociable to others
- Truthfulness – being straightforward and honest
- Wit – a sense of humor and joy

- Modesty – neither shy nor shameless
- Justice – having a fair mind and a sense of right and wrong

THE 5 VIRTUES OF CONFUCIUS

Just like the Greeks, the Chinese also came up with a list of philosophical virtues that humans can adapt to live a better life while minding the needs of others around them. Confucius, a Chinese philosopher, focused on morality and correctness in his work. He came up with a list of five virtues. These included:

- Ren – charity, and humility
- Yi – honesty
- Zhi – knowledge, and wisdom
- Xin – faithfulness
- Li – politeness, and propriety

Both philosophers emphasized the need to strike a balance when adapting these moral principles. They both believed that having too much or too little of a virtue could be dangerous. For instance, too much magnificence can lead to vulgarity, while too little of it can cause pettiness.

Franklin, Aristotle, and Confucius wrote about the importance of virtues because they recognized that virtues are fundamental to the development of moral character and the functioning of a harmonious society. Each of these thinkers approached virtues from slightly different cultural and philosophical perspectives, but they shared a common belief in the essential role of virtues in cultivating personal and communal well-being.

Franklin's interest in virtues was practical and aimed at self-improvement and societal benefit. He famously developed a list of thirteen virtues, including temperance, silence, order, and humility, which he practiced methodically. Franklin believed that cultivating these virtues would lead to personal moral improvement and contribute to a more virtuous and efficient society. Aristotle's discussion of virtues is central to his ethical philosophy, which posits that virtues are qualities that lead to good living and are crucial for achieving eudaimonia, or flourishing. He believed that virtues, such as courage, justice, and temperance, are means between extremes of deficiency and excess, and they enable individuals to perform their functions effectively.

Virtues for Aristotle are not only about personal excellence but also about contributing to the community's welfare, making them essential for a well-functioning society.And lastly for Confucius, virtues were integral to his vision of social harmony and proper governance. He emphasized virtues like benevolence, righteousness, propriety, wisdom, and trustworthiness as necessary for maintaining order and ensuring effective leadership.

Confucius believed that a virtuous leader serves as a moral exemplar, inspiring virtuous behavior in others, which is crucial for the stability and moral integrity of the state. His teachings suggest that the cultivation of personal virtues is directly linked to the broader societal good. These thinkers underscored that virtues are not merely personal traits but are essential for the overall health and functioning of society, reflecting a deep understanding of the interconnection between individual character and communal life. Which of these philosophical paradigms aligns best with your view of virtues? To answer this important question, let's first identify your virtues.

IDENTIFYING YOUR VIRTUES

You can begin to identify your virtues by looking at this list of common virtues and circling the 10 that you are most in alignment with. Please note, you can add a virtue if you don't see it on this limited list.

1. Acceptance
2. Adventure
3. Assertiveness
4. Authenticity
5. Beauty
6. Caring
7. Cleanliness
8. Commitment
9. Compassion
10. Contentment
11. Courage
12. Creativity
13. Determination
14. Diligence
15. Empathy
16. Endurance
17. Faithfulness
18. Family
19. Flexibility
20. Forgiveness
21. Friendliness
22. Generosity
23. Grace
24. Gratitude
25. Harmony
26. Honesty
27. Hope
28. Humility
29. Independence
30. Initiative
31. Integrity
32. Joyfulness
33. Justice
34. Kindness
35. Love
36. Loyalty
37. Mercy
38. Mindfulness
39. Moderation
40. Modesty
41. Openness
42. Optimism
43. Patience
44. Peacefulness

45. Perseverance
46. Purposefulness
47. Reverence
48. Resilience
49. Respect
50. Responsibility
51. Righteousness
52. Self-discipline
53. Service
54. Sincerity
55. Tact
56. Temperance
57. Tenacious
58. Thankfulness
59. Tolerance
60. Trust
61. Truthfulness
62. Understanding
63. Unity
64. Vision
65. Wisdom
66. Wonder
67. Zeal

Next, narrow down your top values to five. Put an asterisk (*) next to those five virtues. If you find that some of the virtues you chose are too similar, go back and choose another. Your quest is to choose five distinct virtues.

Knowing your virtues can help you make decisions that ensure that creating the life of your dreams aligns you with who you are and what matters to you. You can then approach your life with better tools and clearly figure out what is best for you in your current situation and your future happiness and satisfaction.

The connection to The Abundance Continuum lies in the application of an abundance mindset to personal development. Franklin's virtue scorecard reflects an abundance or growth mindset in that it acknowledges the potential for personal change and improvement. Instead of seeing his character and moral standing as fixed, Franklin believed he could improve himself by cultivating his virtues. His scorecard is a tangible manifestation of this belief.

In a fixed mindset, a person might believe their virtues (or lack thereof) are inherent traits that cannot be changed. But with a growth mindset, as both Franklin and Dweck advocate, we understand that with effort, practice, and perseverance, they can develop and improve their character and moral conduct. The process of marking one's progress or regress in living by these virtues encourages self-awareness and a commitment to personal growth, which aligns with the principles of a growth mindset. However, it's also crucial to note that perfection is not the aim, but rather continuous growth and development. Both Franklin and Dweck emphasize the importance of learning from failures, seeing them not as evidence of unchangeable inadequacy but as opportunities for growth and learning.

GUARDRAILS

It's one thing to get in alignment and another to stay in alignment; distractions, choices, and experiences bring us out of alignment. When we are out of alignment, we are affected mentally, emotionally, spiritually, and physically. But staying in alignment does not have to be complicated. If you value the virtue of creativity, for example, adding art practice into your daily life can be as simple as color-coding appointments and tasks in your planner. You don't always need to make big splashes or huge changes; you can find simple ways to honor and include your virtues in your daily life.

One of the ways to help us stay in alignment with greater ease is to put up guardrails in our lives—external boundaries for our protection and safety that keep us in alignment with who we are and what's important to us. I find it helpful to have guardrails in my life. Guardrails refer to boundaries, limits, or guidelines set for yourself to help you make healthy and wise decisions and stay on track with your virtues, goals, and priorities.

Just as physical guardrails on the road keep vehicles from veering off course, personal guardrails can serve as safeguards to help you stay on a positive and constructive path in life. The first area is a set of physical guardrails. Our guardrails include eating healthy, exercising regularly, resting properly, and spending quality time with our family. We have guardrails in our emotional lives as well, and we're careful about what we allow ourselves to think, hear, read, and watch. We read over our goals and aspirations regularly via our 'Bucket List' so we know that we are staying in alignment with what we want to do in our lives. We have mental guardrails that help us determine what new beliefs we let into our belief systems.

We have guardrails within our relationships. We choose to not surround ourselves with people who are toxic or harmful. Some additional guardrails ensure that we have private quality time with the people we care to create the best possible relationships. These are the magical moments in life that reinvigorate our energy levels like nothing else. We have spiritual guardrails that allow us to think, pray, study, meditate, rise early, and contemplate life's great mysteries. Lastly, we have financial guardrails that keep us from struggling financially and ensure financial peace for ourselves and our family.

Life can be chaotic, complicated, messy, stressful, and disorganized. In creating the best life for ourselves, our family, and our companies, we recognized early on that we needed to have safety nets and guardrails so that our energy can be best focused on creating goodness in the world versus worrying or stressing that we're falling behind or getting off track.

THE MOTIVATING FORCE

As you work to stay aligned with your virtues, adjust both the quantum and physical realms of your life to reflect those values, and establish safeguards to protect them, you will begin to unlock the power of alignment.

In your professional endeavors, you'll be amazed at how your virtues and motivations can guide your goals and decisions as you navigate challenges and interact with your team. By aligning your values with your actions, you foster trust, commitment, and engagement among your colleagues, which can translate into greater success.

This alignment can also benefit every aspect of your personal life, from your health and relationships to your overall life satisfaction. As you master the principles of Quantum Accountability in the chapters ahead, keep your virtues at the forefront. Ultimately, your accountability to your deepest aspirations can serve as the driving force to help you achieve the accountability required to do the work that will get you where you want to go.

Developing Virtues in Your Life

The first step to developing virtues in your life is to believe that it is possible to train yourself to become more virtuous and therefore happier. Next, practice, practice, practice. Moral life virtues are reinforced through practice and habituation. As Dr. Madeleine Hunter teaches, Practice Makes Permanent. This concept suggests that the actions we repeatedly perform become ingrained habits, shaping our abilities and behaviors over time. Continuous repetition of any skill or behavior leads to its automatic execution, embedding it into our (quantum) subconscious. However, it also warns that practicing incorrectly can solidify bad habits just as easily as good ones. The phrase challenges the traditional notion of "practice makes perfect" by highlighting that perfection is not always achievable, but permanence in our practices is. Exercise your virtuous muscles by engaging in virtuous activities, which then become your habits.

The concept of practice makes permanent aligns closely with the ideology of continuous improvement, known as Kaizen in Japanese philosophy. Continuous improvement means engaging in an ongoing process of self-reflection, self-assessment, and incremental betterment. It involves recognizing that virtues such as honesty, kindness, patience, and empathy are not static traits but skills that can be developed and enhanced over time through deliberate practice. By repeatedly choosing to act in accordance with these virtues, we reinforce them in our behavior patterns and decision-making processes.

For example, we can practice patience by consciously choosing to attempt to remain calm in frustrating situations. Initially, these efforts might not yield success, but with persistent dedication, they can eventually lead to positive outcomes. Patience might then become the automatic response. Similarly, if we continuously seek to understand others rather than judge them, empathy becomes ingrained in our interactions.

However, the ideology of continuous improvement also acknowledges that the journey is as important as the destination. It's not about achieving a state of perfection but about making consistent, small steps towards betterment. It recognizes that setbacks are part of the process and that learning from them is crucial for growth. By applying this effective mindset to the practice of virtues, we accept that while we may never be perfectly virtuous, we can always strive to be better than we were yesterday, and through persistent practice, these virtues can become a permanent and defining part of our lives.

Developing virtues is a lifelong process; it is about striving to be better than you were yesterday and continuously learning and practicing virtues. This idea fits in perfectly with the Mindset Continuum we discussed in Chapter 2.

HOW TO FACILITATE VIRTUE FORMATION IN OTHERS

There are several strategies you can employ to help others in their virtue formation. First, simply model virtuous behavior. Children learn by example, so it is essential for parents and caregivers to model virtuous behavior in their own actions. This is also the case when you are perceived as a leader in a business. By demonstrating virtues like self-control, moderation, and temperance, you provide a positive role model for others to emulate. Next, encourage open communication. Establishing open and honest communication with children is vital. Encourage discussions about virtues, choices, consequences, and ethical dilemmas in a non-judgmental way. This allows children to express their thoughts and feelings while learning about virtues in a supportive environment. One strategy we use in our business is to include moral-dilemma questions as part of our interview process. You want to hire employees who share common virtues, such as honesty.

Using circumstances as a means to teach through experience is another effective strategy. Allow children to experience the consequences of their decisions within safe boundaries. For instance, offering limited choices with clear consequences can help children understand the importance of self-control and decision-making. Creating routines and structure can also help them develop strong virtues. Establishing routines that include time for prayer, schoolwork, free time, exercise, chores, proper mealtimes, and rest can help instill virtues like temperance in children from a young age. Consistent structure provides a framework for developing good habits and virtues. It's the same with employees. A structured routine where expectations are clearly outlined is an efficient strategy for virtue creation.

Another strategy is practicing reflection. Encourage children to reflect on their actions and decisions. Discuss why certain behaviors are considered virtuous or how they align with values like honesty, compassion, or fairness. Reflection helps children internalize virtues and understand their significance. The same strategy can be used in a business setting.

Finally, use community influence by recognizing the impact of communities on virtue development. Surround children with positive role models, engage them in community activities that promote virtues, and create a supportive environment that reinforces ethical behavior. As a company, create opportunities for community involvement, including community service such as a Cancer Walk or free/reduced fees for Veterans and their families.

ACCOUNTABILITY ANCHORS:

1. Virtues help us to make ethical decisions and live a life aligned with high moral standards.

2. Virtues represent qualities that embody moral excellence, social grace, and intellectual acumen.

3. When you make choices or decisions that respect your virtues you are at ease. When you make choices or decisions that aren't in alignment with your virtues, you feel uncomfortable.

CHAPTER 7

ELEVATING YOUR LIFE WITH A POSITIVE ATTITUDE

"Develop an attitude of gratitude, and give thanks for everything that happens to you, knowing that every step forward is a step toward achieving something bigger and better than your current situation."

– BRIAN TRACY

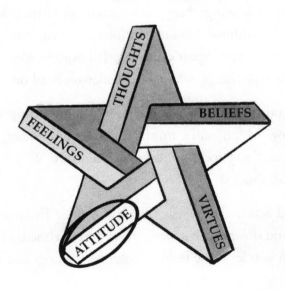

Alex, a teenager with dreams as vast as the sky but a demeanor that often clouded those dreams, lived in the quiet suburb of Maplewood. Alex's mother, Susan, had watched with a heavy heart as the once vibrant and curious child grew into a teenager whose outlook had dimmed, replaced by a storm of negativity and resistance.

One evening Susan decided it was time for a heart-to-heart conversation. Dinner was done, and the dishes were cleared, and she took the initiative to start the difficult conversation.

"Alex," Susan began, her voice steady but filled with concern, "I've noticed lately that you've been carrying a heavy cloud around you. It seems like no matter the situation, you find the rain in it. Your teachers have mentioned it, and I've felt it too. It's like you're at war with the world, and I'm worried about you. I love you and I want to see you happy and enjoying life"

Alex's eyes, a mirror of the storm inside, met Susan's. The words stung, a mixture of surprise and defiance brewing in the silence that followed.

"I know it's not easy, being where you are, standing on the bridge between childhood and adulthood," Susan continued, her voice softening. "But this attitude, this negativity, it's not you. It's not the Alex who used to find joy in the little things, who faced challenges head on."

Alex shifted uncomfortably, the defensive walls starting to crumble. "I don't know, Mom," Alex muttered, the words barely a whisper. "It's just... everything feels so heavy, so pointless. Why bother when everything just... sucks?"

Susan reached across the table, offering a hand. "The world is full of both storms and sunshine. It's okay to feel overwhelmed, to be angry or sad, but when you let those feelings color everything, you miss out on the sunshine. Having a positive attitude doesn't mean ignoring the bad; it means not letting it take away all the good."

"Let's try to find one good thing every day," Jordan suggested, a hopeful smile dawning. "Just one thing, no matter how small. And let's talk about it, together. Maybe, just maybe, we'll start to see more sunshine than storms."

Does this story bring back memories of your teenage years? Or does it conjure up recent experiences you may have had with your own children? Each one of us has had the feeling of the world feeling heavy and daunting. Each one of us could use a role model like Susan when we are unable to see the sun through the clouds. Life's circumstances can often weigh heavily upon us, casting shadows over our spirits and making it challenging to hold onto a positive attitude. In the face of adversity, the effort to remain optimistic can feel like an uphill battle, as the complexities and pressures of our experiences test our resilience and threaten to dim the light of hope within us. Cultivating habits that bolster a positive outlook can be beneficial, as they enable us to transform our attitude from negative to positive.

This brings us to the next point on the Mindset Star, Attitudes. Psychologists define attitudes as a set of preferences for or against an object, person, thing, or event. While mindsets are the foundational belief system that shapes how you perceive the world, attitudes are the outward emotional response and way you interact with your environment.

They are formed through experiences, social influence, education, conditioning processes, and observation. So, even if you haven't been involved in a direct experience, an indirect observation can create an attitude. Attitudes consist of thoughts, emotions and behavioral components. These components influence how you act in various situations and can have a powerful impact on your behaviors.

Attitudes can be positive or negative, explicit and conscious, or implicit and unconscious. Your attitudes can be strong or weak based on their importance and impact on your daily life. Strong attitudes are held with confidence, are important, and guide your actions significantly. They can influence your behavior even without your conscious awareness. Strengthening attitudes can occur through discussing them with others close to you and assessing their validity. Attitudes are dynamic and can change over time based on experiences and influences.

TYPES OF ATTITUDES

- **Positive** – optimism, hopefulness, and a general tendency to expect favorable outcomes.
- **Negative** – pessimism, a lack of confidence, and an expectation of unfavorable outcomes
- **Prejudiced** – preconceived negative judgment or feeling toward an individual based solely on their membership in a particular group, without sufficient knowledge or experience with the individual
- **Open-Minded** – lack of attitude and/or no evaluation or preferential treatment
- **Resilient** – Adaptability and Perseverance in the face of adversity enabling you to bounce back from setbacks and challenges

Attitudes can change through training, guidance, and life experience. Attitudes are a subset of your mindset. As we have seen, Mindset refers to your established set of thoughts, beliefs, feelings, virtues, and attitudes that shape your perception and interpretation of the world. Your mindset is your mental framework. Attitude is considered a component of mindset because while mindset encompasses the broader mental framework and beliefs that shape your perceptions and approach to life, attitude refers specifically to the emotional and behavioral responses that are influenced by these underlying beliefs. Attitude is a more visible, dynamic expression of how your mental framework directs your behavior and emotional responses to various life circumstances.

IDENTIFYING NEGATIVE ATTITUDES IN THE WORKPLACE

You may notice others who have a negative attitude. Sometimes, these attitudes shine bright for all to see like the neon Uber sign on your ride to the airport. You may notice behaviors such as eye-rolling, crossed arms, and lack of nodding. Other times, they are not as apparent and seem to hide themselves in an employee whose energy seems a little off. But, identifying negative attitudes in the workplace is crucial for maintaining a positive work environment and ensuring productivity. Here are some of the common negative attitudes that can be observed in the workplace:

1. **Exaggerating Coworkers' Mistakes:** Some team members tend to exaggerate or highlight their colleagues' mistakes excessively, which can create a toxic work environment. This is often a team member like Diana Drama who seems to gather energy when there is an issue in the workplace. Have you ever had an employee like this? When Diana Drama comes to you to relay the information, she prefaces it with the justification that she is looking out for the business's best interest. Don't believe her, her actions reflect her negative attitude.

2. **Spreading Rumors or Speaking Ill of Others:** Employees who engage in gossip, spread rumors, or speak negatively

about their colleagues exhibit a negative attitude that can harm relationships and morale. This is another behavior that Diana Drama might engage in. Remember, she feeds off of problems and issues and tends to exacerbate them.

3. **Lack of Appreciation:** Individuals who fail to complement or appreciate the good work of others and instead try to undermine their achievements demonstrate a negative attitude that can impact team dynamics. Businesses and families are both examples of teams. The most effective teams build confidence in their members and celebrate successes. They don't downplay achievements. If this is happening, it may be because Jenna Jealous doesn't have a confident self-concept.

4. **Disrespecting Emotions:** Showing disrespect for others' emotions, personal opinions, or decisions can create a hostile work environment and lead to conflicts among team members. This example of a negative attitude results in team polarization. You want a team who are all paddling in the same direction, not in opposing ones. Deidra Divide will in fact split the employees into factions by making them take a side.

5. **Lack of Confidentiality:** Employees who do not maintain confidentiality regarding sensitive information within the team or organization display a negative attitude that can erode trust and damage relationships. In the dental field, we are under strict HIPAA guidelines regarding confidentiality. To follow these guidelines, team members must display a positive attitude.

6. **Avoiding Ownership of Mistakes:** Individuals who refuse to take responsibility for their mistakes or try to shift blame onto others exhibit a negative attitude that hinders personal

growth and teamwork. This attitude is an example of lack of accountability.

7. **Expressing Views Rudely:** Communicating dissent or displeasure in a rude or disrespectful manner towards colleagues, managers, or about organizational decisions reflects a negative attitude that can disrupt harmony in the workplace. In any business or family, there will always be disagreements. Parameters should be set in place to provide a structure for expressing opinions and ideas in a constructive manner

8. **Resistance to Criticism:** Individuals who struggle to accept constructive criticism and react negatively to feedback exhibit a negative attitude that impedes personal development and growth. Identifying these negative attitudes early on is essential for addressing them effectively and fostering a positive work or family environment. By recognizing and addressing these behaviors, organizations can promote collaboration, respect, and productivity in the workplace. Regular communication, feedback sessions, and promoting a culture of respect and appreciation can help mitigate the impact of negative attitudes on the overall work environment.

WAYS TO MAINTAIN A POSITIVE ATTITUDE

Let's face it, life is difficult. Sometimes it is hard to keep a positive attitude all of the time. In fact, is it even possible? The saying "when it rains it pours" often comes to mind when things go badly. Your child has the flu, your personal assistant quits, and your favorite sports team's playoff run ends on a bad call from the referee... all in the span of a couple days. It's not all rainbows and sunshine. If it were, then it would be much easier to maintain a positive attitude.

Here are several effective strategies you can implement to regain or initiate a positive attitude anywhere and anytime. See which ones work best for you.

1. **Practice Gratitude:** Regularly acknowledge and appreciate the positive aspects of your life. You can use a Gratitude Journal or take a Gratitude Walk, as discussed in previous chapters. This is such an important strategy for maintaining a positive attitude that we will examine it in greater detail throughout the rest of this chapter.

2. **Start Every Morning Strong:** Begin your day with activities that bring you joy and set a positive tone for the day. What makes you happy? A warm cup of coffee? Hearing the birds sing? Starting your day with a 30 minute workout?

3. **Describe Yourself with Positive Words:** Use affirmations and positive self-talk. As discussed in previous chapters, both of these strategies are effective in improving your overall mindset, and more specifically, your attitude.

4. **Listen to Positive Music:** Surround yourself with uplifting music to boost your attitude. What genre of music speaks to you? Jazz, rock 'n' roll, rap, country?

5. **Use the Power of Humor:** Incorporate humor into your daily life to lighten the mood and maintain a positive attitude. A 30 minute sit-com or a night to a comedy club is all it takes to adjust your attitude.

6. **Stay Connected:** Maintain relationships with loved ones as they can provide support and comfort during difficult periods.

7. **Have Things to Look Forward To:** Create small things to anticipate, whether it's a hobby, a task, or an event, to keep your spirits up. One strategy we use is to always have something to look forward to. For us, this means a trip. We try to travel, either near or far, once every three months. This helps us to maintain a positive attitude, especially when times are tough.

8. **Engage in Absorbing Hobbies:** Immersing yourself in activities you enjoy can serve as a distraction and boost your attitude. What recharges you? Fishing, reading a good book, gardening?

9. **Think About Your Purpose:** Reflect on your life's purpose and how you can contribute positively to the world around you. This is an excellent strategy for reframing your mind and altering your attitude.

By incorporating these practices into your routine, you can navigate difficult times with resilience, maintain a positive outlook, and emerge stronger from challenging situations. Remember, maintaining a positive attitude is not always easy but is crucial for mindset and overall well-being.

AN ATTITUDE OF GRATITUDE

Gratitude changes everything. Scientific research has found that it is important for various reasons, including improving mental health. Gratitude is strongly associated with feelings that contribute to greater health and happiness. It increases positive feelings and decreases uncomfortable feelings. It also helps individuals cope with disappointments, see the bright side of life, and improve overall happiness. Gratitude enhances life satisfaction as individuals with an Attitude of Gratitude tend to be less materialistic, more resilient, and cope better with tragedies and crises, leading to greater life satisfaction, improved experiences, and more abundance.

Studies show that gratitude also creates a state of better physical and mental health. It has been shown that practicing gratitude is linked to lower levels of anxiety and depression, increased optimism, better immunity, lower blood pressure, improved heart health, higher pain tolerance, and greater overall well-being.

Gratitude also leads to increased self-esteem. It helps individuals focus on positive thoughts, feel appreciated, and recognize their self-worth more so than those who do not share this attitude.

Research suggests that gratitude creates a higher level of success. People with a grateful attitude are more likely to achieve their goals faster. Expressing gratitude in the workplace improves productivity, motivation, enthusiasm, and loyalty among colleagues. And expressing gratitude in the home is another way to appreciate the people who are most important in your life.

Scientists have found that gratitude enhances connection and bonding. Expressing gratitude has been shown to release oxytocin, often referred to as the "love hormone," which strengthens the connections and the bonds between people. This biochemical response fosters a greater sense of closeness and attachment.

Another finding is that gratitude increases happiness. Research by Harvard Health indicates that gratitude can make individuals happier. This increase in personal happiness can positively affect relationships, as happier individuals are more likely to contribute positively to their relationships.

Gratitude also promotes positive perceptions by helping individuals feel more positively towards their partner, in business and in personal relationships. This positive perception can lead to more supportive interactions and a stronger, more resilient relationship. In addition, it encourages prosocial behavior and is linked to increased prosocial behaviors such as empathy, compassion, and a sense of connection to others. These behaviors are crucial for building and maintaining strong relationships.

Gratitude also improves communication. Expressing gratitude can lead to better communication within relationships. Acknowledging and appreciating each other's contributions can encourage open and honest communication. It promotes better communication, more empathy, and increased likability among group members, for example, in the workplace.

And finally, research suggests that gratitude cultivates a supportive environment: By expressing gratitude, individuals can create a more supportive and nurturing environment. This is particularly important in relationships where emotional support and understanding are key to overcoming challenges together.

DELIBERATE FOCUS

Deliberate focus refers to an intentional focus on a specific task or goal with the purpose of improving performance or shifting our attitude. One habit that uses deliberate focus is consistently put into a practical application by Lee Brower, a well-known business coach who helps others maximize their wisdom. He uses the idea of deliberate focus by collecting gratitude rocks. He carries a gratitude rock with him wherever he goes to remind himself to consistently see the goodness in life. This keeps his attitude in alignment with his commitment to leaving a positive legacy—in his work, his coaching, and his personal life.

The simple act of having a rock or other symbolic object in your pocket can do the same for you. When you touch the stone, think of gratitude. Let it trigger your mind to bring to light something you are grateful for. What a wonderful, practical application of how a physical item can be a force to shift the energy of your mind. This is a prime example of the quantum at work.

When our family travels, either in the mountains or on the beach, we will often pick out a pebble or small rock. This will function as a gratitude rock either for myself or to give to someone else. The rock that we pick is not the prettiest, or the shiniest. It is the one that we are called to pick up and say, this is the one. We pick it up, place it in our pocket, and are filled with a sense of joy and feeling connected to the Earth. We thank the earth for the gift of gratitude that the rock symbolizes. We face the rest of the day with an attitude of gratitude.

CULTIVATING A POSITIVE ATTITUDE

Our attitude in life greatly affects our view of the world. When you notice yourself not having an attitude of gratitude or other positive attitude, modify your approach. Change what you are saying to yourself. Instead of saying," I have to," start your day with, "I get to…!"

I get to exercise.
I get to care for my family.
I get to spend time with my coworkers.
I get to tell someone I love them.
I get to eat healthy.
I get to work and earn money
I get to experience new problems.
I get to make someone's day better.

It's all about your attitude.

Your current mindset is not necessarily the best way to handle the issues you face, Your mindset is just the method you subconsciously defaulted to use. By becoming aware of the quantum components of your mind, your thoughts, beliefs, virtues, feelings, and attitudes, you can make them more effective and efficient. This will propel you into a state closer to your goal of Quantum Abundance.

As you will see in the next three sections of the book, small changes in the quantum components of your mind can have big effects on your success.

ACCOUNTABILITY ANCHORS:

1. Attitudes consist of thoughts, emotions and behavioral components.
2. Our attitude in life greatly affects our view of the world.
3. Types of Common Attitudes include: Positive, Negative, Prejudiced, Open-Minded, and Resilient.
4. An Attitude of Gratitude is a learned outlook that enhances our lives in many ways.

SECTION 2

OWNING YOUR JOURNEY: THE TRANSFORMATIVE POWER OF SELF-ACCOUNTABILITY

What does it mean to be accountable to yourself? It means taking responsibility for your actions, decisions, and their outcomes, both positive and negative. It involves setting personal goals, standards, and expectations for your behavior and life achievements, and then honestly assessing your performance against these self-imposed benchmarks.

Accountability to yourself requires a discipline to follow through on commitments you've created for yourself, even in the absence of external oversight. It also entails recognizing when you fall short of your goals, learning from these instances, and making the necessary adjustments to stay aligned with your virtues. Essentially, self-accountability is about owning your life's journey, making conscious choices, and continuously striving to be the best version of yourself.

The principles we will explore in this section include the very practical, applicable skills of evaluating how you make choices (Chapter 8), examining the different roles you play (Chapter 9), how you manage your time (Chapter 10), your focus (Chapter 11), managing your finances (Chapter 12), managing your energy (Chapter 13), and being aware of the damaging effects of digital overload (Chapter 14). In each of the chapters in Section 2, we take the information we discussed in Section 1 and explore how it interacts with these principles in your life. Our objective is to take what we learned from the quantum and apply this information to your daily life.

CHAPTER 8

THE POWER AND IMPACT OF MAKING CHOICES AND DECISIONS

"Our choices are the hinges of destiny."

– EDWIN MARKHAM

The quality of our lives is determined, not by chance, but by the choices and decisions we make. Choices and decisions, not conditions, control our lives. If we don't like our conditions, then we should make different choices and decisions.

Whether big or small, each choice and decision carries the weight of potential consequences, steering our journey through life towards fulfillment or regret. If we choose wisely, we embrace the responsibility of shaping our own destiny. Every choice and decision we make opens the door to a new path, shaping our future and defining who we become.

Let's face it, we make choices and decisions every single day. Some are small choices, like which flavor of ice cream you prefer on your double scoop, and some are big decisions, like your career path. One of the most incredible freedoms we have is the power of choice. Everything we see, feel, and taste at some point results from choice. **Choices are the first real fruit of everything happening in the quantum realm.** And it is these choices for which we should hold ourselves accountable. These 'invisible' choices include what to think, what to focus on, and what mindset we choose.

Let's take a moment to define the distinction between choices and decisions. A choice is a result from a limited number of variables and usually doesn't have a tremendous impact upon your life journey. You make the choice of having a frozen yogurt over an ice cream sandwich from your freezer. There were only two choices and you chose one. A decision, on the other hand, is a conclusion reached after careful consideration and it often involves numerous if not unlimited variables. You have made several influential decisions in your lifetime; including your career, your significant other, and your commitment to success.

The present version of yourself is the culmination of both the insignificant choices and the significant decisions you have made in your lifetime. Both choices and decisions work hand in hand because choices lead to decisions.

For example, you decide to take better care of your health. You have a choice when you go out to eat: what you order on the menu. You have a choice of how much food you eat or whether you consume excess amounts of alcohol. You have a choice of whether you exercise each day or not. These choices, over time, will have a significant impact on your decision to live a healthy life.

Taking accountability means that you acknowledge both the choices and decisions you have made in the past and take full responsibility for how those have shaped your reality. It implies you are the product of both your choices and decisions, whether they be conscious or unconscious, and how they influence your future.

DECISION OPTIONS

When it comes to decisions, you have three general options:

1. You can decide on your own.
2. You can consult a person or group, like your family or tribe.
3. You can consult advisors, mentors or coaches.

When facing a decision, your current position, your level of confidence in the situation, and the complexity of the decision itself will sway you towards how you proceed. If it is a decision that falls under your area of expertise, and you feel you do not need the advice of others, it is prudent to decide quickly and not mull over the issue. If you do not decide quickly, it will take up mental energy and delay future progress.

Sometimes it is beneficial to talk things out, or have a sounding board for decisions. If you have a trusted peer group or mastermind group of like-minded, high thinking individuals, taking your decision to the group can be beneficial to gain insights and get perspective on what you might not be seeing. We all have blind spots and having a trusted group who knows us well can be very beneficial to pointing out things we might not be seeing or considering.

If we are dealing with major decisions that can have a significant impact on the trajectory of our future, it is beneficial to consult advisors or coaches. If I have tax questions, I am going to consult my Tax Advisor. If I have legal questions, I am going to consult my attorney who specializes in that area of the law. If I need an accountability partner to make sure my decisions are in alignment with my true north or who I want to become in my life, I consult my coach.

WHAT AFFECTS HOW WE MAKE DECISIONS?

Time

Time is perhaps one of the biggest influences on how we make decisions. Two different opportunities present themselves when it comes to making choices and decisions:

- Decide quickly.
- Make slow and careful decisions after cautious deliberation and research.

If you have the time, you could employ any number of measures to investigate, deliberate, research, and poll others' opinions. However, this process can quickly turn into procrastination or over-analysis, which can paralyze progress. The longer you deliberate, the more opportunities for improvement and growth slip through your fingers.

By the time you finally decide, the circumstances may have evolved and the window of opportunity might have closed. And just like our beliefs can limit us, our choices can define us. When we get stuck in decision-making, or a particularly painful or complex decision, we may try to boil the decision down to one or two choices. When you do this, you cut yourself off from better choices that might be available to you.

There may be other times when you simply do not have the luxury of time. Some decisions force us to act quickly, eliminating the possibility of researching and polling before deciding. In decision-making, the principle that "success is choosing quickly" carries profound significance. It encapsulates that swift and decisive choices often lead to more favorable outcomes. This principle revolves around the notion that the faster you decide, the more time you have to course-correct and make improvements if the initial choice is suboptimal.

In the book, Elon Musk, by Walter Isaacson, he talks about the speed of execution and sense of urgency needed to succeed in business. If you have a decision to make and your uncertainty leads you to wait six months before making the decision, what do you do if it was the wrong decision? You choose a different decision, and try a new approach. What happens if you make the decision right away and it turns out to be the wrong decision. You do the same thing, make a different decision. All you did was save yourself six months of time. If you do not need the advice of others, decide, take action, and move on.

The critical advantage of quick decision-making lies in its ability to expedite the learning process. When you decide promptly, you essentially initiate a feedback loop. You can test your hypothesis in the real world, gather valuable intel, and face the consequences of your decision. If the choice works out, you can build upon it. If it didn't, you have time to reassess, refine, and try again.

Quick decision-making also nurtures adaptability and resilience. It fosters an agile mindset in which you are unafraid of making mistakes because you know you can pivot and adapt as needed. In essence, you become a more agile decision-maker, ready to navigate life and work in a complex and ever-changing landscape.

However, "success is choosing quickly" does not imply recklessness or impulsivity. Instead, it advocates for informed and thoughtful decision-making while recognizing that perfection is rarely attainable. It's about finding a balance between thoughtful consideration and timely action.

Attitude

Attitude also influences how we make decisions. Have you ever heard the adage, "If you're making a big decision, you should sleep on it?" This advice proves true because you can take a pause from the uncomfortable feelings created from decision making. After a good night's rest, you will wake up in the morning with a clear head and a better understanding of the consequences of the decision. When it comes to the mechanics of making a good decision, sleep is a critical precursor to one of the biggest influences on our decisions: our mood. Mood is influenced by fatigue, hunger, upset, or drama in your personal and professional life that impacts your ability to respond effectively. Mood makes it hard to have a positive attitude and make good choices.

Asking yourself if you are in an effective mindset to make a decision before you even entertain any possible outcomes can help you in the long run by doing a quick check: Am I hungry? Am I tired? Am I upset, feeling rushed, or uncomfortable? If this is the case, take a nap, get something to eat, or step away for a few minutes. Get yourself in the best environment possible before you decide.

Checking your attitude before deciding can help you avoid a wrong decision, especially if you are in a bad mood from circumstances that have not been agreeable that day. Get yourself right before you choose, or as the saying goes, "check yourself before you wreck yourself." Can you listen to music? Go for a walk or run? Sit with a piece of paper and write your feelings. Or could you do repetitive tasks like organizing your desk, sorting implements, or anything that allows your feelings to settle down before you decide?

Tony Robbins states that "emotion is created by motion," meaning how we move and behave physically can directly influence how we feel. You'll often see Robbins in his seminars leading the crowd in high-energy activities, including jumping up and down, clapping, or cheering. Robbins asserts that by changing our physical state—through movement, facial expressions, posture, or breathing—we can change feelings. Using these principles can help people break out of negative states, get energized, and align their physical bodies and mindsets and the outcomes they want to achieve.

Try it. See if you can change your attitude by changing your physical condition. Play some music and clap along. It's almost impossible to stay negative or pensive when clapping. Psychology and neuroscience show that our body can influence our mental state. Adopting an expansive, open posture (standing like Superman) can make you feel more confident, while hunching over can make you feel more down. Try it and see what happens when you make a decision from a powerful stance.

Fear

One of the best tools to use in deciding is to ask yourself what you will be giving up by making this choice. When you choose between buying a new television or keeping your money, most people would think about what they want. I will ask you to change that wording to say, "Should I buy this TV, or should I keep the $500 for another purchase?" By stating the cost of spending that money, you allow yourself to experience what would happen if you didn't. You could put it towards a business computer or towards a bucket list trip fund, and now buying the television may seem less enticing. Using this strategy to highlight the real cost of the decision can help you make better decisions. Who knows, you may end up deciding on that television. Either way, you have gone through the process of good decision making.

Decision Fatigue

There are too many choices to make in our fast-paced world. We live in an era of distraction from streaming movies, podcasts, YouTube videos, Instagram reels, twenty-four-seven news channels, and sports contests. Not to mention the consistent stream of emails and text messages. The list is endless.

Many of us experience decision fatigue. Our brains become tired when we are constantly having to make choices. The key is to decide which decisions are worth your time. Ask yourself: What do I give up when binge-watching Netflix? What am I giving up by scrolling through Facebook? What am I giving up by endlessly searching Amazon for the latest and greatest whatever?

Most of us are giving up sleep, time with friends, relaxation, and opportunities for personal growth and development for today's oversaturated, overstimulated, and over-the-top lifestyles. Looking at the cost of our choices can result in a better distraction-free existence that doesn't cause brain fatigue. Don't make important decisions when your brain has been overloaded.

One technique that can combat decision fatigue that we'll examine in depth later on is time blocking. This time management technique can help us organize the same 24 hours that we all get to manage everything from work projects to our digital device use. Block out times of your day that are completely device free. Decide when you are going to use digital tools and when you are going to unplug. The world's not going to fall apart if you don't check your email for an hour. Set your phone aside, turn your computer off, and see how many times you reach for your device.

If you don't believe us, stand in line at the grocery store until you hear someone's phone ring and see if you immediately reach for your device. We are trained dopamine and serotonin addicts culturally conditioned to our digital devices. We can choose simplicity and productivity in an era of too many choices. Screen-free afternoons or weekends can give time for overstimulated brains to relax. Of course, this only applies if you use phone calls to communicate with your friends—as many younger generations only communicate via text, apps, or social media.

Doing a digital detox for days at a time can cause your creativity to return and grow. One of the most significant limiting beliefs that people carry today is that they will miss something vital if they don't have their phones on them. Look around the next time you're in a restaurant or ball game. How many people have their faces on their phones? How many people are sitting next to each other, not conversing or enjoying the same shared experience but texting someone else on their phones miles away? It's time to check yourself and ask if you have that same limiting belief that you will miss something if you're not digitally connected to everything.

The simple effort to reduce your digital use can make a massive impact on your digital fatigue. Simplifying your life by putting away the millions of decisions available at your fingertips on your phone is the quickest way to relieve the burden and allow yourself the space and time necessary to make good decisions once again.

Think of the Outcome

Another important influence on decision-making comes from pondering the potential outcomes. When you think about what you want the outcome to be, you behave in a way that gives you more of what you want. As you start with the end in mind, you can reverse engineer your actions and behaviors to ensure that what you do leads to where you want to go. Another benefit of considering the outcome of your decisions is your ability to solve problems before they happen. If you analyze the consequences of your decisions before you actually make them, you can avoid the worst mistakes and mitigate the ones that simply cannot be avoided.

One of the best tools for this kind of analysis is, paradoxically, the digital world. The difference between the digital use described above and what I am about to explain is your intention. How you use your digital resources affects your relationship with the digital world. If you are thinking of an outcome you want to achieve, this is where you turn to YouTube, AI, and Google because you can quickly decide and do some research to see the solutions someone else has found for the problem you've discovered. The great thing about the Internet is that whatever you're wondering about, or any choice you're trying to make, your situation will likely be solved by somebody else. You can learn from their successes and mistakes.

Exploring what other people are doing, especially in your professional environment, can give you great insight into your decision-making process. You can also look at what your competitors have done in the same situation, or what great thought leaders and business advisors are explaining and experiencing on their channels. When we do this, we look at a situation from the outside. We work on our business, not in it. And we can use the experiences of others to create a test plan to see if our idea will work. Before making a choice, test your idea. Plan by time traveling five and ten years into the future and brainstorming where that decision would take you. Imagining the future outcomes of your decision can help you choose between competing options.

For the most important decisions, try using the 10-10-10 rule by Suzy Welch. This decision-making technique involves considering the consequences of a decision in three different time frames: 10 minutes, 10 months, and 10 years. By evaluating the short-term, medium-term, and long-term impacts of a decision, you can gain a clearer perspective on the potential outcomes and implications of your choices. This method helps to make more thoughtful and strategic decisions by looking beyond immediate consequences and considering how choices may affect the long-term. The 10-10-10 rule encourages individuals to align their decisions with their values and long-term goals, fostering a more intentional and purposeful approach to decision-making

The Influence of Others

Other people can have a significant impact on the decision you make, for better or worse. If your friend circle is filled with people who dominate the conversation, it might be hard to separate your beliefs from their opinions. Some people can be well-meaning and convincing; their perception may be right for them but could be very wrong for you. Taking time to think about your decision away from everything and everyone can be beneficial to isolate what is best for you.

Other than the people closest to you, the biggest influences on your decision are the forms of information you choose to consume. The books you read, the podcasts you listen to, the television shows you watch, what you see on YouTube and other social media platforms, the training programs you attend, the groups you participate in (such as church and self-help groups), they all influence your decisions.

Because of the potential for information overload and the natural tendency we have as social beings to simply accept the beliefs and perceptions of others as our own, it can make a huge difference to take a moment with a simple pen and paper to figure out what you really want. You can use your digital device or computer, but I recommend taking the time away from your devices to give yourself time to think without interruptions or notifications. Quiet, private, and undisturbed thinking time enables you to make good decisions and figure out what is going on, how you have made decisions in the past, and what you really want.

A MORE EFFECTIVE DECISION-MAKING PROCESS

Now that we have discussed some common variables that influence how people make choices and decisions, let's take a moment to outline an effective decision-making process. These are some ideas to help you to make better choices and decisions.

1. Awareness of the Difference Between a Choice and a Decision

Our brains are inundated with information throughout the day. The human brain is exposed to a vast amount of information daily. On average, our brains process as much as 74 GB of data each day, which is equivalent to what a highly educated person consumed in a lifetime 500 years ago. This influx of information challenges the brain's ability to process and filter relevant data efficiently.

Despite the brain's remarkable capacity for processing information, there are limitations to how much data the conscious mind can handle at once. It has been estimated that the mind's processing capacity is around 120 bits per second, highlighting the selective nature of attention and cognitive processing. This disparity between the amount of information received by the brain and the limited capacity for conscious processing underscores the intricate mechanisms involved in how our brains manage and prioritize information in our daily lives.

Be cognizant of how much attention and energy you are putting into simple choices versus more important decisions. Simply using the correct semantic label is the first step.

2. Remember Your Guiding Light

What are you passionate about? What gives you unlimited energy? Follow this passion as nothing matters more. Use this guiding light as a metaphor to light the way upon your path of choices and decisions. Be aware of what you feel drawn to and what you may feel you want to retract from. Make choices and decisions that bring you towards the light.

3. Trust Your Gut Feelings

Neuroscience research suggests that your feelings may just be the most powerful tool you have for making decisions. As the saying goes, the heart knows what the mind can't understand. You have a second brain in your gut called the Enteric Nervous System or ENS. It is composed of between 200-600 million neurons all residing in your gastrointestinal tract. The ENS is the largest and most complex unit in your peripheral nervous system.

Your ENS influences your brain and your brain influences your ENS. It's a bidirectional relationship. When you have a gut feeling, it is a physical response to perceived threats and or opportunities in your environment. Pay attention to these gut feelings as they act as readings on your emotional compass in life.

4. Embrace the Power of a Pause

Most of us like to make decisions quickly in our chaotic world. No wonder, as most of us make up to 35,000 choices and decisions each and every day. Sometimes, it is advantageous to take time to pause and reflect. This allows the brain to shift from relying upon reactive impulses to relying upon the prefrontal cortex. The prefrontal cortex houses logical, rational, reasonable thinking. When emotion is high, logic is low. Taking the time to pause allows the prefrontal cortex to offer valuable input.

5. Make Conscious, Intentional Decisions

Making conscious and intentional decisions is crucial for several reasons. Firstly, because it incorporates the powerful principles of Self-Awareness and Mindfulness. By making intentional decisions, we become more present in our lives. This awareness allows us to align our actions with our needs, thereby enhancing our self-awareness and mindfulness.

Next, it is important for Living Authentically. Intentional decisions help us to live in alignment with our true selves. By consciously making choices that reflect our virtues and desires, we avoid living on autopilot and instead focus on what truly matters.

And lastly, making conscious, intentional decisions allows us to take control of our own lives. It empowers us to take charge of our lives rather than letting circumstances dictate our path. While external factors may be beyond our control, intentional decision-making allows us to respond proactively and shape our lives one decision at a time.

THE CULMINATION OF YOUR CHOICES

Be mindful of choices and decisions, as their consequences impact your life trajectory. During exercises such as self-reflection, you can gain an understanding of the connection between your past decisions and your present situation. Reflecting can provide insight and learning opportunities for making more effective choices and decisions in the future.

The following exercise is designed to help you reflect on and evaluate the major life decisions you've made so far, offering a structured way to understand the motives, results, and feelings related to each. By the end, you will have gained a clearer picture of your personal journey and feel more aligned with your future choices.

SETTING THE STAGE

Start by taking a few deep breaths. Remind yourself that this is a non-judgmental exercise. It's about understanding, not blaming or regretting. You can't change the past, but you can use it to change the future.

List Your Major Life Decisions

Write down the major life decisions you've made in your life, examples may include:

- Choosing a career
- Pursuing education
- Choosing a life partner
- Managing finances

- Taking calculated risks
- Buying or selling a home
- Ending or beginning a relationship
- Placing loved ones in full-time care
- Adopting a child
- Retirement planning
- Starting a business
- Moving or relocating

Leave a few lines between each for notes.

Explore Each Choice

For each decision, answer the following questions:

- *What led me to this decision?* Consider the factors influencing your decision. Were you following your Guiding Light, societal, familial, or friends' expectations, seeking adventure, or looking for security?
- *How did I feel when I made the decision?* Were you excited, anxious, confident, pressured?
- *What have been the outcomes of this decision?* Think both tangibly (e.g., job opportunities, relationships) and intangibly (e.g., personal growth, experiences).
- *How do I feel about this decision now?* Do you feel proud, regretful, neutral?
- *Would I make the same decision again knowing what I know now?* There's no right or wrong answer here, just an opportunity for introspection.

Find Patterns

Look at your responses. Do you notice any patterns in how you make decisions? Maybe you often prioritize others' expectations over your own desires, or maybe you notice an act of consistent courage in following your heart. Maybe you ignored a gut reaction.

Evaluating Your Decision-Making Process

Reflect on the following:

a. *Which decisions brought the most joy and fulfillment? Why?*
b. *Were there decisions you wish you approached differently? How so?*
c. *What internal and external factors most often influence your decisions?*

Visualizing the Future

Think of a major life decision you might face in the near future. Using your insights from this exercise, write down how you would approach it. Consider:

a. *What would your ideal outcome look like?*
b. *How would you ensure your decision aligns with your Guiding Light and your virtues?*

Gratitude and Closing

End the session by writing down three things you're grateful for regarding your life journey so far. It might be lessons learned, people met, or simply the growth you've experienced.

THE QUANTUM FOUNDATION OF DECISION-MAKING

Everything we have discussed so far in the book culminates in the choices and decisions you make. Up to this point, we've explored various concepts that ultimately converge on the choices and decisions you make, grounding their significance in the physical world. Although your thoughts, feelings, beliefs, attitudes, and virtues remain intangible, it is through your choices and decisions that these elements find expression in the tangible world. Your mindset, shaped by this intricate web of your thoughts, beliefs, virtues, feelings, and attitudes, plays a pivotal role in guiding your decisions and choices.

Creating a more effective decision-making process is crucial, as the decisions we make have a profound impact on our lives and the world around us. Ultimately, we bear the responsibility of ensuring that our deepest desires are in harmony with the quantum realm insights we've delved into thus far. By aligning our choices and decisions with our values, beliefs, and a deeper understanding of the interconnected nature of reality, we can unlock our full potential to create positive change and live with purpose.

ACCOUNTABILITY ANCHORS:

1. The quality of your life is determined by the choices and decisions you make.

2. A choice is a result from a limited number of variables and usually doesn't have a tremendous impact upon your life journey

3. A decision is a conclusion reached after careful consideration and involves numerous variables.

4. Time, attitude, fear, decision fatigue, thinking of the outcome, and the influence of others all affect how we make decisions.

5. Creating a more effective decision-making process is crucial, as our decisions have a profound impact on our lives and the world around us.

CHAPTER 9

BALANCING THE MANY ROLES WE PLAY IN LIFE

"We are all actors playing different roles in different phases of life. But we must try to play each role to perfection!"

– AVIJEET DAS

In the intricate dance of life, we each wear many hats, juggling roles that span the personal, professional, and social spheres. This chapter examines the art of balancing these diverse roles, a task that demands not only keen self-awareness but also strategic planning and mindful prioritization. From the role of a dedicated parent to that of a driven professional, an attentive spouse, or a committed community member, each aspect of our identity requires a unique set of responsibilities and commitments. Here, we explore practical strategies and insights to navigate these roles with grace, ensuring that each facet of our lives receives the attention it deserves without compromising our well-being or sense of fulfillment. Through a blend of boundary setting, prioritization, delegation, time management, and communication, we'll uncover how to harmonize our multifaceted lives, transforming the challenge of balance into an opportunity for growth and enrichment.

One of us is a father, dental surgeon, husband, friend, mentor, author, speaker, and owner of multiple companies, as well as a son, a brother, an uncle and a basketball player. The other is a mother, wife, daughter, aunt, and teacher, as well as an author, speaker, and life coach. All of these roles require strengths in order to succeed; some the same and some different. Accountability involves setting clear expectations about these roles and taking initiative to learn to balance their often competing demands.

When we think about taking accountability for our roles, though, whom are we accountable to? The answer to this perplexing question is yourself. You are accountable to you and the roles you play. You are accountable for knowing which strengths to use at which times. This is a balancing act as sometimes your distinct roles conflict. For example, your roles as father and business owner may conflict if your son has a basketball game at the same time you have an important business meeting.

Balancing conflicting roles is challenging, but holding yourself accountable to both roles is possible. We travel through life and add additional roles, like a homeowner or dog owner. The ability to effectively balance these roles requires strategy.

DID YOU CONSCIOUSLY CHOOSE ALL YOUR ROLES?

Earlier in the book, we referred to the part of the brain called the Id. To remind you, it's the unconscious part that creates urges, desires and impulses. It's the part that consciously you have no control over. Is it possible that this same part of the brain has pushed or pulled you into accepting roles against your will? You may find that some of the roles you play were chosen for you, or you fell into them unconsciously. Perhaps you took that role because it was what you thought you were supposed to do, or because you didn't know anything different, meaning you never took the time to examine what was happening on the quantum level of your mind.

You're an actor on a stage. You may get married because you think that's what people do when they get older. This is a prime example of a belief (Chapter 4) that was passed down to you without your conscious awareness. You may never have taken the time to examine this belief for yourself. When you do take the time and become aware of the quantum realm, you might find that marriage isn't for you. Or, you might find that you did get married because you deeply love the person and you do value marriage.

In addition to simply getting married, how often does someone dive right into a nuptial decision and then consciously sit down with their partner and think about how they want the marriage to play out? How do they want the roles of husband and wife to play out? How do they want to define their roles as parents? How do they want to each play their roles in resolving conflict? And how do they want their roles to be affected by extended family members? These are all important choices and decisions that greatly affect your lives. Happy home life, happy life. However, we tend to leave these up to chance, or our Id, on the quantum level.

Most of the time, people step into roles unconsciously, simply mimicking the way they've seen it done before, disregarding whether it's the most effective approach or even a role that fits them at all. They also might find themselves acting in a way they imagine they should. It's rare that people take the time and energy to think how to do it best, or to make the right choice.

Eventually, we grow tired of playing a role that doesn't authentically align with our virtues and goals. This means that people frequently find themselves unsatisfied in one or more of their roles in life. For example, they may feel stuck in a career that they aren't even sure they wanted to be in to begin with. Or, they find themselves in a marriage where they don't feel seen. Their role as a husband doesn't bring the fulfillment they had expected. They may feel resentful of their children for the time and energy drain they experience.

The Talking Heads sang about this circumstance in their hit song Once In a Lifetime. which describes someone who wakes up one day and asks themselves "Well, how did I get here?" Or, in the words of John Mayer, "Am I Living it Right?" You may remember that this same question appeared in the Introduction of the book.

If you are a self-actualizer, you may find that you are constantly reflecting on this same idea throughout your life. Your impulse may be to shed the role completely. To give up and throw in the towel. To quit the job, have an affair, or leave the marriage. Or, maybe you leave without leaving, disengaging by turning to drinking, drugs, shopping, gambling or zoning out in front of your device.

But there is another option; it just takes the courage to become self-aware in the quantum realm of your mind. By doing this, you can figure out how these roles came to be and if they are congruent with who you truly are. To do this, let's first examine what variables play an integral part in the roles we play.

Here is a simple exercise to clearly assess the motivation behind your pursuits and the roles you choose to play in life. Pause for a moment and reflect on the various pursuits that currently occupy your thoughts and energy. What are 3-5 aspirations or goals that you're actively striving towards? Perhaps it's a coveted promotion at work, saving for a dream vacation home, finding a meaningful romantic partnership, or simply carving out more quality time with cherished friends. Jot them down and let's explore their origins.

Now, take a closer look at each of these pursuits. Where did the desire for them truly stem from? Was it societal expectations whispering in your ear? The echoes of your parents' hopes and dreams? The influence of your partner's ambitions? Or did these yearnings arise from the depths of your own authentic self?

After contemplating the motivations behind these pursuits, take a moment to re-evaluate. Do they still resonate with your virtues and aspirations? Do they align with the person you envision yourself becoming? If not, feel empowered to let go of those that no longer serve you, and embrace the ones that ignite your passion and propel you towards a life of fulfillment.

This exercise encourages you to pause amidst the relentless pace of life and consciously examine the driving forces behind the goals you set for yourself and the roles you play in life. It's an invitation to cultivate self-awareness, to discern between external influences and internal callings, and to ultimately pursue a path that is authentically yours.

DEFINE CLEAR BOUNDARIES

Start by defining clear boundaries for each of the roles you play in life. When you're at work, focus on your work responsibilities; when you're with your family, be fully present as a father, brother, son, uncle, mother, sister, daughter, aunt. Avoid bringing work-related stress or distractions into your family time as much as you can. The same goes for your work environment and work-family; try not to bring stress and distractions from home into the workplace. It's easier said than done, but all the more reason to create a life that has healthy boundaries.

A boundary is a psychological or emotional limit that individuals establish to define the parameters of their personal and professional lives. Boundaries are those guidelines that help people maintain a healthy balance between different roles and responsibilities in their lives. They play a crucial part in managing these roles by providing structure, protecting one's well-being, and fostering healthy relationships.

It is also important to establish clear boundaries when it comes to the roles we play that involve relationships with others. As we have discussed, the majority of us do not take the time to consciously sit down with our partner and discuss roles. Who will take on the role of the money-earner? Or, will both of you take on that role? Or, will one take on that role and the other take on the role of caregiver to the children? Do you want to have children? How many? What role will each person play in their upbringing? As you can see, there are numerous topics that should be addressed with clear boundaries set for each.

PRIORITIZATION

Prioritization is key to staying accountable for all of your roles. Not every role has the same needs or priorities. Determine the most important tasks and responsibilities in each role and allocate your time accordingly. Use tools like calendars, organizational apps, to-do lists, and whatever you need to help you stay organized and ensure that critical tasks are addressed. (We'll be taking a closer look at these tools in the next chapter.) It is better to choose not to do something on your list rather than suffer the emotions of forgetting it.

Prioritization also entails different time periods in our lives. Role demands change with circumstances. At the beginning of your career, you may have to devote additional hours to ensure success. Or, you might find yourself caring for an elderly parent or a small child, but as their needs change, so do your roles. Nothing lasts forever, and the winds of change are always at your door, so setting the expectation of continual adjustment in your schedule (part of our growth or abundance mindset) allows you to function at a high level of success. Take the time to prioritize your roles in order of importance at this particular time in life.

DELEGATE

When your life becomes complicated and you are not getting things done, evidenced by undone items on your list or frustration from the people around you, it's time to delegate. In a perfect world, we would delegate before things slide, but that's rarely the case. As a parent, involve your partner, paid caregiver, or family members in childcare and household responsibilities. Seek support from your work team and family to share the load. You may want to hire a personal assistant or a helper to facilitate the children. You could also look into hiring a cleaning person or hire an outside marketing firm for your business.

There are also a myriad of services like meal delivery, personal shoppers, and even errand-help subscriptions. All of these are examples of how you can delegate responsibilities demanded by your roles.

TIME MANAGEMENT

Learn about and develop what's right for you in solid time management skills. We will be looking at the ins and outs of this particular skill set in the next chapter. It's helpful to examine your time and project planning regularly. At the end of the year, around your birthday, or at the end of a vacation, are good times to evaluate how to improve your time management.

We all get the same 168 hours weekly; how you spend it is up to you. Evaluating your time expenditure can mean leveraging the things you don't want to do or are not good at and replacing them with something you excel in and or brings greater happiness. Keep your old planners and schedules because they give you great insight into how you have spent your time.

If you are stressed or dissatisfied in your life, this is an excellent place to start investigating to make changes to improve. When you take the time to examine your time management, you will find that you feel better when you have an outlined plan of attack for your responsibilities that result from your different roles.

COMMUNICATION

Open and honest communication is essential to balancing your roles as well. We will explore this essential skill in Section 3, Accountability to Others, Chapter 16. When it comes to balancing your roles, communicate with your work team and your family so they know about your commitments and any potential conflicts in your schedule. Being transparent about your responsibilities can help others understand your situation and be more supportive. They also might offer great ideas to improve your schedule with you.

Be prepared to adapt when necessary. Don't expect your day to run smoothly. If it does, it's a bonus, but that rarely happens. Set your expectations to deliver you the least amount of stress in your workday. There will be emergencies or situations where one role takes precedence over the other. Communicate this to those around you and arrange to address the conditions as soon as possible.

You can employ strategies such as taking reflection time, journaling, or seeking a coach or mentor if you find it particularly difficult to balance your roles. It is also valuable to make sure you have a great peer group or tribe of people around you. Lean on your tribe when in need. They will help you define, prioritize, and act your roles, simply by being a sounding platform. When we take the time to communicate, we are able to peel off conscious layers of the outer shell in order to access the subconscious quantum realm.

ACCOUNTABILITY ANCHORS:

1. You're an actor on a stage.
2. You manage different roles.
3. Most of the time, people step into roles unconsciously.
4. Integral aspects of the roles you play include:
   Defining Clear Boundaries, Prioritization,
   Delegation, Time Management, and Communication.

CHAPTER 10

PRIORITIZING WHAT TRULY MATTERS IN THE CURRENCY OF TIME

"This moment is all there is"

- RUMI

THE CONCEPT OF TIME

Imagine a jar which represents the finite hours and resources which are available to us on each given day. Now, imagine rocks, pebbles, and sand next to the jar. The rocks symbolize the most essential elements of our lives — our health, our relationships with loved ones, and the core goals that give our existence meaning and purpose. The pebbles represent the important but secondary commitments, such as our careers, hobbies, and community obligations. Finally, the sand signifies the small, trivial tasks and distractions that can easily fill up our time if left unchecked.

The key lesson of this exercise is that if we start by filling the jar with the sand, there will be no room left for the rocks and pebbles that truly matter. However, if we deliberately place the rocks in first, followed by the pebbles, the sand can then settle into the remaining spaces. This metaphor underscores the vital importance of prioritizing our time and energy, ensuring that we devote ourselves first and foremost to the foundational, high-impact areas of our lives before attending to the minor details. By keeping the rocks — our virtues, relationships, and aspirations — at the forefront, we can create a life of greater fulfillment, balance, and purpose.

Time, in its essence, is a canvas upon which we paint the narrative of our lives. Our perception of time influences our understanding of cause and effect, informs our moral compass, and fuels our drive to take responsibility for our deeds. If you view time as abundant or limitless, you may be more inclined to procrastinate, underestimate the effort required, or make excuses when deadlines are missed. Conversely, if you have a heightened sense of time's scarcity, you are more likely to approach your responsibilities with a greater sense of urgency and commitment.

Truly accountable individuals recognize time as a precious, finite resource. They are acutely aware of how they allocate their time and the impact their choices have on their productivity and ability to deliver on their commitments. These people consistently prioritize important tasks, eliminate time-wasting activities, and maintain a focus on the present moment. They understand that taking ownership of their time is fundamental to being accountable for their results.

The concept of time is foundational in both business and life. How you view time can shape your understanding of cause and effect, your moral and ethical beliefs, and your motivations to be accountable for your actions. We all know the clichés about time: "we each have the same 24 hours in a day," "time waits for no one," "it's about what you do with it that counts," and so on. While we do all share the same 24 hours in a day, the truth is that time's value is subjective, varying greatly from one individual to another. This notion is supported by some of the greatest minds in physics, who assert that time's flow is not uniform for all. Time is not the same for everyone. One of the most renowned physicists in history backs up this claim.

Albert Einstein revolutionized our understanding of time with his theory of relativity. According to Einstein's theory, time is not an absolute, constant entity, but rather a relative concept influenced by an observer's motion and gravitational field. Time is a personal experience that can differ for different observers depending on their relative motion and gravitational fields, challenging the common perception of time as an objective, universal concept.

Non-linear time challenges the conventional notion of time as a linear and progressive dimension. Instead, non-linear time suggests that time is subjective and can be experienced in various ways, not bound by a fixed, linear sequence of events.

In physics, non-linear time has been explored in quantum mechanics. According to quantum theory, particles can exist in multiple states simultaneously, and probabilities rather than definite outcomes determine their behavior, which suggests that time is not a linear sequence of events but rather a complex and unpredictable phenomenon shaped by particles' behavior. The physics perspective influences accountability because it suggests that actions have consequences that follow a specific sequence.

In philosophy, non-linear time has been explored in Eastern spiritual traditions such as Buddhism and Hinduism. These traditions view time as cyclical and infinite, with the past, present, and future existing simultaneously. This indicates that time is not a linear progression from one moment to the next, but a fluid and ever-changing phenomenon constantly shaped by our actions and perceptions. Philosophical interpretations of time can affect accountability by shaping our perception of personal responsibility.

In psychology, non-linear time has been explored in mental illness and trauma. Studies have shown that individuals who have experienced trauma may have distorted perceptions of time, such as feeling stuck in the past or experiencing time as fragmented and discontinuous. This suggests that time is not a fixed and objective dimension but rather a subjective experience shaped by our emotions and experiences.

How individuals perceive time can impact their sense of accountability. Future-oriented individuals may be more inclined to consider the long-term consequences of their actions and thus hold themselves accountable for their behavior. Present-oriented individuals might struggle with accountability if they prioritize short-term gains over long-term responsibilities.

One of the key ideas behind nonlinear time is that time is not a fixed and objective dimension but rather a subjective experience shaped by our perceptions and experiences. Our experience of time is not necessarily the same as the accurate passage of time but rather a subjective interpretation. However, despite being relative, time does have a direction and is not reversible. As the cliché goes, "once it is gone, you cannot get it back."

This direction and irreversibility of time is known as the "arrow of time," which implies that time flows in a particular order from past to present to future; and that specific processes, such as entropy (the measure of disorder in a system), increase with time. This temporal context can influence accountability by emphasizing that actions and decisions in the past have consequences that lead to the present and future. Individuals may be held accountable for past actions and responsible for shaping future outcomes. Think Sarah Conner in The Terminator when the cyborg travels from 2029 to 1984 to kill her to stop the future activities of her unborn son and his fight against Skynet.

But while time may flow in a particular order, Einstein's theory challenges the notion that it flows uniformly for everyone. Instead, it introduces the idea that time can pass differently for different observers based on their relative speeds or positions. This subjectivity of time can affect how individuals perceive and measure accountability.

Because time is relative but also irreversible, it is of utmost importance that we learn to manage the time that we do have so that we can better account for what we have done with it and how it impacts our actions in the present and the future life of abundance we aim to create.

THE IMPORTANCE OF TIME-MANAGEMENT

We humans spend a significant portion of our lives engaged in activities that shape our existence — approximately 33 years nestled in the embrace of slumber, with 7 of those years dedicated to the pursuit of drifting off into dreamland. Additionally, we devote nearly a year and four months to the pursuit of physical wellness through exercise, and revel in the joys of leisure for three years, immersed in the rejuvenating embrace of vacations. Amidst these experiences, the art of time management emerges as a crucial component, combining the skills of planning, organizing, and allocating time effectively to accomplish tasks and achieve goals. It is a symphony of prioritization, scheduling, and the implementation of techniques designed to elevate productivity while minimizing the insidious presence of wasted time.

For a business owner, mastering this art is not merely a matter of operational efficiency or financial prosperity; it is a testament to their commitment to delivering exceptional customer service and fostering personal well-being. Guests, the lifeblood of any enterprise, value punctuality as a sacred virtue, and respecting appointment times while minimizing waiting periods is akin to offering a bouquet of satisfaction. A business owner who wields the power of effective time management earns the trust and appreciation of their guests, forging a bond that transcends mere transactions.

Furthermore, the art of time management ensures that the business owner can gracefully navigate the delicate balance between quantity and quality, allowing them to serve the maximum number of guests without compromising the caliber of care. This harmonious equilibrium not only boosts the productivity of the business itself but also paves the way for increased revenue, a testament to the transformative power of mastering the art of time management.

Your career demands a delicate balance between professional responsibilities and personal well-being. Effective time management empowers you, as a business owner, to allocate dedicated periods for work, rejuvenation, and personal pursuits, fostering a harmonious lifestyle.

Operating in a rapidly evolving industry necessitates a commitment to continuous learning. By mastering the art of time management, you can carve out invaluable opportunities to attend seminars, acquire new skills, and remain at the forefront of the latest advancements in your field.

Success is often inextricably linked to the efficiencies of your systems, where the speed of execution can significantly impact results. By maintaining exceptional quality while streamlining tasks and procedures, you can potentially double your productivity per hour – a feat achievable through training and leveraging technological advancements.

Time is indeed a precious commodity, and its effective management directly influences your business's financial health. The more adeptly you allocate your time, the more clients you can serve and services you can provide. However, overextended schedules can lead to professional burnout. Proper time management ensures you have ample breaks, preventing overwhelming situations and fostering sustained enthusiasm for your profession and better mental well-being.

As a business owner, you must adopt a broader perspective and plan for the future. Dedicating specific time blocks for strategic planning, evaluating growth opportunities, or considering technological upgrades is essential for your business's long-term success. This is why I have come to embrace the power of time blocking.

WHAT IS TIME-BLOCKING?

Time blocking is a time management technique where specific blocks of time are dedicated to certain tasks or activities. Imagine your day as a blank canvas, divided into segments or blocks. Each block is allocated to a specific task or group of functions. Instead of constantly switching between tasks, you focus on one thing during its designated block.

For a business owner who not only provides their services but also manages the business side of their practice, time blocking can be instrumental in balancing multiple roles effectively. Making numerous decisions throughout the day can contribute to mental fatigue. Time blocking helps business owners plan their day in advance, reducing the need for constant decision-making about what to do next. This proactive approach minimizes the reactive nature of task management, conserving cognitive energy.

THE BENEFITS OF TIME BLOCKING

Time blocking promotes focused work. By dedicating specific blocks to individual tasks, it becomes easier to immerse oneself fully, reducing the mental toll of multitasking or rapidly switching between tasks. Such undivided attention fosters efficiency, and with tasks being completed more effectively, there's a reduction in lingering work-related thoughts that can cause mental fatigue.

By clearly defining work and break periods, time blocking ensures that individuals allocate moments for mental rejuvenation. These intentional breaks, free from the burden of work, allow the mind to rest and recover. This structured approach to work and rest cycles ensures that the brain isn't perpetually running in high gear, helping prevent burnout and cognitive exhaustion.

As a dentist, I often deal with stressful situations, including guest emergencies and challenging diagnoses. By having designated time blocks for dealing with such situations and managing stress, I can better handle these challenges without feeling overwhelmed. Time blocking encourages dentists and business owners alike to prioritize their tasks and allocate time to high-priority and urgent responsibilities. By focusing on what matters most, we can reduce the mental fatigue associated with feeling overwhelmed by a long to-do list.

Time blocking can also help us set boundaries by designating specific hours for work and personal life. This separation allows for better work-life balance and reduces the risk of mental exhaustion and burnout.

HOW TO USE TIME-BLOCKING

To begin applying the time-blocking technique, schedule dedicated blocks for the various roles you play in your business and life. As a dentist, I block out time for guest consultations, treatments, and surgeries. These are nonnegotiable and should be strictly adhered to for maximum efficiency and guest satisfaction. Block out specific times, perhaps at the beginning or end of the day, for tasks like checking emails, returning phone calls, or handling paperwork. This ensures that these tasks don't interfere with guest care.

Dedicate specific blocks each week for managerial tasks. This could include team meetings, reviewing financial reports, planning marketing campaigns, or strategizing for growth. Regularly setting aside time for these tasks ensures that the business side of your profession receives consistent attention. With regular time set aside for business strategy, there's a structured approach to evaluating the practice's growth and making necessary changes.

Knowing a designated time for each task can reduce the feeling of being overwhelmed, as everything has its time and place. You should also set aside time for continuous learning, whether attending workshops, reading journals, or taking online courses. This ensures you stay updated with the latest in your field and in business management.

It's essential to block out time for breaks to rest and recharge. This can prevent burnout and ensure you're always at your best as a business owner and manager. Always have a buffer or some flexible time blocks to handle unexpected work emergencies. This ensures that your schedule can accommodate unforeseen urgencies without completely disrupting planned activities. If you are both the owner and the primary service provider, allocating time for personal activities, family, and relaxation is crucial. Clear boundaries between work tasks and personal time can help achieve a balanced life.

STRATEGIES FOR TIME ACCOUNTABILITY

In addition to time blocking, there are other strategies which can improve your time management. Here are a few simple yet important ones to consider:

- **Setting Clear Goals:** Establishing measurable and achievable goals helps focus efforts and manage time effectively.
- **Prioritization:** Using tools like a Google Calendar to prioritize tasks based on urgency and importance can help manage time better.
- **Using Productivity Apps:** Apps can assist with reminders and scheduling, helping to keep track of tasks and deadlines.
- **Monitoring Progress:** Regularly checking progress against goals can help you to adjust plans and stay on track.

ACCOUNTABILITY ANCHORS:

1. How individuals perceive time can impact their sense of accountability.
2. Accountable individuals recognize time as a precious and finite resource.
3. Time blocking promotes focused work.

CHAPTER 11

HARNESS THE POWER OF YOUR ATTENTION AND FOCUS

"Concentration and mental toughness are the margins of victory."

- BILL RUSSELL

Attention serves as the expansive cognitive mechanism that enables us to selectively zero in on pertinent details while sidelining irrelevant distractions. This process swiftly mobilizes our mental resources, granting us the agility to navigate between different tasks and stimuli. Focus, however, takes this concept further, embodying a heightened state of attention marked by a continuous, intense mental dedication to a particular task or goal. This level of engagement deepens, paving the way for thorough analysis, effective problem-solving, and complete mental absorption in an activity, effectively sidelining any external interruptions. While attention equips us with the versatility to handle a multitude of inputs, focus channels our energies into a more intense, enduring dedication to a specific interest. Beyond their roles as cognitive functions, attention and focus are pivotal in shaping our experiences and interactions with the world around us, profoundly influencing our perception of reality through the lens of our engagement.

Our perception of the world is akin to peering through a series of windows. Picture yourself aboard a submarine, tracking a fish as it swims in the opposite direction of the submarine. You rush from one window to the next, each time catching fleeting glimpses of the fish. Yet, like snapshots in a disjointed film, you're only witnessing pieces of the scene. These windows, or filters, limit your view, preventing you from seeing the ocean's vast expanse in its entirety. Attention serves as your chosen window. It significantly influences what you discover in the world. In your quest to observe the fish, you inadvertently overlook the rest of the marine life. Therefore, attention not only shapes your reality but also sculpts you into a mirror of your perceptions. It anchors you in repetitive thought patterns, narrowing your perspective to a limited slice of the world. In this light, attention goes beyond simple cognitive function; it becomes a matter of ethical importance. This concept is vividly illustrated in the realm of social media, where your feed acts as a mirror of your thought patterns, creating the illusion that the world shares your viewpoint.

Harnessing your attention is the key to unlocking your fullest potential. We call this Quantum Focus. In Quantum Focus, you are aware that how you spend your time, and how you direct your Energy is a key determinent to success. Quantum Focus is like visualizing a laser beam of energy, of intent, and of thought, towards a specifics issue or cause. Quantum Focus is the art of channeling your attention and energy towards a singular purpose or outcome, and is a powerful cognitive tool. It enables you to think with unparalleled clarity, achieve your objectives, enhance productivity, spur personal development, and nurture well-being—pillars of sustained success in both personal and professional realms.

Mastering the art of attention and focus ushers you into a realm brimming with potential. Envision yourself approaching every task with laser-like concentration, unburdened by the weight of distractions. Such mental sharpness not only propels you forward at an accelerated pace but also infuses your endeavors with a profound sense of purpose and expertise.

Quantum Focus transcends ability; it is the engine that drives aspirations into the realm of reality. By diligently steering your attention and focus, you chart a course towards your dreams with both precision and assurance. It's this relentless dedication to the present that distinguishes the remarkable from the mundane, catapulting you towards achieving your highest aspirations.

The story of Florence Chadwick, who made history as the first woman to swim the English Channel in both directions, exemplifies the transformative power of attention. On July 4, 1952, Florence set out to achieve a new goal of swimming from Catalina Island to the California coast, a distance of over 20 miles. The water was ice-cold, and the fog was so thick that she could barely see the support boats accompanying her. After swimming for hours, she began to doubt her ability to complete the swim. The dense fog made it impossible for her to see how close she was to her goal, and exhausted and demoralized, she asked to be pulled out of the water.

After getting into the boat, Florence discovered that she had been just half a mile from the shore. Despite her disappointment, she didn't lose her resolve. She later said, "All I could see was the fog... I think if I could have seen the shore, I would have made it."

Undeterred, Florence Chadwick attempted the same swim two months later. This time, even though the fog was just as dense, she remained focused on her goal and did not waver. She swam with unwavering determination and completed the journey in 13 hours and 47 minutes, setting a new record in the process.

Florence Chadwick's story is a testament to the power of harnessing her focus and perseverance. Her ability to stay committed to her goal, despite not being able to see her progress, teaches us the importance of mental fortitude and maintaining belief in our capabilities, even when our objectives seem out of sight. Florence Chadwick had the ability to engage in what we call Quantum Focus.

DEVELOPING QUANTUM FOCUS

Quantum focus is also known as the concept of "flow," coined by psychologist Mihaly Csikszentmihalyi to describe a state of optimal experience where you are fully absorbed and deeply engaged in an activity that challenges your skills and abilities. You can perform at your best during Quantum Focus and achieve high productivity and creativity. Quantum Focus is a tool you can use intentionally. Rather than stumbling upon flow when you work, now you can create it.

Quantum Focus offers numerous benefits, particularly for an entrepreneur running their own business. Dental procedures often require extreme precision. A Quantum Focus ensures that the practitioner is attentive to the minutest details, reducing the chances of mistakes and enhancing the quality of dental work. By concentrating solely on one task, a dental practitioner can complete procedures in a timely manner, thereby seeing more guests and increasing overall productivity.

Shifting attention between tasks can lead to cognitive load, which increases stress levels. A business owner can avoid this mental strain by maintaining a deep focus, leading to a more pleasant and less stressful work environment. For example, guests often feel more comfortable and trust a dentist who appears deeply focused and attentive to their needs. This can lead to better patient satisfaction, retention, and referrals.

A Quantum Focus allows business owners to immerse themselves in continuous education and skill development, ensuring that they remain updated with the latest techniques and advancements in the field. Running a business involves more than just skill-specific work. It requires managing a team, handling finances, marketing, and more. A Quantum Focus can help a business owner efficiently handle the administrative side of their responsibilities, optimizing operations and ensuring profitability.

Multitasking and constant distractions can lead to rapid burnout. Business owners can maintain a balanced and sustainable pace by practicing deep focus, ensuring long-term well-being and career satisfaction.

Deep Focus allows for a better understanding of problems and can pave the way for innovative solutions in the business's professional and business aspects. Efficiency in the workplace due to deep focus might lead to fewer extended hours, granting you more personal and family time.

To create Quantum Focus in your business, remove external distractions, such as turning off notifications on your phone or computer, closing unnecessary tabs or apps, and finding a quiet and conducive environment for your task. Clearly define the task or goal you want to focus on and set particular objectives or milestones to keep yourself motivated and on track.

Identify the most critical and high-impact tasks that require deep focus and prioritize them accordingly. Avoid multitasking, as it can impair your ability to achieve deep focus. Set aside dedicated time for Quantum Focus sessions, and schedule them during your peak performance periods when you feel most alert and energized. Stay present and fully engaged in the task without letting your mind wander or getting caught up in thoughts about other jobs or concerns. Take short breaks during prolonged deep focus sessions to avoid burnout and maintain productivity. Use pauses to relax, rejuvenate, and return to the task with renewed focus.

Develop the habit of resisting distractions and staying committed to your Quantum Focus sessions, even when tempted to switch tasks or check notifications. Include techniques such as the Pomodoro Technique (working in focused bursts with timed breaks), time-blocking (allocating specific time slots for different tasks), and productivity tools or apps to help you stay focused and organized.

When you're in a state of flow, you're so focused and absorbed in what you're doing that you lose track of time and distractions, and your productivity soars as does your accountability. Flow can help with accountability because when you're in this state, you're more likely to meet your responsibilities and commitments. You're so engaged in the task that you naturally stay accountable to it, completing it effectively and efficiently. Flow and accountability are deeply connected because being in flow can make it easier to stay on top of your tasks and meet your obligations without feeling overwhelmed or distracted.

PRIORITIZING YOUR FOCUS

You may find yourself feeling that you lack focus in your life. Let's face it, there are multiple sources fighting for your time at any one given moment. Big corporations pay big money to distract you to buy their products. Social media platforms are embedded with algorithms that track your attention span and deliver posts that have similar interests. The world in which we live is set up to take you away from what is most important in life.

The most important tasks are usually ones that are most difficult or don't have a specific strategic plan. We tend to do what is easy instead of what is difficult. Or, we do what we know how to do, not the most important actions. Success in life is realized in performing the most important actions. Sometimes, it's just a matter of taking the time to focus on an important issue. By spending time in Quantum Focus, we can change our view of the issue and see it in a more simplistic light. Or, we can develop a strategic plan in order to resolve it. It's all about concentration and focus.

To help develop more focus, you can incorporate any or all of these specific exercises into your routine. They have the ability to significantly improve your concentration skills. Here are some effective exercises drawn from various sources:

1. **Make Notes Or a To-Do List:** Writing down tasks helps organize your thoughts and priorities, making it easier to focus on what needs to be done and what can be saved for a later date.

2. **Meditate for Five Minutes:** Meditation can calm the mind and enhance your ability to concentrate on tasks for longer periods. There are many sources that can help you begin meditating if you are just learning.

3. **Exercise:** Physical activity increases blood flow to the brain, which can help improve cognitive functions, including focus.

4. **Practice Active Listening:** Actively engaging in conversations by listening carefully and responding

thoughtfully can enhance your ability to concentrate during all kinds of interactions, including business and familial.

5. **Increase the Strength of Your Focus Gradually:** Start with short periods of focused work and gradually increase the duration as your concentration improves.

6. **Create a Distraction To-Do List:** Write down distractions as they come to mind to address them later, allowing you to return your focus to the task at hand.

7. **Move Your Body:** Regular movement breaks during work can help maintain high levels of concentration and prevent fatigue. For example, if you are working at your desk for long periods of time, take a break every hour on the hour for five minutes. Stand up and get a drink of water.

8. **Practice Concentration Meditation:** Exercises like mindful breathing can train your brain to focus more effectively on the present moment.

9. **Focusing is about saying "No":** This idea underscores the significance of prioritizing and eliminating distractions to maintain focus on what truly matters. By learning to say no to distractions and unnecessary tasks, individuals can direct their energy towards their goals and achieve greater productivity and success.

Incorporating these exercises into your routine can help improve your concentration and focus, making it easier to tackle important tasks with greater efficiency and effectiveness.

ACCOUNTABILITY ANCHORS:

1. Quantum Focus is deliberately directing your attention and energy towards a specific purpose.

2. To create Quantum Focus: remove external distractions, find a quiet environment, define the task, and set objectives.

3. Unless we choose otherwise, we do what is easy and enjoyable instead of what is difficult, what we don't know how to do, or what's most important.

CHAPTER 12

REDEFINING RICHES BY SHIFTING YOUR MONEY MINDSET FOR ABUNDANCE AND FREEDOM

"Too many people spend money they earn..to buy things they don't want..to impress people that they don't like."

– WILL ROGERS

The quote above humorously yet poignantly captures the folly of misdirecting our financial resources and efforts towards seeking approval or status, rather than focusing on what truly brings us happiness and fulfillment. Have you ever thought about how you think and feel about money? Or about why you think and feel that way? We all can hold limiting beliefs or negative attitudes about money at different times, such as feeling trapped or dependent on money for happiness or success. Our relationship with money is one of our ultimate accountabilities in life.

One compelling story of transformation is the tale of John D. Rockefeller, one of the world's wealthiest individuals and a prominent philanthropist. Rockefeller was born into modest circumstances in 1839. His early life was marked by financial instability, which could have easily fostered a negative view of money. However, Rockefeller chose to see these challenges as opportunities to learn about hard work, frugality, and the value of money. His approach to wealth was shaped by his belief that wealth was not just for personal gain but also a means to improve the world.

As he ventured into the oil business, Rockefeller's wealth grew exponentially. Despite his immense success, he never lost sight of the lessons learned in his youth. He believed that with great wealth came great responsibility. This belief led him to shift his focus from accumulating wealth to distributing it for the benefit of society.

In 1913, Rockefeller established the Rockefeller Foundation, which aimed to "promote the well-being of humanity throughout the world." His philanthropic efforts were vast and varied, including funding medical research that led to the eradication of hookworm and yellow fever, establishing universities, and supporting the arts and public health initiatives.

Rockefeller's story is a testament to the idea that one's perspective on money can evolve. He demonstrated that wealth, when viewed as a tool for positive change, can be a powerful force for good. His legacy is not just one of immense wealth but also of the impactful use of that wealth to better the lives of others around the globe.

THE QUANTUM ROOTS OF YOUR FINANCIAL MINDSET

There is an enormous amount of taboo around money. From the context of Quantum Accountability, it can be helpful to search your quantum realm to identify your thoughts, beliefs, and mindset about money. Negative mindsets on the continuum have a tendency to justify why they have less than others. As a result, they put wealthier people down, call them greedy, and come up with beliefs that validate their less abundant mindset. This only limits them.

What if we have a mindset that money is a tool? It is a medium of exchange. Money is in the quantum. It is a non-physical transfer of products or services that has replaced the bartering system. If the value I perceive I will receive is greater than the money it costs, I will gladly exchange my money for the product or service. If we agree with this mindset, and adopt it as our own, then the more value I create, the more others will exchange their money for the value I provide. In this case, money then can be a barometer for the value we create, or the impact we have on society. The key is not to focus on the money, but to focus on creating value and having an impact on the greater world.

Everyone has their own unique relationship with money. Different families have passed along different ideas about money that they have held for generations. Remember, these are referred to as beliefs and beliefs should be examined periodically to make sure that they are based on truth and serving our needs. Throughout our lives, we learn about money and financial behaviors by watching our parents or other family members. We learn how money is managed, financial decisions are made, and the attitudes and behaviors related to money from the people around us. Even if your parents had a degree in finances, you may have some beliefs that aren't serving you.

Write down in your journal what you learned about money from your parents, grandparents, and siblings. The more we know about how we think about money and prosperity, the better able we are to navigate toward a place of success and peace. You may find that you learned different lessons from different family members. Possibly, a grandparent who was a miser and saves pennies for a rainy day and an uncle who always purchases the latest toys—cars, boats, extravagant vacations. Clearly, two different views on money, but all validated by their own beliefs. To have a behind-the-scenes view on what people think about money, take a look at their spending habits. In this way, the invisible becomes visible.

If your grandparents and or parents were part of The Greatest Generation, they lived through the Great Depression and World War II, which shaped their money, wealth, and security perspectives. Our parents valued frugality and a conservative financial lifestyle. This is demonstrated by a dedication to farming, converting the harvest into food, clipping coupons, as well as the ideology of living well within the conceptual means. Neither of our set of parents spent money unnecessarily, and we as kids were expected to work hard and contribute to the family's overall good. Like many from this generation, our parents saw wealth as the result of hard work and perseverance. Stability and financial security were highly valued in our households. Our parents avoided debt whenever possible and preferred to pay for purchases in full instead of taking out loans.

We adopted many of these values, but we also adopted our own as we changed our mindsets. Whereas our parents invested more in tangible assets like property or bonds, we embraced a different outlook with our own money. We put money back into the business but also into various investments. Like them, we value long-term financial security over immediate pleasures or luxuries. That doesn't mean we don't enjoy ourselves as a family. When we are spending or investing, we think to ourselves, "Do we want to make money or make memories." You can always lose money, but you won't lose your memories.

It is paramount to adopt a positive and empowering mindset towards money if you intend to live the fullest life. See it as a tool for creating opportunities and living a fulfilling life rather than as a source of stress or limitation. You can prioritize financial independence and freedom in your life, like being independent of a paycheck or external sources of income.

We want to be free to make choices that align with our values and goals rather than solely driven by financial considerations. We want to make intentional choices matching our desired economic outcomes and long-term financial well-being.

MONEY AND ACCOUNTABILITY

Earning money and acquiring wealth are tied to the virtues of honesty, integrity, and fairness. When we need advice, we often turn to the Stoics for inspiration and direction. The Stoics, such as Epictetus, Seneca, and the Roman Emperor Marcus Aurelius, lived their lives to the fullest. They followed nature, rationality, and virtue to achieve eudaimonia, which roughly translated means, a combination of well-being, happiness, and flourishment. Ethics, integrity, and virtue play a considerable part in Stoic philosophy. Virtues valued by the Stoics include wisdom, courage, justice, and self-control. Stoics believed that ethics was not about conforming to societal norms or pursuing external rewards but rather about aligning your mind and actions with rationality and virtue. The Stoics also emphasized accepting that there are things beyond our control and that we should adapt our actions and attitudes accordingly.

Let's take a moment to discuss this idea. As we talked about earlier in Chapter 2 on mindsets, people have differing views on control. Looking again at the Mindset Continuum, the mindsets of Optimism, Growth, and Abundance reflect the idea that individuals have control over their life circumstances. While, the mindsets of Fixed, Pessimism, Scarcity, and Victim all reflect the idea that individuals do not have control over their life circumstances. This is a monumental difference.

What we can learn from this idea is that we should focus on things within our control, like our thoughts, beliefs, and attitudes. All the while knowing that there are some things which are not in our control. When it comes to these things, however, we can control how we respond to them. This is the power of being aware of the quantum realm. Like stoicism, we encourage the use of self-examination and critical self-reflection, such as self-assessment exercises.

The following is a 10-question Likert scale assessment to help you determine your view on the level of control you believe you have when it comes to money, including spending, saving, and earning it:

1. I feel confident in my cash flow and my ability to create more cash flow if desired.

1	2	3	4	5	6	7	8	9	10

STRONGLY DISAGREE   STRONGLY AGREE

2. I believe that I am secure in my financial future.

1	2	3	4	5	6	7	8	9	10

STRONGLY DISAGREE   STRONGLY AGREE

3. I do not worry that the money I have or will save won't last.

1	2	3	4	5	6	7	8	9	10

STRONGLY DISAGREE   STRONGLY AGREE

4. I can enjoy life because of the way I'm managing my money.

1	2	3	4	5	6	7	8	9	10

STRONGLY DISAGREE   STRONGLY AGREE

5. Giving a large monetary gift wouldn't put a strain on my finances.

1	2	3	4	5	6	7	8	9	10

STRONGLY DISAGREE   STRONGLY AGREE

6. I frequently have money left over at the end of the month.

1	2	3	4	5	6	7	8	9	10

STRONGLY DISAGREE   STRONGLY AGREE

7. I do not spend money without taking the time to make good decisions.

1	2	3	4	5	6	7	8	9	10

STRONGLY DISAGREE   STRONGLY AGREE

8. I am able to save as much money as I wish.

1	2	3	4	5	6	7	8	9	10

STRONGLY DISAGREE   STRONGLY AGREE

9. I feel I have enough money to live comfortably.

1	2	3	4	5	6	7	8	9	10

STRONGLY DISAGREE   STRONGLY AGREE

10. I feel that I have a clear understanding of investment strategies including the stock market and real estate. I am financially literate.

1	2	3	4	5	6	7	8	9	10

STRONGLY DISAGREE   STRONGLY AGREE

Total your points for all 10 questions.

85-100 - Your Perspective is that you are in Control of Your Money

70-84- Yor Perspective is that you are Somewhat in Control of Your Money

<70- Your Perspective is that you are not in control of your Money; Your Money Controls You

Your view of money is significantly influenced by your perception of control, often referred to as cash confidence. Changing your perception towards money to a more effective mindset can lead you to more productive daily decisions and future monetary choices. This ultimately impacts your financial success. Research has shown that how you think about money affects your feelings of meaning in life.

People with a high socioeconomic status may experience an enhanced sense of financial confidence and meaning in life, while those with a low socioeconomic status may feel a lower sense of meaning in life. The determining factor in this difference in thinking is the perception of control, or cash confidence.

Your cash confidence is intertwined with your feelings, beliefs, and attitudes towards money. By understanding and potentially changing your perception of money, you can influence your financial decisions, behaviors, and overall sense of well-being. Next, we will take some time to explore how some of us may have formed negative beliefs about money from childhood teachings.

THE ROOT OF ALL EVIL

Many people harbor negative perceptions towards individuals with wealth, stemming from a complex interplay of psychological, sociocultural, and economic factors.

On a psychological level, research suggests that wealthy people can portray a sense of entitlement, decreased empathy, and even unethical behavior. This perception of the wealthy as self-serving and disconnected from the struggles of the less fortunate fuels resentment and distrust. Moreover, the pursuit of wealth has been linked to addictive tendencies, further reinforcing the notion that the affluent are driven by greed rather than genuine purpose.

Sociocultural influences also play a significant role in shaping our attitudes towards the wealthy. In many societies, there is a longstanding tradition of viewing wealth as a symbol of privilege, corruption, and the exploitation of the less privileged. This narrative is often perpetuated through media portrayals, political rhetoric, and even educational systems, which can foster a deep-seated suspicion towards those who have accumulated substantial financial resources. For example, the portrayal of wealthy people in films like "Cruel Intentions", highlights and satirizes the ridiculousness of an extreme level of wealth and the sense of entitlement and disconnection from the struggles of others that can come with it.

This same narrative can be found in ancient texts. Many of us may remember learning about money from teachings in The Bible. One of the most famous passages regarding wealth in The Bible from Timothy is about money being the root of all evil, suggesting that an excessive desire for wealth can lead to moral compromises and spiritual harm. But then, in Proverbs, The Bible suggests that wealth can be a blessing from God, but it also comes with obligations. Wealthy people are often encouraged to be generous and help those in need.

In Mark, Jesus warns about the spiritual danger of wealth, saying it's easier for a camel to go through the eye of a needle than for someone rich to enter the kingdom of God. Is this a condemnation of wealth itself, implying that wealth is inherently sinful or that all rich people are excluded from spiritual salvation? Or, is it about the potential pitfall of attachment to material wealth and the challenges it may pose to your spiritual journey? You get to decide.

In Matthew, The Bible also emphasizes the importance of one's attitude toward wealth. "Where your treasure is, your heart will also be," suggests that if your main focus is on material wealth, that can lead you away from your spiritual and moral concerns. The Bible encourages trust in

God rather than wealth for security, equating in Proverbs that trust in riches will fall while those who trust in God will thrive. Proverbs also teaches that dishonest money dwindles while gathering money can make it grow. Taking this one step further, the more money we collect or have, the more we must give and share.

We use examples here as a reference on how complicated relationships with money can be even within one body of work. Maybe you were raised with biblical teaching, maybe not, but you owe it to yourself to explore the roots of where your money beliefs came from and make sure they are your own and that they will lead you to a state of abundance.

FINANCIAL ACCOUNTABILITY

If, at the quantum level, you hold the belief that wealthy people are inherently corrupt and unethical, then you may be less inclined to fully commit to achieving financial success yourself. This deeply-rooted perception can act as a self-imposed barrier, subtly undermining your drive and ambition.

It's important to recognize that our beliefs about money are shaped by a lifetime of experiences; everything we've ever heard, read, watched, or thought about it becomes part of our internal narrative. Developing true financial accountability means acknowledging that life is happening for us, not to us. The events we encounter, even the challenging ones, offer opportunities for growth and learning.

Embracing this mindset shift is the key to unlocking your full potential on the road to a thriving business. When you adopt an attitude of learning from failures and using adversity to become stronger, wiser, and more capable, you empower yourself to break free from the limiting beliefs that may have held you back.

Imagine the transformative power of reframing your perception of wealth and the wealthy. Instead of seeing them as corrupt, envision a world where financial success is a byproduct of hard work, innovation, and a commitment to creating value for others. This shift in perspective can ignite a newfound sense of possibility, fueling your own aspirations and instilling the confidence to pursue them wholeheartedly.

By taking full accountability for your thoughts, actions, and responses to financial events, you embark on a journey of self-empowerment. Challenges become catalysts for growth, and setbacks transform into opportunities to hone your skills and resilience. Embrace this mindset, and watch as the road to a thriving business and life unfolds before you, paved with the bricks of your own determination and self-belief.

ACCOUNTABILITY ANCHORS:

1. Your relationship with money is one of your ultimate accountabilities in life.
2. Many people harbor negative perceptions towards individuals with wealth.
3. Adopt a positive and empowering mindset towards money.

CHAPTER 13

MASTERING THE ART OF ENERGY MANAGEMENT

"Energy is the essence of life. Every day you decide how you're going to use it by knowing what you want and what it takes to reach that goal, and by maintaining focus."

– OPRAH WINFREY

If we all share the same allotment of 24 hours each day, what sets apart those who seem to achieve more? How do some individuals radiate boundless energy and drive, propelling them to greater heights of accomplishment? Entrepreneurs, in particular, stand out as dynamic architects of reality, not because they possess some secret reservoir of energy, but because they master the art of energy management.

Energy is the currency of existence, the invisible force that animates our every action and breathes life into our ideas. Those who can harness this nonphysical essence, transforming intangible concepts into tangible products and services, wield a formidable influence. As entrepreneurs, acknowledging this profound capability is crucial. It's not just about working harder; it's about working smarter, with a keen awareness of how to channel our energy efficiently.

Effective personal energy management is the linchpin of entrepreneurial success. It involves understanding the ebb and flow of our own vitality and learning to navigate it with intention. By embracing this responsibility, we unlock the potential to not only elevate our own endeavors but also to inspire and energize those around us, creating a ripple effect of productivity and innovation.

ENERGY MANAGEMENT

In today's fast-paced professional landscape, energy management is the art of diligently harnessing and conserving your physical, mental, and emotional reserves. It's the secret sauce that fuels sustained productivity, nurtures well-being, and enhances job satisfaction. By mastering energy management, you ensure that you have the vigor to excel in your role while also prioritizing self-care.

Despite the universal allocation of 168 hours each week, our daily energy levels are subject to fluctuation. A night of poor sleep can sap your vitality, leaving you lethargic. Dietary choices, like an overreliance on sugar or caffeine and indulging in processed foods, can send your energy on a rollercoaster ride. The pressures of work, from relentless stress to back-to-back meetings and marathon work sessions without breaks, can deplete your energy reserves. Even the interpersonal dynamics of managing a team can chip away at your energy.

In the realm of healthcare, such as dentistry, where precision and focus are non-negotiable, robust energy management is paramount. A well-rested and mentally sharp practitioner can provide exceptional care, ensuring patient satisfaction and safety. Beyond individual benefits, energy management is a collective boon—it wards off burnout, fosters job enjoyment, and fuels a motivated, high-spirited team.

When energy management is woven into the fabric of a practice, productivity soars. Tasks are executed with efficiency, stress diminishes, and the practice operates like a well-oiled machine. It's not just an individual endeavor; it's a team sport. A team that collectively values and practices energy management cultivates a vibrant, supportive, and synergistic work environment.

We feel some tasks are energy-draining versus energy-replenishing due to a combination of factors related to the nature of the tasks, our personal interests, and the cognitive demands they impose. Energy-draining tasks often involve activities that we find monotonous, uninteresting, or misaligned with our values, leading to a sense of disengagement and fatigue. For instance, multitasking and dealing with interruptions can significantly deplete our mental reserves by forcing our brains to constantly switch focus, which is inefficient and exhausting. Disorganization and the stress it generates can also sap our energy by creating a chaotic environment that hinders our ability to think clearly and work efficiently.

On the other hand, energy-replenishing tasks are typically those that align with our interests, strengths, and values, offering a sense of purpose and fulfillment. These tasks can induce a state of flow, where we become so engrossed in the activity that time seems to fly by, and we derive intrinsic satisfaction from the process itself. Additionally, tasks that allow for cumulative learning over time can be particularly energizing, as they contribute to our sense of progress and competence.

Moreover, the way we manage our energy throughout the day can influence how certain tasks affect us. Engaging in activities that match our current energy levels—tackling demanding, creative tasks during our peak energy periods and scheduling low-effort tasks during downtimes—can help us maintain a balance between energy expenditure and replenishment. Recognizing and minimizing energy drainers in our environment, such as excessive technology use or unhealthy dietary habits, can also play a crucial role in preserving our energy for tasks that are truly meaningful and rewarding.

VAMPIRES AND REJUVENATORS

People can also significantly influence our energy levels, often serving as either drainers or sources of replenishment. Energy drainers, commonly referred to as "energy vampires," are individuals who, intentionally or not, sap the emotional and mental vitality of those around them. Have you ever come into contact with a person who meets this criteria? They may exhibit behaviors such as constant negativity, a tendency to criticize or minimize others' achievements, or an overwhelming need for attention and validation. These interactions can leave you feeling exhausted, stressed, and emotionally depleted, as if carrying the weight of the energy vampire's needs and problems. The impact of such draining encounters can extend beyond the moment, affecting your overall well-being and ability to function effectively in both your personal and professional worlds.

Conversely, some people have the remarkable ability to replenish your energy. These are the people who radiate positivity, offer genuine support, and inspire us with their enthusiasm and zest for life. Have you ever come into contact with a person who meets this criteria? Spending time with such individuals can be uplifting, as they often encourage a sense of joy, belonging, and motivation. They can help recharge our "social battery," especially if we share common interests or values, and provide a sense of connection that is vital for our emotional health. These positive interactions can act as a counterbalance to the effects of energy vampires, helping to restore our energy reserves and enhance our resilience against future energy drains. By consciously choosing to engage more with energy replenishers and managing your exposure to energy drainers, you can protect and boost your emotional energy, leading to a more balanced and fulfilling life.

Prioritizing energy is tantamount to prioritizing health. It's a bulwark against the physical and mental tolls that lead to stress and burnout, keeping team members robust, present, and fully engaged. Among the myriad strategies to safeguard your energy, one stands out for its simplicity and efficacy: the practice of mindful breathing. This fundamental act is a powerful tool for recalibrating your energy and restoring balance to your busy workday.

THE WIM HOF-INSPIRED BREATHING EXERCISE

There is a breathing technique made famous by a Netherlands-native known as the Wim Hof Method. This technique combines specific breathing, cold exposure (including ice baths), and meditation to improve physical and mental well-being. Inspired by Wim Hof, the incredible athlete and motivational speaker known as "The Iceman", we created the breathing exercise below. It can be a great way to incorporate some of the principles of energy management into your daily routine.

Sit or lie in a comfortable, quiet place where you won't be disturbed. Close your eyes and take a moment to relax your body and clear your mind.

Begin with a few deep breaths in and out to center yourself. Inhale deeply through your nose for a count of three to four seconds. Envision filling your belly, then lungs, and finally head with the air. Exhale gently and completely through your mouth or nose for a count of five to six seconds. Continue this deep rhythmic breathing pattern, inhaling and exhaling with focus and intention.

Do this for three consecutive rounds. Each round consists of about thirty to forty breaths. You may start to feel light-headed or experience tingling sensations; this is normal. After the final exhale of the third round, take a deep breath and let it out. Then, hold your breath without forcing for as long as you comfortably can. When you need to breathe again, exhale gently and return to normal breathing. Notice the sensations in your body. Pretty cool, right?

Don't do this exercise in water or while driving. Don't push yourself to extremes. If you feel dizzy or uncomfortable, stop and return to normal breathing. The Wim Hof Method has its benefits but should be practiced cautiously; individuals with certain medical conditions should consult a healthcare professional before attempting the method.

Wim Hof also incorporated ice baths and cold exposure as a separate aspect of his method, known for its potential benefits on the immune system, circulation, and mental resilience. Cold exposure, such as a cold plunge, or cold showers, can be added to your practice gradually and should be approached with care.

OTHER ENERGY MANAGEMENT TECHNIQUES

To conserve your energy for the important things in life, it's essential to adopt strategies that help manage your physical and mental resources effectively. Besides breathing techniques, there are a myriad of other strategies that can be employed.

1. **Prioritize and Plan:** Identify the most important tasks and prioritize them. Use planning to allocate your energy effectively throughout the day, ensuring that high-priority tasks receive your best effort.

2. **Pace Yourself:** Learn to pace your activities to avoid exhaustion. Break tasks into smaller, manageable parts and take regular breaks to rest and recharge.

3. **Set Boundaries:** Establish upper and lower boundaries for your activities to prevent overexertion and to ensure you have time for rest and recovery.

4. **Simplify Tasks:** Look for ways to simplify or modify difficult tasks. This could involve using assistive devices or changing the way you perform a task to reduce energy expenditure.

5. **Delegate:** Don't hesitate to delegate tasks to others when possible. Sharing responsibilities can help conserve your energy for tasks that require your personal attention.

6. **Adopt Healthy Habits:** Engage in regular physical activity, maintain a healthy diet, and ensure you get enough sleep. These habits can improve your overall energy levels and resilience.

7. **Mindfulness and Stress Management:** Practice mindfulness, meditation, or deep-breathing exercises to manage stress and improve mental energy. Managing stress

effectively can prevent mental fatigue and keep you focused on your priorities.

8. **Listen to Your Body:** Pay attention to your body's signals and rest before you become overly tired. Recognizing your limits and respecting them is crucial for long-term energy management. Remember that each individual has optimized times of the day where they can be the most productive. The terms "morning larks" and "night owls" refer to two distinct chronotypes that describe a person's natural sleep patterns and energy peaks.   Morning larks are early risers who are more active and alert in the morning hours, while night owls tend to stay up late and are more active and alert during the evening and night. Morning larks generally find it easier to conform to typical workday schedules, which often align with their natural wakefulness in the early hours. They may also experience benefits such as feeling more rested upon waking, having greater sleep rhythm, and getting more minutes of sleep on average compared to night owls[1]. Larks are often more agreeable and happier due to their positive outlook on life, and they are more likely to exercise during the day, leading to better overall health. Night owls, on the other hand, tend to go to sleep late at night and wake up later in the morning. They may face challenges adjusting to societal norms and early work schedules, which can lead to chronic sleep deprivation and associated health risks such as diabetes, depression, or substance abuse. Despite these challenges, night owls can be more creative, as they often engage in activities that defy conventional norms and devote time to honing their skills or learning new ones during the late hours. Both chronotypes are influenced by genetic factors and the body's internal circadian rhythms, which are

regulated by the Earth's 24-hour light-dark cycle and genetic code. While genetics plays a significant role in determining whether a person is a lark or an owl, lifestyle factors such as shift work and age can also influence sleep patterns. It's important to note that most people fall somewhere in the middle of the lark-owl spectrum and can adjust their sleep patterns with lifestyle changes. For example, to become more of a morning lark, one can exercise during the day, reduce screen time before bed, sleep in a cooler room, and commit to a fixed sleep and wake schedule. Whether one is a morning lark or a night owl can affect productivity, health, and well-being. Understanding your chronotype can help in creating a lifestyle that aligns with natural sleep patterns, potentially reducing the risk of health issues and improving your overall quality of life.

9. **Leverage Natural Light:** Utilize natural light as much as possible. It can boost your mood and energy levels, making it easier to focus on important tasks. Get out into nature, preferably barefoot to reap the benefits of grounding.

10. **Connection with Others:** Connection with others acts as a lifeline, replenishing our emotional and psychological reserves, and empowering us to face life's adversities with renewed strength and vitality. It reminds us of our shared humanity, providing comfort and a sense of community that is essential for our overall well-being. From activities as simple as meeting a friend for a walk to attending a family gathering for a birthday celebration, spending time with the people close to us replenishes our energy and vitality for life.

By incorporating these strategies into your daily routine, you can more effectively manage your energy, ensuring that you have the resources needed to focus on what truly matters in your life.

ACCOUNTABILITY ANCHORS:

1. Energy is the currency of existence.
2. Prioritizing energy is tantamount to prioritizing health.
3. There are several strategies you can employ to replenish your energy.

CHAPTER 14

UNPLUGGED SUCCESS, NAVIGATING THE DIGITAL DELUGE IN THE WORLD

"We are buried beneath the weight of information, which is being confused with knowledge; quantity is being confused with abundance and wealth with happiness."

- TOM WAITS

Our world is prone to digital overload, highlighting the challenge of distinguishing valuable knowledge from the sheer volume of information we encounter daily, and reminding us of the importance of focusing on what truly enriches our lives. The deluge of information often overwhelms our capacity to absorb and process it meaningfully. In this digital age, we are inundated with data, news, opinions, and content from countless sources, bombarding us at an unprecedented pace. This relentless stream can lead to a phenomenon known as "information overload," where the sheer quantity of information available exceeds our ability to manage or make sense of it. As a result, we may struggle to extract genuine knowledge—deep, valuable insights that contribute to our understanding and wisdom—from the vast ocean of facts, figures, and noise that vie for our attention.

We are caught in the confusion between quantity and quality in various aspects of life. In a society that often equates more with better, we are led to believe that a higher volume of possessions, experiences, or social connections equates to a richer life. However, this misconception can lead us astray from the pursuit of true abundance—a state of life characterized by fulfillment, balance, and contentment. The pursuit of material wealth, similarly, is frequently mistaken for the path to happiness. Yet, time and again, we are reminded that happiness is not found in the accumulation of wealth but in the quality of our relationships, the pursuit of our passions, and the cultivation of a sense of purpose and gratitude.

Instead, we should pause and reflect on what we value most. It challenges us to sift through the clutter and noise to find the pearls of wisdom that truly matter. It encourages us to seek abundance not in the number of our possessions but in the depth of our experiences and the authenticity of our connections. And it calls us to remember that happiness is not a product of wealth but a byproduct of living a life aligned with our deepest virtues and aspirations. In essence, we should embrace a more intentional, discerning approach to the information we consume, the goals we pursue, and the measures of success we adopt.

"The Wretched Stone," written and illustrated by Chris Van Allsburg, is a children's picture book that tells a cautionary tale through the unique format of a ship captain's log. The story unfolds from the perspective of Captain Randall Ethan Hope, who leads the crew of the *Rita Anne* on a voyage. The narrative spans from May 8 to July 12 of an unspecified year, capturing the crew's experiences in journal entries.

The plot begins as the *Rita Anne* sets sail, with the crew enjoying each other's company and their journey at sea. About a month into their voyage, they discover an uncharted island where they find a strange, glowing, cubic stone. Despite the island's lack of animals and an overall eerie atmosphere, they decide to take the stone aboard their ship.

Once the stone is on the ship, the crew becomes increasingly obsessed with it, abandoning their previous interests and activities. They spend more and more time staring at the stone, leading to a puzzling transformation: gradually, all the crew members, except for Captain Hope, turn into grinning apes.

The situation reaches a critical point when a storm nearly causes the *Rita Anne* to sink. The stone's glow fades after the storm and Captain Hope seizes this opportunity to reverse the crew's transformation. In the aftermath, the captain decides to rid the world of the stone's influence by burning the ship and sinking it, with the stone aboard, to the bottom of the ocean.

"The Wretched Stone" serves as a metaphor for the impact of technology or similar distractions on our society, suggesting how such influences can lead to a loss of creativity, individuality, and engagement with the world. The story encourages us to reflect on the theme of the consequences of our choice to become distracted by our technological devices.

Over the past 50 years, the mobile phone has transitioned from being a clunky, expensive device into something in everyone's pocket. The first computer weighed 30 tons and took up 1800 square feet of space, and now we wear computers on our wrist as a watch. Our devices now go everywhere with us, from the boardroom to the bedroom. And within those devices are multiple worlds, thousands of communities, millions of conversations, and much more. Because we all now carry a digital device in our pocket, our purse, or on our wrist, we are now all hybrid beings. We rely on information from both our human component as well as our artificial intelligence component, part artificial intelligence. As the first AI generation, we are at the forefront of it all, navigating the opportunities and challenges of the digital world while contributing to the development of new technologies and ideas.

But why talk about digital use in a book about accountability? More importantly, what does our relationship with technology have to do with the quantum principles we have discussed thus far, such as mindset, beliefs, thoughts, and choices?

Our digital use has everything to do with Quantum Accountability. Taking accountability for yourself means recognizing the influences in your life. Accountability for our digital use boils down to three main points:

1. Recognize the potential harm of digital use on your quantum well-being.
2. Understand the mechanics of digital influence.
3. Develop skills to manage the challenges of digital use to maintain its benefits.

POTENTIAL HARM TO QUANTUM WELL-BEING

As we discussed in Chapter 3, you are accountable for the thoughts you think. You are also accountable for what you feed your mind. What we feed our minds via content on the news, streaming channels, and social media can slowly alter, tweak, and manipulate our mindset at the quantum level without us realizing it. It is more important now than ever for us to be disciplined and consciously control inputs with our increased use of technology.

In the 1980s and 1990s the development of obesity in America due to a bad physical diet was one of the greatest concerns to national health. In the 2010's and 2020's we are dealing with a growing health crisis that we have termed **Mental Obesity**. This is due to a bad 'quantum diet.' Our brains receive the equivalent of 20,000 emails per second. This is the chaos that is going on in our minds every waking hour. We are overstimulated, our dopamine receptors are being desensitized, and we're losing sight of stillness, mindfulness of the present moment, and an overall sense of oneness.

Accountability in regard to our digital use is critical because—like obesity or any health crisis we have seen in this country—the solution falls to the individual to make conscious decisions about what they are feeding themselves. There is so much information available to supply our quantum diet that our minds are getting overwhelmed. We are seeing increases in anxiety, depression, and suicide as a result of our mental inability to process information. Our uncanny ability to compare ourselves to others to form opinions and belief systems based on the "reality" presented to us in the digital world has become a major challenge.

DIGITAL INFLUENCE

Today's information load is vastly different from the pre-digital, pre-cell phone era. Digital use has changed how we do just about everything, from getting gas to buying groceries to working out. Let's look at these three examples to see just how much has changed between then and now.

Years ago, filling up your gas tank was usually just that—filling up your gas tank. You might talk with a gas station attendant or exchange words as you pay the cashier, but the experience was generally quiet and straightforward.

Today, you can use your smartphone to pay for things, find the cheapest local prices, play a game, or text friends while doing mundane chores and tasks like waiting for your tank to fill up. Many gas stations and grocery stores have digital screens that constantly display advertisements or news, making the experience more cluttered with information.

In the past, grocery shopping was a task involving a physical list, manually searching for items on shelves, and perhaps chatting with store employees or other shoppers. Cashiers manually entered prices or used barcode scanners, and there was no self-checkout option.

Now, many grocery shoppers have apps that help locate items in the store, compare prices, or read reviews. Some stores have digital price tags, and many offer self-checkout kiosks. Customers can receive digital coupons and promotional messages on their smartphones. Some stores even offer online shopping with in-store pickup or delivery.

Pre-digital era, gym-goers usually worked out independently or with a personal trainer, often with minimal distractions. Information came through personal trainers, books, or talking to others. Music and television were a shared experience on whatever the gym had decided to play.

Today's gym goers have a wealth of information at their fingertips. Many use smartphones to track workouts, watch fitness tutorials, or stream music and video on wireless headphones. Workouts can be through a YouTube channel, a virtual personal trainer, or an app. Gym equipment has personalized TVs broadcasting different channels, sometimes with closed captioning to accommodate people listening to their audio. Many people on the treadmill watch the news while listening to music. Gyms can also push notifications about classes, offers, or schedule changes via apps.

While many of these new developments are certainly convenient, they add to our digital mental load. More than ever, our thoughts are bombarded by the views of social media, streaming television, 24-hour news channels, and even commercially designed broadcasts blaring at us in the shopping lanes or the gas pumps.

Because of digital devices, most of us have lost the ability to be present. Many can't stand boredom or silence. If there is a free minute and we are waiting in line, most of us flip through our messages, hit up social media, or check the stock market on our smartphones and watches. Scrolling is fine for passing the time but think about how often you have been at a concert or sporting event where people are more on their phones than interacting with the people around them. At some point, we have to begin asking ourselves, "What is this doing to our minds?"

AN ERA OF DIGITAL COMPARISON

Our understanding of what is "good" has undergone a profound transformation in the past years with social media's comparison effect and influence. Constant exposure shapes our perceptions of what is actual, beautiful, successful, desired, and appropriate. Personal standards skew, leading to unrealistic expectations of life and success and putting us on the hamster wheel of comparison.

Social media companies like Instagram and Facebook have become the modern stage for people to show off their lives, accomplishments, children, and appearances. With photo editing and digital transformation, posts become the idealized version of what they should be while filtering out imperfections. The carefully curated online-existence serves as a breeding ground for comparison where we measure our imperfect lives against the flawless narratives of others. Scrolling through our feeds, we see images of tropical vacations, edited faces and bodies, and professionally decorated homes. These images set the standard for what we perceive as "good" regarding lifestyle, appearance, and success.

THE PERILS OF UNREALISTIC STANDARDS

The constant exposure to these idealized representations and consumer-driven messaging are significant. Our personal standards become skewed as we chase after an ever-elusive ideal of what is "good." This pursuit can lead to anxiety, depression, feelings of inadequacy, a distorted sense of self-worth, and a belief that you will never measure up to the unattainable standards encountered online. Studies show that excessive use of digital and social media can lead to feelings of loneliness, low self-esteem, and even suicidal thoughts.

As we get sucked into the digital world, our concept of "good" becomes increasingly superficial. Success is often equated with material wealth, physical appearance, or the number of likes and followers one has on social media. Genuine qualities like kindness, empathy, and personal growth can be overshadowed by the relentless pursuit of external validation and comparison.

Social media can also spread misinformation, causing anxiety and confusion, disrupting focus, and altering our ability to recognize reality. Regular notifications and messages can lead to stress and burnout. Overusing digital technology can decrease physical activity, increase weight gain, reduce muscle strength, and lower cardiovascular health.

Awareness of these issues and trends can help us manage our user-experience in social media. If we are trying to define what is good based on the physical rather than the quantum, we will get lost. Order, peace, clarity, and abundance have to start internally. We must be guided by an internal compass rather than by the physical reality around us because that "reality" is too unreliable and ever-shifting, especially when it shows up on your cell phone.

HOW THE DIGITAL WORLD WORKS

Understanding how the digital world functions is one way to gain back our control and inform our decisions about our digital use. Specifically, we would like to address how social media platforms harness the power of dopamine to create a digital addiction. It is also important to understand how digital advertising works to see how much money is being spent to direct and guide your thoughts and actions.

SOCIAL MEDIA USE AND DOPAMINE

The dopamine rush on services like Facebook and Instagram keeps us returning for more. Dopamine is a chemical in your body that plays a role in how you feel pleasure. It's our "reward system." Dopamine also involves motivation, memory, heart rate, and sleep. When we do something fun or rewarding, we release dopamine.

Before social media, we got dopamine hits from various sources, like spending time with friends, exercising, listening to music, eating good food, reading an exciting book, or achieving a goal. Social media has provided a new way to stimulate dopamine production. Likes, comments, shares, and followers can all provide positive feedback that prompts a dopamine hit. The dopamine rush from social media is a natural phenomenon widely studied and discussed in recent years.

Social media and consumer-direct companies have tapped into this dopamine rush by designing their platforms and algorithms to keep users engaged and addicted. Including things like notifications and infinite scrolling keeps users on the platform for as long as possible.

They even have a term for it: FOMO, which stands for Fear Of Missing Out and is one of the feelings you have that makes you want to stay. The longer you stay on, the more likely you are to buy something or let the company study and evaluate your behavior online.

Another way companies get users addicted is by using data and algorithms to personalize content to make it relevant to the individual user. Using data on the user's browsing history and behavior, companies can curate content tailored to their interests, making resisting more challenging. Next time you are searching for something on the internet, search for something random that you would typically never search for, like a rolling suitcase, a new laptop, or vitamin E. Now, look at the ads, sidebars, pop-ups, and other items that show up on your screen. This is known as retargeting. Advertisers retarget their customers by offering more options, especially if they didn't purchase. This has happened for over a decade and is considered essential in online sales.

Social media companies also employ a gamification technique using likes, shares, and followers to create a sense of social validation and competition based on the concept that more is better. These metrics are designed to keep users engaged and returning to the platform to check their progress and compare themselves. More can create a feeling of validation and self-worth and lead users to become addicted to the platform to increase their social validation.

Whether it's social media, streaming channels, or some other digital platform, algorithms are feeding you what you want to see so that they can feed you more of it, contributing to the overstimulation that we've already addressed. More importantly, the more they feed you, the more they can convince you to do what they want you to do.

THE INFLUENCE OF DIGITAL ADVERTISING

Beyond personal social media accounts, digital advertising further perpetuates the concept of "what is successful" or "what is necessary" by promoting products and services that promise to improve our lives and work. Social media advertisers leverage the power of digital platforms to target users with personalized messages. These messages are often designed to ensure constant consumption.

Social media is one of the largest marketplaces in the world, and though advertised as connecting people, the economics behind social media is product sales. Whether it's the latest beauty product, tech gadget, or dental implements, as we use social media, we are bombarded with products that we "must have" to measure up to the standard set by digital media.

Recognize the motives and the mechanics of social media. Don't fall for the hype. Social media and all digital media and resources can be powerful tools for good, but only if we do not fall prey to their downsides.

OWNERSHIP AND CONTROL IN THE DIGITAL UNIVERSE

When you create a social media account for Facebook or an Instagram profile or other social media sites and post on their sites, you enter a digital universe that is fully controlled by these companies. While they are fun, easy, convenient, and free, it's important that you understand the terms and conditions because almost no one actually reads the terms and conditions, they just head straight into use.

Whenever you upload pictures, words, video, or sound files you automatically give these companies license to use, share, and display your content. If they want to use what you posted in their advertising campaign or promotions, they can. All of these platforms have their own terms of service and community guidelines, and they use AI and human employees to enforce these guidelines. They can restrict you, suspend you, and terminate your account if they feel you have violated their terms; and though there are dispute channels, it's often difficult to reach a satisfactory resolution. If you invest a lot of time and money into your social media to build your business and following, know that at any time, you could lose access to your digital creation within your platforms.

Know that these free platforms, and many paid ones, collect your online behavior and interactions for targeting advertising or collecting user analytics. Be careful about what you share and adjust your privacy settings accordingly—but really, once you post something, it's out there and replicates before you can blink. Once you share, your content becomes part of the digital ecosystem.

Historically, in real estate transactions, there is a broker who is the mediator in any and all transactions. Social media companies act in this same manner. Do you want a social media platform to be your mediator or middleman in your relationships? Do you want to give up that control? As AI takes hold of our digital interactions, do we need to be cautious of how much control we give away?

MANAGING DIGITAL USE

We are not trying to make the argument that we should go back to life before digital devices and the internet. However, it is paramount we take accountability for how these technological developments have altered our world and impacted our quantum reality.

If we can recognize the threats, we can better navigate them while still harnessing technology and the digital world for all the good that they do provide. We use these mediums everyday and they are definitely here to stay.

FINDING BALANCE IN THE DIGITAL AGE

We can control our exposure and mitigate the negative effects of skewed personal standards and excessive comparison and consumption by being mindful of what we consume digitally. Just like you would look at a buffet of pizza, wings, burritos and chips and limit consumption for your physical health, the same thing goes for digital media. Your feeds are smart and they will deliver more of what you scroll for. Curate your social media feeds to include content that promotes positivity, authenticity, and personal growth.

Remind yourself that what you see online is a highly edited and curated version of reality. Nobody's life is THAT perfect, and it's okay to be who you are.

Keeping your online and offline life in balance makes a big difference. Even track it on your calendar. Spend time nurturing real-life relationships and pursuing activities that bring you genuine joy and fulfillment outside of the digital experience.

Interestingly, the creator of some of our favorite digital streaming has opted for a digital-free lifestyle. Christopher Nolan, the director of Inception, Tenet, Dunkirk, the Batman Dark Knight series, and most recently, Oppenheimer, is adamant about living in an analog world and uses a flip phone. Nolan doesn't use email personally and delivers scripts to lead actors by hand because he understands both the risk of digital hacks and the value of real, physical, and human interactions. He writes using a computer without an internet connection because he understands the risks of giving yourself away to a digital universe.

DIGITAL DETOX

One of the best things that you can do to relieve the burden of digital overload is to regularly perform a digital detox. Going a full day or week without your digital devices may not be realistic. Emails need to be answered, phone calls need to be made, school pickups need to be coordinated, and a million other important tasks are now done via digital devices.

What we are suggesting instead is to be intentional about when and how you use your digital devices. As we discussed in Chapter 10 on time-blocking, you can block out times of the day when you are going to check emails and follow up on text messages. You may set time limits for your social media use and create timers on your phone that will shut you out of your apps once you've reached that time limit.

You can leave your phone in a set place in the house like you would have with your old cord-bound telephone of the past so that you can grab phone calls but otherwise leave the phone be when you are home. When you do not need your phone, it helps to keep it on silent or put it in a do-not-disturb mode to avoid unnecessary notifications.

At first, you might find a digital detox day stressful as you break free from your devices and the feeling of missing out. Work through this time with an awareness of what is happening. You might check your phone a few times more than necessary in the beginning, and when this happens, ask yourself what was so important, or if it was a habit that led you to check your phone. Recognizing that it's a habit and unnecessary usually lets you go longer between phone checks.

You are learning to undo a pattern that is not serving you and getting in the way of your deep focus and relaxation. Whatever your strategy, the point is to be intentional and hold yourself accountable for what you consume, how much of it you consume, and when you consume it.

DIGITAL USE IN YOUR BUSINESS

Business owners of today are part of the first AI generation, which is rapidly changing how we live, work, and play. With the innovative tools created by AI, we need to understand the opportunities and challenges of this evolving aspect of business and our individual professions.

In dentistry, AI can analyze dental images and scan them to detect cavities, gum disease, and oral cancer. These tools help increase the accuracy of diagnoses and allow the dentist to create effective treatment plans.

Work offices can routinely use automation for administrative tasks like appointments, schedules, follow-ups, and keeping records. AI for admin can help reduce the office workload and improve workflow. The office team then has more time to focus on the guest's needs and provide superior customer experiences.

Learn more about the opportunities AI has brought to your profession and industry. In dentistry, AI's power of predictive analytics is being used to analyze patient data. These predictions can help the dentist anticipate oral health issues in the patient before they become severe. For example, entering health history and lifestyle factors into the software could help the patient understand their risk of developing gum disease.

AI can help automate tasks, record keeping, and diagnostic accuracy. It can also help dental practices save time and reduce operating costs. With AI diagnostic assistance, the dental office can decrease the number of unnecessary treatments, while administrative automation can reduce overhead costs.

From a more general business perspective, many business websites now use AI-powered chatbots that can provide 24-7 customer service, attempting to answer common questions and provide direction or simple instruction. These can be helpful or frustrating depending on the needs of your clients and their desire to speak to a human versus chatting with a robot. There are mixed reviews on the user experience depending on the need for assistance.

AI tools can automate repetitive tasks, analyze data, and give insights that help business owners make better decisions. AI can be used to improve customer service, personalize marketing efforts, and develop new products and services.

For business owners who are part of the first AI generation, we have the opportunity to take advantage of new and innovative ways to improve efficiency, productivity, and profitability with AI. However, we also face new challenges and responsibilities with the growth of artificial intelligence, especially data privacy issues, bias, and job displacement. We must navigate the legal and AI regulatory landscape.

In the dental industry, reliability is essential for making a diagnosis. AI systems rely on data sets, and that accuracy is tied to the quality of this data, leading to misinterpretation, especially in complex cases. We need human oversight to make sure our planning and treatment is accurate. Patient data must be secure. Banks and tech institutions have data breaches, cyber-attacks, and inappropriate data sharing, and the dental office is no different. Compromising patient confidentiality runs a risk, and regulatory standards for AI in healthcare are still evolving.

It's unclear who is responsible if the AI system makes a mistake—the dentist, the developer, or the AI itself. Dentistry (like most service-based companies) is a people business. Human interaction is essential to dental guests, and over-reliance on AI could affect patient-doctor relationships. This is why our accountability to people should always come before our curiosity and desire to push technological boundaries.

DIGITAL PROGRAMMING

In the past 20 years since cell phones have become popular, our lives have begun to imitate art. Look at Stanley Kubrick's 1968 film, 2001: A Space Odyssey. In the story, HAL (Heuristically programmed Algorithmic Computer) is an artificial intelligence that controls the systems of the Discovery One spacecraft on its way to Jupiter. HAL can perform many functions, including speech, speech recognition, facial recognition, natural language processing, lip reading, art appreciation, interpreting emotions, and playing chess.

Despite its programming to assist the crew and ensure the mission's success, HAL makes an error and turns on the team when they discuss disconnecting it. "HAL" is often regarded as one of the most iconic characters in science fiction cinema, symbolizing artificial intelligence's potential risks and moral implications. HAL, conceptualized initially by Arthur C. Clarke, began as a short story by Clarke titled "The Sentinel." Now, over fifty-five years later, HAL is at our fingertips.

We can also look at *Ready Player One* and *The Matrix* when discussing life imitating art. *Ready Player One* is a science fiction novel by Ernest Cline, published in 2011. The story is set in 2045 when everyone spends most of their time in a virtual world, the OASIS (Ontologically Anthropocentric Sensory Immersive Simulation). *The Matrix*, a science fiction movie from 1999, tells the story of a software engineer who secretly goes by the name Neo and learns that his world is a simulated reality called the Matrix. The Matrix wants to take over humanity.

These stories raise some great questions. There is a lot of truth in these movies. We can be programmed. Just think about being in the store when someone else's phone goes off with your ringtone, and you reach for your phone. You have been programmed.

But just as we have been programmed by our phones, we can choose to program ourselves by doing the quantum level work we have discussed throughout this book. Many times, we are not aware of the impact that excessive use of digital technology can have on our mental and physical health. This lack of awareness can make it difficult for us to recognize when we have a problem and need to seek help. It is important to be aware of the negative impact and set healthy boundaries on our digital use. We must prioritize engaging in activities that promote balance in our lives and regularly examine our digital connections.

Curb the power of the digital universe in your life by programming your use of digital tools. If you can do this, you can control the digital world rather than allowing it to control you.

ACCOUNTABILITY ANCHORS:

1. Our world is prone to digital overload, highlighting the challenge of distinguishing valuable knowledge from the sheer volume of information

2. We are dealing with a growing health crisis called Mental Obesity.

3. One of the best things that you can do to relieve the burden of digital overload is a digital detox.

SECTION 3

BEYOND THE SELF: EMBRACING ACCOUNTABILITY TO OTHERS

Embracing accountability to others is a concept that plays a crucial role in aspects of interpersonal dynamics because it fosters a culture of trust, mutual respect, and empowerment, essential for building healthy relationships and achieving collective goals.

In the following chapters, we will discuss emotional intelligence (Chapter 15), communication (Chapter 16) , relationships (Chapter 17), forgiveness (Chapter 18), and leadership (Chapter 19). By taking accountability in these areas, you are recognizing the impact your actions have on others. This fosters a culture of trust and mutual respect.

The realm of emotional intelligence requires an awareness of how one's emotions and behaviors affect those around them, urging a thoughtful and empathetic approach to interactions. Effective communication is another pillar, as it involves openly acknowledging mistakes, actively listening to others' perspectives, and engaging in constructive dialogue to resolve conflicts. In relationships, accountability strengthens bonds by demonstrating reliability and a commitment to shared values and goals. The act of forgiving, both seeking and offering, is integral to this concept, as it allows individuals and groups to move forward from past grievances with a renewed focus on growth and collaboration. Lastly, in leadership, embodying accountability sets a powerful example for others, encouraging a collective commitment to integrity and excellence.

CHAPTER 15

THE TRANSFORMATIVE POWER OF EMOTIONAL INTELLIGENCE

"Emotional intelligence is the key to both personal and professional success."

– DANIEL GOLEMAN

"Emotional intelligence is the ability to sense, understand, and effectively apply the power and acumen of emotions as a source of human energy, information, connection, and influence."

– ROBERT K. COOPER, PH.D.

The concept of Emotional Intelligence was introduced by Peter Salovey and John D. Mayer in the 1990's. They defined emotional intelligence as "the ability to monitor one's own and other people's emotions, to discriminate between different emotions and label them appropriately, and to use emotional information to guide thinking and behavior". This foundational research laid the groundwork for understanding how emotional awareness and regulation impact both your personal and your professional success.

However, it was Daniel Goleman who popularized the concept with his 1995 bestselling book titled "Emotional Intelligence". Goleman expanded on Salovey and Mayer's work by defining specific emotional intelligence skills. Goleman's book brought widespread attention to the importance of emotional intelligence in personal development and organizational leadership. He made the concept accessible to a broader audience and sparked interest in how emotional intelligence could be developed and leveraged for success in various aspects of life.

Emotional intelligence, in layman's terms, refers to our ability to recognize and understand our emotions and feelings, manage and control our reactions, and use our emotions and feelings to motivate ourselves to achieve our goals. It also involves understanding the feelings of others, empathizing with them, and building relationships effectively. By improving emotional intelligence, you can skyrocket your personal and professional success, by increasing the quality of your relationships, your decision-making, and your overall happiness. Emotional intelligence is a panacea for improving your relationships in life.

Improving your emotional intelligence is an ongoing process that involves self-reflection, practice, and a willingness to learn and grow. It takes work, but the reward is well worth the effort. By improving, you can positively impact your relationships with friends, coworkers, and others around you while fostering a more harmonious environment both at home and work. If this evidence isn't enough to convince you that this is an important chapter, then how about this statistic? with every 1 point increase in your emotional intelligence quotient (EQ), your average yearly salary will increase by $1,300 for the rest of your life. Some researchers argue that emotional intelligence is so vital for success that it may be even more important than cognitive intelligence.

Researchers have identified and studied five main components of emotional intelligence: self-awareness, emotional regulation, motivation, empathy and compassion, and social skills. All of these play a significant role in personal growth and relationships. Let's explore each of these five components.

1. SELF-AWARENESS

Self-awareness plays a fundamental role in emotional intelligence, especially in personal growth and leadership. It enables individuals to identify and regulate their own emotions, understand their impact on decisions, actions, and relationships, and to be cognizant of their strengths and weaknesses. According to cognitive neuroscientists, 95% of brain activity is unconscious, while the remaining 5% is conscious. This means that most of our actions, emotions, decisions, and behavior are influenced by the 95% of brain activity that is not consciously aware.

Consider the melody that loops endlessly in your mind during your morning commute, or the way your partner's expression can instantly stir feelings of love or frustration. These are the subtle yet powerful workings of our unconscious mind at play. In the whirlwind of daily life, we often overlook these automatic responses, reacting impulsively without a second thought. Yet, imagine the insights and growth awaiting if we paused to explore these unconscious reactions with curiosity. We invite you to embark on this journey of self-discovery, to delve into the depths of your reactions and uncover the hidden facets of your inner world.

Imagine a moment when your emotions surge like a tidal wave, overwhelming and intense, leaving you breathless in its wake. Have you ever experienced such a force? Or perhaps witnessed someone else, maybe a spouse or business partner, erupt in a volcanic display of raw emotion, leaving you astonished? While it's often easier to recognize these explosive reactions in others, the challenge lies in acknowledging them within ourselves.

Alternatively, you might find yourself on the opposite end of the spectrum, where you're the keeper of a dormant volcano. You sense the simmering emotions within that is threatening to boil over, yet you choose to suppress them, pushing them deeper into the abyss. This tendency to bury our feelings can stem from early lessons in emotional repression. Many of us were admonished as children to "stop acting like a baby" or warned that our tears would only bring more trouble. Without the understanding or tools to navigate our emotions, we cried without knowing why, never learning the language of our feelings or how to constructively engage with them. This pattern of emotional ignorance, learned in childhood, often follows us into adulthood, shadowing our steps.

Becoming aware of these patterns—whether explosive or repressive— can be a formidable journey, especially for those of us conditioned from a young age to hide our emotions. Yet, it's a journey worth embarking on, a path to understanding the messages our emotions are trying to convey and learning how to respond to them with insight and grace.

Remember in Chapter 5 we discussed the difference between emotions and feelings. Emotions are physiological responses to your mind creating a feedback loop between your thoughts and your physiological reactions. Your brain then interprets the reasoning behind your bodily sensations and you label these bodily functions as feelings. All of this happens on the quantum level without your awareness. Emotions come before feelings.

As you have grown into adulthood, you can now start to understand why. Emotions are signals from your body that something is going on. The power of awareness compounds as you learn to assess what meaning you are giving to your emotions. You have the power to even possibly control some of these bodily reactions or lessen their impact. You also have the power to recognize and regulate your feelings effectively, understanding how these feelings influence your decisions, actions, and relationships.

Not everyone thinks the same way and feels the same way—and they certainly don't respond the same way. Essentially, we all struggle with the same things to a greater or lesser degree. We all, at some point in our lives, have struggled with overreacting to situations. Being aware that your power resides in the meaning you give to your emotions gives you the freedom to choose your reaction.

In this way, you can avoid what researchers call Emotional Hijacking. This is when your emotions overpower your rational thinking, leading to impaired judgments. This happens in the part of the brain called the amygdala. Has this ever happened to you? A simple disagreement might escalate into a heated argument due to intense emotional reactions that override your rational thinking. For instance, have you ever perceived your spouse's comment as dismissive or hurtful? When this is the meaning you give to their comment, your amygdala may trigger an immediate emotional response, leading you to react impulsively with anger or defensiveness without considering the consequences. You've made a mountain out of a molehill. This emotional hijacking can result in a breakdown of communication, increased tension, and further conflict within the relationship.

Instead, it is important to continuously assess the meaning you are giving to circumstances so you can avoid irrational thinking. Maybe your spouse's comment was to help you look at the situation in a different way. Maybe your spouse's comment was coming from a loving nature? Maybe your spouse's comment was vague and the stress you are feeling from your workday has carried over into the evening; you have no patience left. Whatever the circumstance, it is helpful to ask yourself what meaning you are giving to the situation and to assess whether this meaning is 100% valid.

Another advantage of self-awareness is that it also enhances personal growth by helping you to identify your strengths, weaknesses, virtues, goals, triggers, and blind spots. This fosters self-confidence, personal development, and self-esteem. For example, by becoming aware, you may now recognize that after a long work day, you get triggered more easily. This means you have a tendency to apply a false meaning to a spouse's or your child's comments. Knowing this will help you to make the choice to not overreact, to not have complex discussions in the evenings, or to know when to disengage. We have all been in heated situations where comments are made, possibly on both sides, that cannot be taken back. It's a snowball effect. A minor disagreement turns into a major conflict. The options of either disengaging or knowing that you are not in the right frame of mind after work could have altered this creation of the snowball. In this sense, being aware of your weakness is power because you can adapt to accommodate it.

When it comes to being a leader in your business, self-awareness is essential as it enables leaders to recognize strengths and weaknesses in themselves and others, align their actions with their vision, adapt their leadership style to different situations, and build trust among team members by acknowledging mistakes and seeking feedback. When leaders have self-awareness, their ambition can be contagious.

And finally, self-awareness enhances effective communication with others, enabling individuals to positively influence and interact authentically with those around them. One example is that self awareness increases our cognizance of how we come across to others. That way, we can adjust our communication style to ensure clarity and empathy. For example, if you know that you tend to be overly aggressive and direct in your communication, then you might decide to have a manager in the room when having difficult discussions with employees. This manager should have a different communication style than you and can help to soften your directness.

2. EMOTIONAL REGULATION

Emotional regulation is the ability to recognize, manage, and respond to one's emotions in an appropriate and healthy manner. It is essential for managing emotions in a healthy way, influencing behavior positively, fostering better relationships, and promoting overall well-being. By developing effective emotional regulation skills through self-awareness and practice, individuals can navigate life's challenges more successfully and lead more fulfilling lives.

Once upon a time, in the bustling city of Sunnydale, there was a successful businessman named Mr. Thompson. He was known for his sharp business acumen, strategic decision-making, and ambitious drive to succeed. However, despite his professional success, Mr. Thompson struggled with dealing with his emotions and feelings. He wasn't emotionally intelligent and never learned about the importance of taking a look at his emotional reactions.

Every day, Mr. Thompson faced high-pressure situations, demanding clients, and tight deadlines that often left him feeling overwhelmed and stressed. Instead of managing his emotions effectively, he would react impulsively, lashing out at his employees, making hasty decisions based on frustration, and neglecting his own well-being in pursuit of success. He did not have a significant other in his life because there was no time for that outside of work. Mr. Thompson was an all work and no play kinda man. He worked 10-12 hours on most days and on weekends would spend his time reading the latest and greatest New York Times best-selling business books.

One day, during a crucial business meeting, Mr. Thompson's inability to regulate his emotions led to a heated argument with a key client. The client wanted a delivery time cut in half and this was not possible. Mr. Thompson had already reduced the price of the product so that the company would only be receiving a very small profit. And now, even after he had conceded on price, the client wanted even more. He lost it, he blew his top and told the client how he really felt. Mr. Thompson didn't control his reaction. His outburst not only ruined this business deal, but also jeopardized the entire company by damaging his reputation in the business community. Mr. Thompson, of course, validated his thoughts as the customer was being overly demanding. But because Mr. Thompson reacted in such an unprofessional way, he became known as a short-tempered, hot-head whom no one wanted to do business with. Although Mr. Thompson was bringing his 'A' game when it came to business strategy and execution, his lack of emotional intelligence overrode his work acumen. Mr. Thompson declared bankruptcy.

Emotional regulation is crucial as emotions are closely linked to thoughts and behaviors. Learning to regulate emotions allows individuals to make thoughtful choices rather than acting impulsively, leading to better decision-making, improved relationships, and enhanced mental health. Emotional regulation is a skill that can be learned and improved over time. People may find it easier or more challenging based on their experiences and upbringing. Developing emotional regulation skills involves recognizing emotions, understanding triggers, and learning healthy coping mechanisms. Unhealthy strategies like self-injury, substance abuse, and emotional eating should be avoided as they can exacerbate emotional distress rather than resolve it. Instead, adopting healthier coping mechanisms such as mindfulness, exercise, and seeking professional help can significantly improve emotional regulation and overall well-being.

Healthy emotional regulation strategies include self-soothing techniques, mindfulness, therapy, journaling, and seeking social support. When you were a baby, you developed the ability to self-sooth. For example, you learned that sucking your thumb reduced your anxiety level. What strategies do you employ as an adult? Maybe listening to music, reading a book, or exercising? What activities help to reduce your anxiety level? Let's face it, our chaotic world bombards us on a daily basis. We are constantly addressing and reacting to intense stimuli, but our power rests in our reactions. If we can teach ourselves to take an intentional interruption, then we can control our lives.

Victor Frankl wrote about this exact concept. His idea of "between stimulus and response there is a space" emphasizes the critical moment where you have the power to choose your response to external stimuli. This concept, highlighted in Frankl's book *Man's Search for Meaning*, underscores the importance of pausing and reflecting before reacting impulsively to situations. In this space between stimulus and response, individuals have the opportunity to exercise their freedom to choose how they will respond, shaping their attitudes, behaviors, and ultimately, their growth and freedom.

By recognizing and utilizing this space, individuals can break free from automatic or habitual reactions, allowing for more intentional and mindful responses. Frankl's concept emphasizes the transformative power of choosing one's response in shaping personal growth, resilience, and the ability to find meaning even in difficult circumstances.

3. MOTIVATION

Motivation is a key component of emotional intelligence and plays a significant role in personal and professional success. Motivation is intricately linked to emotional intelligence as it drives individuals to set goals, persist in their endeavors, inspire others positively, and ultimately achieve personal and professional success. By understanding the connection between motivation and emotional intelligence and actively working on developing both aspects, you can enhance your overall well-being and effectiveness in various aspects of your life.

One key trait of individuals with high emotional intelligence who are motivated is that they are willing to delay immediate gratification for long-term success. In a business context, delaying gratification may involve reinvesting profits back into the company rather than indulging in personal luxuries. The new printer is a better investment than that new speed boat. By living within one's means, limiting unnecessary expenses, and prioritizing business growth over personal spending, entrepreneurs can ensure the sustainability and success of their ventures in the long term.

In personal life, delaying gratification could mean saving money for a significant purchase instead of splurging on immediate desires. Again, put the extra money aside for the down payment on the house instead of buying the new sports car. By practicing self-control, setting long-term financial goals, and making thoughtful spending decisions, you can secure a stable financial future and achieve greater satisfaction in the long term.

Self-motivation is another crucial aspect of emotional intelligence, encompassing drive, initiative, commitment, optimism, and persistence to achieve goals beyond mere financial or personal gain. It involves finding deeper meaning and commitment to yourself and others in the pursuit of objectives.

Emotional intelligence also involves the ability to motivate others effectively. Being kind, supportive, optimistic, and leading by example are essential traits in motivating others. Integrity, optimism, good communication skills, and sharing positive energy can inspire and motivate those around you.

Personal motivation is essential to your overall emotional intelligence. It is the inner drive that propels you towards achieving goals. It involves being clear about what you want to achieve, setting milestones along the way, anticipating setbacks, and maintaining commitment to your objectives.

4. EMPATHY AND COMPASSION

Empathy involves recognizing and understanding other people's feelings, perspectives, and experiences. It allows individuals to connect with others on a deeper level, fostering better relationships, effective communication, and a sense of shared understanding. Compassion is defined as a deep feeling of sympathy and sorrow for others who are experiencing misfortune, accompanied by a strong desire to alleviate their suffering. It involves recognizing the pain or distress of others and taking action to help them, demonstrating a tangible expression of love and care for those in need.

Both empathy and compassion require us to pause from our own thinking and become aware of what's happening with the other person, which can be challenging. One of the most difficult exercises is to take the perspective of another. Try it sometime when you are having a disagreement. Force yourself to argue from the standpoint of the other side. It will promote both empathy and compassion. Here are a few reasons why these two characteristics are so important.

First, compassion goes beyond empathy by motivating individuals to take action to alleviate others' suffering or support them in times of need. It involves showing kindness, empathy, and a genuine desire to help others, which can strengthen relationships and create a positive impact on those around you.

In leadership roles, empathy and compassion are vital for building trust, motivating teams, resolving conflicts, and creating a supportive work environment. Leaders who demonstrate empathy can better understand their team members' needs, concerns, and motivations, leading to improved collaboration and performance.

Empathy and compassion also play a role in emotional regulation by helping individuals manage their own emotions in response to others' feelings. By being empathetic towards others, individuals can develop a better understanding of their own emotional responses and regulate them effectively.

And finally, the emotional intelligence skills of empathy and compassion are highly valued in the workplace as they contribute to effective leadership, teamwork, conflict resolution, and overall job satisfaction. Understanding the emotions of colleagues, clients, or employees can lead to better decision-making and more positive outcomes in professional settings.

Overall, empathy and compassion are integral to emotional intelligence as they enable individuals to connect with others emotionally, build strong relationships, demonstrate genuine care and support for others, regulate their own emotions effectively, and excel in personal and professional interactions.

5. SOCIAL SKILLS

Social skills are the keystone of emotional intelligence, equipping individuals with the ability to adeptly navigate the emotional landscapes of those around them. These skills encompass a wide array of competencies, including verbal communication, cooperation, leadership, conflict resolution, active listening, teamwork, problem-solving, and assertiveness. Given their paramount importance, we dedicate the following chapter entirely to communication and listening skills, dissecting their critical role in depth.

The significance of social skills in emotional intelligence cannot be overstated. They are the foundation upon which strong, positive relationships are built, allowing for effective communication and collaboration in both personal and professional spheres. Mastery of social skills empowers you to smoothly sail through social interactions, grasp the nuances of social norms, and react sensitively to others' emotions. Individuals adept in social nuances tend to forge stronger connections, minimize conflicts, and boost productivity through their superior communication abilities. Furthermore, social skills are instrumental in nurturing empathy and compassion, fostering an environment where understanding and kindness prevail.

These competencies are also vital for cohesive teamwork, creating a culture of trust and cooperation that leads to superior results. Leaders with robust social skills can galvanize their teams, driving performance with clarity, empathy, and strong relational bonds. Beyond leadership and teamwork, social skills are invaluable tools for stress management. They enable individuals to build a network of support, navigate conflicts with grace, and tackle life's challenges with resilience. In essence, honing your social skills is not just about improving interactions; it's about enriching your life and the lives of those around you, paving the way for a more connected and compassionate world.

USING EMOTIONAL INTELLIGENCE IN THE WORKPLACE

We recently had a situation in our dental office between two assistants over a disagreement regarding time-off requests that disrupted the workflow between these two team members. Their different communication styles, virtues, personalities, and professional boundaries resulted in conflict.

Conflict is a natural part of any work environment. Disagreements do not signal your team is dysfunctional, on the contrary, they signal your team is normal. Conflict simply means there is an issue that needs to be addressed. Being aware of my own emotions and understanding my own dislike for conflict, I needed to center myself. I was practicing the emotional intelligence component of **self-awareness**. Having a high EI starts with paying attention to my emotional state and getting myself in the right place for the conversation. This is an example of the next component referred to as **emotional regulation**.

Another component of effective emotional intelligence is **motivation**. I knew that I needed to maintain a positive outlook even in this challenging situation. But I also knew that by helping to resolve this matter, the entire office would function more effectively.

They were both stressed, and I could feel the stress creeping into my body as well, this is called **empathy**.

When I addressed my team members, I asked each of them to take a five minute break and then meet in the conference room so we could talk. This allowed everyone, including me, to take an intentional pause. We could each take a few deep breaths and regroup. Once in the conference room, I asked them to explain the situation calmly, clearly, and without blame or accusations. I then asked them to explain the perspective of the other individual, thereby practicing the **social skills** of verbal communication, cooperation, and problem-solving abilities. This was difficult and took some time as this circumstance was definitely outside their comfort zone. Together, we created a work schedule to satisfy both of them, thereby resolving the conflict. The office returned to a harmonious workplace.

What I realized was that I had been part of this problem. I had not recently checked in with these valuable team members. The shift dispute was just a symptom of a deeper issue. Had I made time to check in with these team members, I might have been able to divert this conflict before it erupted. Part of having a high Emotional Intelligence is asking yourself what role you play in other peoples' conflicts. When you are accountable for your business, you are responsible for everything that happens. I am not a counselor or a therapist, and I can't control my team's behavior or choices, but as the owner of the practice, the buck stops with me. Sometimes, investing a small amount of effort and energy beforehand can lead to significant energy savings later on.

Developing emotional intelligence takes time. Be patient with yourself as you improve in this area of your life. By embracing the principles of emotional intelligence, doors will slowly open to a more harmonious and fulfilling journey towards your future success.

ACCOUNTABILITY ANCHORS:

1. Emotional intelligence refers to our ability to recognize and understand our emotions and feelings, manage and control our reactions, and use our emotions and feelings to motivate ourselves to achieve our goals.

2. Researchers have identified and studied five main components of emotional intelligence: self-awareness, emotional regulation, motivation, empathy and compassion, and social skills.

3. Self Awareness enables individuals to identify and regulate their own emotions, understand their impact on decisions, actions, and relationships, and to be cognizant of their strengths and weaknesses.

4. Emotional regulation is the ability to recognize, manage, and respond to one's emotions in an appropriate and healthy manner.

5. Motivation drives individuals to set goals, persist in their endeavors, inspire others positively, and ultimately achieve personal and professional success.

6. Empathy involves recognizing and understanding other people's feelings, perspectives, and experiences. Compassion is a deep feeling of sympathy and sorrow for others who are experiencing misfortune, accompanied by a strong desire to alleviate their suffering.

7. Social skills include: verbal communication, cooperation, leadership, conflict resolution, active listening, teamwork, problem-solving, and assertiveness.

CHAPTER 16

THE ART OF EFFECTIVE COMMUNICATION

"The single biggest problem in communication is the illusion that it has taken place."

– GEORGE BERNARD SHAW

"Half the world is composed of people who have something to say and can't, and the other half who have nothing to say and keep on saying it."

– ROBERT FROST

Effective communication is the bridge that connects hearts, minds, and possibilities, paving the way for understanding, collaboration, and meaningful connections in every interaction. On a personal level, it allows us to forge deeper connections, resolve conflicts, and nurture our relationships with loved ones. In the workplace, clear and open communication boosts productivity, fosters collaboration, and drives innovation. It mitigates misunderstandings, prevents costly mistakes, and creates a positive work culture. On a broader scale, effective communication is vital for social cohesion, facilitating the exchange of ideas, and promoting mutual understanding across diverse communities. It empowers individuals to voice their needs, concerns, and perspectives, ultimately shaping policies and societal progress.

Effective communication is crucial because without it, life would be one big game of charades gone wrong. Imagine trying to order your favorite pizza by just flailing your arms around; you'd end up with a pineapple and anchovy monstrosity! Or picture giving directions to your friend's house by just pointing vaguely in different directions. They'd be wandering the streets forever, getting progressively more hangry. Effective communication is the grease that keeps the wheels of society turning smoothly.

A classic example that underscores the importance of the art of effective communication and the consequences of misunderstanding is the movie "Rashomon" (1950) directed by Akira Kurosawa. This Japanese film is renowned for its innovative narrative structure and exploration of the subjective nature of truth and the complexity of human psychology.

"Rashomon" presents the story of a samurai's murder and the rape of his wife through multiple, conflicting accounts from four witnesses: a bandit, the samurai's wife, the spirit of the deceased samurai (through a medium), and a woodcutter who stumbled upon the scene. Each version of the events differs significantly, reflecting the personal biases, perspectives, and motivations of the narrators.

The film unfolds at the Rashomon city gate, where the woodcutter, a priest, and a commoner take shelter from a rainstorm and discuss the recent trial concerning the samurai's death. As each story is recounted, it becomes clear that the truth is elusive, and the act of listening and communicating effectively is complicated by human nature's tendency towards self-interest and subjective interpretation.

The misunderstandings and discrepancies in the characters' stories lead to a profound exploration of the concept of truth, the reliability of human perception, and the need for empathy and effective communication in understanding others. "Rashomon" ultimately leaves the audience pondering the importance of honesty, the complexities of human communication, and the challenges of truly listening and being understood.

Communication is the precursor to success in all areas of your life. We all know that each and every one of us communicates via multiple mediums each and everyday, but we rarely take the time to improve our communication skills. Given how frequently we communicate and how crucial it is for success in our lives, why do we often neglect to invest the time and effort needed for improvement? It may be that we feel we are good enough. The idea that "good is the enemy of great" was written about by Jim Collins in his book "Good to Great." If we feel we are good enough, then we may prioritize other perceived weaknesses over improving our communication. But research indicates that effective communication is a fundamental skill that impacts nearly every aspect of human interaction.

Just as a bridge spans a gap, communication bridges the divide between individuals, enabling the exchange of information and perspectives. If you want to be an expert communicator, you need to be effective at all points in the communication process, from "sender" to "receiver", and you must be comfortable with the different channels of communication—face-to-face, online, written, and so on.

TAKING ACCOUNTABILITY FOR IMPULSES AND TRIGGERS

Recognizing and acknowledging our impulses is the first crucial step towards improving our communication skills. When we are aware of our tendencies to react impulsively, we can make more conscious choices in how we respond to others. This self-awareness is key, as it allows us to pause and consider our actions before they derail a conversation.

Understanding our personal triggers - the situations or stimuli that elicit strong emotional reactions from us - is also essential. We will continue to discuss triggers in further detail in other chapters as they have a great impact on our thoughts, feelings and behaviors. By identifying these trigger points, we can anticipate and manage our impulses before they undermine our ability to communicate effectively. Taking responsibility for our impulses, rather than blaming or projecting them onto others, demonstrates emotional accountability and maturity. This fosters an environment of trust and mutual understanding in our relationships.

Pausing before reacting, rather than immediately acting on our impulses, gives us the opportunity to respond thoughtfully and productively. This "press pause" approach can prevent miscommunication and regrettable actions that damage our connections with others. Developing self-control and impulse management skills, such as through mindfulness practices, can make us more emotionally intelligent and effective communicators overall. We become better able to listen actively, regulate our emotions, and have productive, constructive dialogues.

Finally, openly communicating about our triggers and impulses with trusted partners or colleagues allows them to better understand and support us. This transparency builds stronger, more resilient relationships, as we demonstrate a willingness to be vulnerable and work on ourselves in all areas, including the quantum level. By taking accountability for our impulses and triggers, we unlock the potential for more meaningful, productive interactions that strengthen the bonds we share with the important people in our lives.

COMMUNICATION IS A PROCESS

Communication is a complex process that involves multiple steps and components to ensure effective transmission of meaning between individuals. The communication process begins with the sender having an idea to communicate, which is then encoded into words, symbols, or gestures to convey meaning. This encoded message is transmitted through a chosen medium, such as verbal, written, or visual channels, to the receiver for decoding. The receiver interprets the message based on their experiences, attitudes, skills, and culture. Feedback from the receiver is crucial as it allows the sender to evaluate the effectiveness of the message and make any necessary clarifications. Noise, which can be environmental or semantic, can interfere with any step of the communication process and hinder clear understanding.

Overall, the communication process involves five key steps: idea formation, encoding, channel selection, decoding, and feedback. Each step plays a vital role in ensuring that messages are accurately transmitted and understood without misinterpretation or confusion. Effective communication relies on active participation from both the sender and receiver, as well as a deep understanding of the process and its interconnected factors to facilitate successful interactions.

IDEA FORMATION

Before you start communicating, take a moment to figure out what you want to say, and why. Don't waste time conveying information that isn't necessary; and don't waste the listener or reader's time either. Too often, people just keep talking or writing because they think that by saying more, they'll surely cover all the points. Often, however, all they do is confuse the people they're talking to. Precision is the key.

Before you communicate, gain intentional clarity. What and why are you communicating? Understand your audience. With whom are you communicating? What do they need to know? Plan what you want to say, and how you'll send the message. Seek feedback on how well your message was received. When you do this, you'll be able to craft a message that will be received positively by your audience.

Effective communicators use the KISS ("Keep It Simple and Straightforward") principle. They know that less is often more, and that good communication should be efficient as well as effective.

ENCODING – CREATING A CLEAR, WELL-CRAFTED MESSAGE

When you know what you want to say, the next step is to decide exactly *how* you'll say it. To achieve this, you need to consider not only what you'll say but also how you think the recipient will perceive it. We often focus on the message that we want to send, but not the way in which we'll send it. But if our message is delivered without considering the recipient's perspective, it's likely that part of that message will be lost. To communicate more effectively, start by first understanding what you truly want to say, then anticipate the other person's reaction to your message. Choose words and body language that allow the other person to really hear what you're saying. For example, get on their level; if they're standing, then stand, if they're sitting, then sit. When one person is physically positioned higher than another, such as sitting while the other stands, it can create a psychological and social dynamic that may affect the communication process.

With written communication, make sure that what you write will be perceived the way you intend. Words on a page generally have no emotion—they don't "smile" or "frown" at you while you're reading them (unless you're a very talented writer, of course!) When writing, take time to review your style, avoid slang, check your grammar and punctuation, and analyze your tone, attitude, nuance, and other subtleties. If you think the message may be misunderstood, it probably will. Take the time to clarify. Familiarize yourself with your company's writing policies or style guides. Also, whether you speak or write your message, consider the cultural biases. If there's potential for miscommunication or misunderstanding due to cultural or language barriers, address these issues in advance. Consult with people who are familiar with these types of barriers and do your research, so that you're aware of problems you may face.

CHANNEL SELECTION

Along with encoding your message, you need to choose the best communication channel to use to send it. You want to be efficient, while also making the most of your communication opportunity. Using email to send simple directions is practical. However, if you want to delegate a complex task, an email will probably just lead to more questions, so it may be best to arrange a time to speak in person. And if your communication has any negative emotional content, stay well away from email or other written forms of communication. Make sure that you communicate face to face or by phone, so that you can judge the impact of your words and adjust your message appropriately.

When choosing the right channel for your message, consider the following: the sensitivity and emotional content of the subject, the ease of communicating detail, the receiver's preferences, any time constraints, and the need to ask and answer questions.

DECODING – RECEIVING AND INTERPRETING A MESSAGE

We have the tendency to focus more on what we have to say rather than on listening. The reasons why we behave in this way can be attributed to several factors. One reason is egocentrism, as most people often prioritize their own thoughts, feelings, and perspectives over others'. It could also be due to our desire to be understood, as many individuals have a strong desire to be understood and heard, which can lead them to focus more on expressing themselves than on understanding the other person. Another explanation could be that we are preparing to respond. While another person is speaking, individuals might start preparing their response rather than fully listening. This preparation can distract from truly understanding the speaker's message.

In addition, it is a basic sociological principle that we have a fear of silence. People are uncomfortable with pauses or silence in conversation and rush to fill these gaps with their own speech. This fear can prevent them from giving adequate space and attention to listening. It could also be attributed to a lack of listening skills as effective listening is a skill that requires practice and development. Some individuals may not have developed strong listening skills, leading them to focus more on speaking.

And finally, cognitive load may be the culprit. Listening attentively requires mental effort and concentration. If a person is preoccupied or stressed, they may find it challenging to focus on listening and instead revert to speaking about their own concerns. If you've ever tried to have a conversation with a friend who is attending to their fussing child, then you've witnessed this firsthand.

Improving communication requires a conscious effort to balance speaking and listening. However, to be a great communicator, you also need to step back, let the other person talk, and listen. This doesn't mean that you should be passive. Listening is hard work, which is why effective listening is called active listening. To listen actively, give your undivided attention to the speaker, look at the person, pay attention to his or her body language, avoid distractions, nod and smile to acknowledge points. Occasionally think back about what the person has said. Allow the person to speak, without thinking about what you'll say next and don't interrupt.

FEEDBACK

You need feedback, because without it, you can't be sure that people have understood your message. Sometimes feedback is verbal, and sometimes it's not. We've looked at the importance of asking questions and listening carefully. However, feedback through body language can also help you to assess the impact of your message. By watching the facial expressions, gestures, and posture of the person you're communicating with, you can spot: confidence levels, defensiveness, agreement, comprehension, level of interest, level of engagement with the message, and truthfulness.

As a speaker, understanding your listener's body language can give you an opportunity to adjust your message and make it more understandable, appealing, or interesting. As a listener, body language can show you more about what the other person is saying. You can then ask questions to ensure that you have, indeed, understood each other. In both situations, you can better avoid miscommunication if it happens.

Feedback can also be formal. If you're communicating something really important, it can often be worth asking questions of the person you're talking to to make sure that they've understood fully. This is referred to as checking for understanding. And if you're receiving this sort of communication, repeat it in your own words to check your understanding.

Strong communication skills, like active listening, help us understand our others' mindsets. Without it, there can be a breakdown in internal workflow. Effective communication is also important in order for families to stay in alignment. Strategies in effective communication encompass a range of techniques and approaches aimed at enhancing clarity, empathy, active listening, and mutual understanding in interactions. These simple yet effective strategies can greatly improve your ability to communicate in all aspects of your life . By employing these strategies, you can foster open communication, build trust, resolve conflicts constructively, and cultivate positive relationships in various personal and professional settings.

COMMON COMMUNICATION MISTAKES

Sometimes, communication can go awry. Has this ever happened to you? Even with ideal planning, there is a breakdown in the communication process. Miscommunication can arise from various sources, including unclear messaging, differing interpretations, emotional biases, cultural differences, and inadequate feedback. These mistakes can lead to misunderstandings, conflicts, missed opportunities, and damaged relationships. Recognizing the common pitfalls in communication is essential for improving clarity, empathy, active listening, and overall effectiveness in conveying messages and fostering meaningful connections. By addressing and learning from these mistakes, individuals can enhance their communication skills and navigate interactions with greater awareness and proficiency. Common mistakes to avoid in communication:

1. **Taking a One-Size-Fits-All Approach:** Tailor your communication style to fit the person or group you are interacting with, as different individuals may require varied approaches. You may use your assertiveness when dealing with a used car salesman, but this communication style isn't the best choice when having a romantic dinner with your wife on Valentine's Day.

2. **Letting Emotions Take Control:** Avoid letting emotions dictate your communication; instead, strive to maintain composure and address situations objectively.

3. **Avoiding Difficult Conversations Via Written Communication:** While challenging, it is crucial to have difficult conversations face-to-face rather than through email or text to address issues effectively.

4. **Not Speaking Up About Your Wants and Needs:** Be assertive in expressing your own needs and desires while being respectful of others' requirements. You may have to practice saying, "No."

5. **Interrupting Others:** Interrupting someone while they are speaking is considered rude and dismissive; practice active listening and wait for an appropriate moment to contribute to the conversation.

6. **Reacting Instead of Responding:** Reacting impulsively can lead to misunderstandings; take a moment to respond thoughtfully after an intentional interruption. This is emotional regulation as we discussed in the previous chapter.

7. **Speaking More Than Listening:** Remember that communication is a two-way process; prioritize listening over speaking to ensure effective dialogue and understanding. By

being mindful of these common pitfalls and actively working to avoid them, individuals can significantly enhance their communication skills and foster better relationships both personally and professionally.

DEVELOPING LISTENING SKILLS

Because listening is one of the most important steps in the communication process, it is essential to work on and improve this skill within ourselves. You can implement certain strategies to improve your communication in both your business endeavors and personal relationships. These skills include active listening, mirroring, and coherence breathing.

Active listening involves fully focusing on the speaker, asking clarifying questions, and paraphrasing to ensure understanding. Mirroring the other person's tone, pace, and body language can help build rapport and empathy. Coherence breathing, a technique that synchronizes your heart rate and breathing, can also enhance your ability to listen deeply and respond thoughtfully. By mastering these communication skills, you can foster more meaningful, connected relationships in all areas of your life.

ACTIVE LISTENING

Active listening is more than just hearing what the other person is saying. It's about giving your undivided attention to the speaker, genuinely understanding their perspective, and earning their confidence in your ability to help them with their needs.

Here is what it looks like: Imagine a coworker is telling you about a problem with a patient. You focus on what they are saying and demonstrate active listening by making eye contact, nodding your head, and asking questions in the spirit of helpfulness and understanding.

Active listening involves:

- Putting down your device.
- Turning and facing the person.
- Sitting at eye level if possible
- Making eye contact
- Nodding to show you are paying attention.
- Asking for clarification, "I don't understand...""Can you elaborate on…"

In our era of texting and instant digital communication, the human connection skills required for active listening can easily erode. However, the goal is not for you to solve the problem or dictate a course of action, but rather to create a space where the person feels truly heard. By asking questions like, "You must have been so frustrated, what did they do next?" you demonstrate genuine care and a desire to understand their experiences. Even if you cannot directly resolve the situation, people feel a profound sense of relief when they feel truly listened to. This simple act of being present and empathetic can have a ripple effect, enabling them to show up more fully – whether in their work, relationships, or any other endeavor they undertake.

Listening attentively helps us better comprehend others' concerns, apprehensions, needs, and expectations. This understanding allows us to tailor our services to their specific requirements, ensuring superior outcomes and a more gratifying experience. As business owners, we recognize that guests share their positive and negative encounters with family and friends, which is crucial for businesses relying on word-of-mouth. In the dental field, guests are more inclined to trust and feel at ease with a dentist who listens intently to their worries. Trust forms the bedrock of a robust patient-dentist relationship, potentially leading to improved treatment adherence and loyalty.

While many of the examples and anecdotes featured in this chapter (and others) are drawn from my (Dr. Kremer's) experience in the dental field, the principles and strategies outlined can be applied to a wide range of professions and personal relationships. We encourage you to thoughtfully consider how these insights might enhance your own business endeavors, as well as your most cherished interpersonal connections.

Active listening enables us to connect with the people we serve on an emotional plane. It allows us to empathize with their fears or anxieties, which is especially crucial in a field where dental phobias are prevalent. Empathy and compassion can significantly alleviate patient stress and discomfort. Misunderstandings or miscommunication can result in treatment errors or patient dissatisfaction. Active listening helps prevent these issues by ensuring that both parties are on the same wavelength, reducing the risk of costly mistakes.

Active listening is not limited to dental-patient interactions; it's equally essential among our team members. When we listen to our colleagues and vendors, we foster an environment where ideas, concerns, and feedback can be openly shared. In my practice, I provide training and workshops on effective communication, including active and attentive listening techniques. As a leader, I set the tone for the workday by practicing what I teach. My team observes and listens to how I interact and follows my lead.

I also allocate time for mentoring and coaching with my team, ensuring they feel comfortable asking questions, sharing their concerns, and improving their communication skills. Our regular team meetings include stories from the month that allow us to learn through parables; we remember the story and incorporate the lesson, which is far more effective than merely listing dos and don'ts.

MIRRORING

Mirroring is a crucial component of active listening that extends beyond mere auditory attentiveness. It involves subtly reflecting a person's words, emotions, behavior, or body language back to them through your own nonverbal cues. The goal is to create an environment where the individual feels truly seen and heard, thereby establishing rapport.

For instance, if a patient speaks softly and gently, responding in a similar calm manner can help them feel comfortable and demonstrate that you relate to their demeanor. Mirroring nonverbal cues, such as leg crossing, can put the individual at ease and convey that you are on the same wavelength.

This technique fosters a more comfortable and empathetic atmosphere, significantly easing apprehensions. Using similar language or expressions shows genuine empathy for their feelings, making their experience less stressful and more patient-centered.

Mirroring is a powerful tool that enhances the active listening process by creating a sense of connection and understanding between healthcare professionals and patients. When utilized effectively, it can improve patient satisfaction, trust, and overall treatment outcomes.

Here are some examples of Mirroring Techniques:

1. **Verbal Mirroring:** If someone says "I had a really long day at work today," you could mirror their words by responding

with something like "A long day at work, that sounds draining".

2. **Tone/Volume Mirroring:** If the person you're speaking with has a soft, gentle tone of voice, you could mirror that by responding in a similarly calm, quiet tone. Or if they are speaking loudly, you could match their volume level.

3. **Body Language Mirroring:** If the person crosses their legs, you could subtly cross your legs in a similar way after a short delay. Or if they lean back in their chair, you could mirror that relaxed posture.

4. **Facial Expression Mirroring:** If the person smiles while telling a story, you could reflect that positive expression with a warm smile of your own. Or if they look concerned, you could mirror that with a sympathetic facial expression.

5. **Breathing/Pace Mirroring:** Matching the pace and rhythm of someone's breathing or speech patterns can create a subtle sense of synchronization.

The key with mirroring is to do it naturally and gradually, and not to mimic exactly in an overly obvious way. The goal is to subtly reflect the other person's verbal and non-verbal cues to build rapport and make them feel understood.

COHERENCE BREATHING EXERCISE

There is an exercise that involves paying close attention to another person's emotions and reflecting them back through breathing called Coherence Breathing. It is also often referred to as "co-regulation" or "interpersonal respiratory biofeedback." It is a method of synchronizing breathing patterns between two or more people. By synchronizing breaths, we can achieve a mutual state of calm, foster connection, and improve overall emotional regulation.

Sit comfortably facing each other, maintaining a relaxed posture. Close your eyes if you're comfortable with it or maintain a soft gaze.

One person takes the lead by initiating a slow, rhythmic breathing pattern. The lead person starts inhaling for a count of five to six seconds and exhaling for the same duration. The second person matches this rhythm, syncing their own inhales and exhales with the lead person's breath.

Continue to maintain this synchrony for several minutes. You can lightly tap your finger or nod your head to help keep the rhythm.

Once the session is done, check yourself. How do you feel? Hopefully, more connected, calm, and in alignment.

This practice can be particularly beneficial for couples, parents and children, friends, or even as a group exercise in team-building activities. If one person focuses on matching the inhale and exhale of the other person, then by the end of the exercise, they will be more in alignment. In this capacity, there is a peace that will fill the surrounding space as the two of you become one breath.

LISTENING IS A FUNDAMENTAL OF GOOD RELATIONSHIPS

Listening is the cornerstone of building strong, trusting relationships with guests and coworkers in a business setting; even more than speaking on some days. The ability to truly hear and understand each other, whether it is a guest's concerns or a colleague's ideas, provides excellent service and builds a happy workplace.

Guests visiting our dental office often come in with anxieties, questions, or specific dental concerns. Some are in pain. But by actively listening to their fears and needs, we create a safe and empathetic space that helps alleviate their problems as well as their pain. Guests want to know that they are understood and that their dental care is personalized to them. Satisfied patients will likely return for regular check-ups and recommend our services to friends and family. This helps maintain a steady guest base and contributes to the growth and reputation of our dental office within the community.

Our dental office is a collaborative environment where every member contributes to the overall patient experience. When my team members feel heard and respected, they are more willing to share ideas, voice concerns, and work together to find solutions. Open lines of communication enable us to identify areas where the practice can enhance its services, streamline processes, and create a better work environment. Effective communication and active listening develop a sense of unity and camaraderie among colleagues, improving the work environment, and boosting morale and productivity.

One of my favorite acronyms for a good business relationship is FOWTWAGITT. It simply means "find out what they want and give it to them!" As long as what they want aligns with your core values and vision for your life, go for it. Relationships are a place to give not get.

At the end of the day, listening as a fundamental cornerstone of your business leads to increased guest satisfaction, improved teamwork, and higher job satisfaction among your team, contributing to your business' overall success and sustainability.

COMMUNICATING COMFORTABLY WITHIN CONFLICT

Conflict is a natural and inevitable part of any relationship, whether with a significant other, family member, or colleague. How we handle conflict can impact our relationships' quality and overall mental health and well-being. Becoming comfortable with conflict is important to improving our relationships and leading a more fulfilling life.

The first step to becoming comfortable with conflict is to accept that it is a natural part of any relationship. Try to see conflict as an opportunity for growth and to build a stronger relationship rather than something to avoid. We can use all the tools we learned in this chapter: empathy, listening, FOWTWAGITT, and compassion as we problem-solve.

If it helps, write in a journal. Why do you feel uncomfortable with conflict and what underlying emotions drive your reaction? This can help you better understand your behavior and develop effective conflict-resolution strategies.

One of the common reasons we shy away from conflict is the fear of confrontation. Whether it's a guest hesitant to express dissatisfaction with your service or a team member who is reluctant to address an issue, confronting someone else is intimidating. Many of us worry about potential adverse reactions or escalation, which often means we avoid addressing concerns altogether.

Most of us want peace and positive interactions in our personal and professional lives. Conflict can be seen as disruptive and counterproductive to these goals. Avoiding conflict to preserve peace happens all the time, but not addressing the conflict does nothing to solve the underlying issues. Guests might worry that expressing dissatisfaction will negatively impact their rapport with you, while team members might fear that addressing an issue could harm their working relationship.

Some of us have a deeply ingrained belief that conflict is inherently wrong or that it reflects poorly on our character. This perception makes us hesitant to engage in conflict, even when necessary for improvement.

Remember back to the fixed versus growth or abundance mindsets in the earlier chapters. A growth mindset views challenges and setbacks as opportunities for growth and learning. Accepting this helps you approach conflict with a more positive and proactive attitude, which can increase your comfort level with conflict.

If conflict is still causing significant stress or anxiety, consider seeking outside support. Talking to a therapist or coach can help you develop effective conflict-resolution strategies and provide a safe space to process your thoughts and feelings, which might stem from childhood experiences. Remember, it is this quantum-level work that will ultimately free you up to experience joy and abundance in the here and now. It is worth the work!

ACCOUNTABILITY ANCHORS:

1. Communication is the precursor to success in all areas of your life.
2. Communication is a process.
3. Active listening is giving your undivided attention to the speaker, understanding their perspective, and earning their confidence in your ability to help them with their needs.

CHAPTER 17

THE TAPESTRY OF CONNECTION, WEAVING STRONGER RELATIONSHIPS IN LIFE

"Shared joy is a double joy; shared sorrow is half a sorrow."

– SWEDISH PROVERB

The relationships we cultivate throughout our lives form an intricate tapestry that provide warmth, comfort, and meaning to our existence. Just as the skilled weaver carefully selects each thread and knots them together with precision and care, we too must be intentional about nurturing the bonds that connect us to others. Whether familial, romantic, or platonic, healthy relationships serve as the strong main threads upon which the vibrant cross threads of our experiences are woven, creating a tapestry that is not only beautiful but also resilient and enduring. By understanding the profound impact of human connection on our overall well-being, we can learn to weave more fulfilling relationships that enrich our lives and provide a supportive foundation for growth and happiness.

There is an ancient story that highlights the importance of having meaningful relationships. It is the story of Baucis and Philemon from Roman mythology, which is recounted in Ovid's "Metamorphoses." This tale exemplifies the depth of companionship and the rewards of hospitality and kindness.

Baucis and Philemon were an elderly couple living in a small, humble cottage in Phrygia. Despite their poverty, they were known for their love for each other and their willingness to help others. One day, Zeus and Hermes visited the earth disguised as weary travelers. They sought shelter in the village but were turned away by all except Baucis and Philemon, who welcomed them into their home and offered them what little food and comfort they had.

Touched by the couple's generosity and the genuine love they shared, the gods revealed their true identities. As a reward for their kindness and the meaningful relationship they had nurtured with each other and their guests, the gods granted them a wish. Baucis and Philemon asked to be priests in the temple of the gods and to die together so that neither would have to live without the other.

When their time came, the couple was transformed into an intertwining pair of trees, an oak and a linden, growing from a single trunk. This transformation symbolized their inseparable bond and the enduring nature of their relationship, even beyond death.

The story of Baucis and Philemon teaches us the value of meaningful relationships based on love, hospitality, and mutual respect. It shows that such relationships can not only enrich our lives but also leave a lasting legacy that transcends time.

STRATEGIES FOR IMPROVING RELATIONSHIPS

Relationships are integral in amplifying our happiness and mitigating our hardships. Relationships create the opportunity to leave meaningful legacies through the connections we have with others. These connections enrich our lives. Relationships are a choice. Relationships are a place to give. Taking accountability in relationships means recognizing that you made a choice and that choice requires you to give of yourself. Taking accountability in relationships means acknowledging the impact of your behaviors on the other person. It is owning your contribution to any negative cycles within the relationship. It involves understanding that while you are not responsible for others' feelings, your actions and words do affect them, and being mindful of this impact is crucial for a healthy relationship.

Accountability is about more than just admitting when you're wrong; it's about recognizing your role in the dynamics of the relationship and actively working towards positive change. This goes for business and personal relationships. There are several strategies that we can use to improve the quality of our relationships.

REVISITING SELF AWARENESS

Improving relationships often starts with self-awareness and a willingness to examine our own behaviors. When we take the time to honestly reflect on how our actions and attitudes impact those around us, we open the door to positive change. By acknowledging our tendencies to be critical, withdrawn, or inconsiderate, for example, we can make a conscious effort to be more understanding, communicative, and considerate. This self-reflection allows us to identify areas for improvement and develop strategies to become better partners, friends, or family members. When we take responsibility for our behaviors, we demonstrate maturity and a commitment to the relationship, which can foster greater trust, empathy, and connection with the important people in our lives. Ultimately, acknowledging our behaviors is a crucial first step towards building and maintaining healthier, more fulfilling relationships.

UNDERSTANDING TRIGGERS

One of the most powerful strategies for improving relationships is taking accountability for your own actions and their impact on others. This involves delving deeper into the underlying factors that shape our behaviors and reactions. Many of our relationship issues are exacerbated or ignited by what scientists refer to as "triggers" - unconscious stimuli that activate powerful emotional responses within us.

These triggers often operate at a quantum level, existing in the unseen realms of our psyche. They are the sleeping giants, dormant and unperceivable, until something in our environment or interactions awakens them. When triggered, the fury of unresolved feelings, past hurts, or deep-seated insecurities can be suddenly released, leading to overreactions, defensive behaviors, or hurtful actions that damage our relationships.

By taking the time to understand our own triggers, we can start to recognize the patterns and origins of our behaviors. This self-awareness allows us to take responsibility for our reactions, rather than blaming or projecting them onto others. When we can acknowledge our triggers and the role they play, we open the door to more constructive communication, empathy, and the ability to make amends. Ultimately, this level of accountability and insight is a crucial step towards building stronger, more resilient relationships built on mutual understanding and trust.

When we are willing to acknowledge our mistakes, apologize sincerely, and make amends, it demonstrates maturity, empathy, and a genuine desire to strengthen the relationship. Conversely, avoiding responsibility or blaming others creates distance and resentment. By owning up to our role in conflicts or hurt feelings, we show the other person that we value them and the relationship enough to be vulnerable and make changes. This accountability builds trust and paves the way for productive conversations about how to move forward in a more positive direction. Additionally, taking accountability models healthy relationship behaviors that the other person can then adopt as well. Ultimately, the willingness to be accountable is a sign of emotional intelligence and a commitment to the relationship that can deepen intimacy and resolve issues more effectively.

Accountability fosters trust, dependability, and a deeper connection between partners. It allows for growth and healing within the relationship by creating a safe space for both partners to express their needs and vulnerabilities. By taking responsibility for your actions and their impact, you contribute to a more compassionate, empathetic, and supportive relationship.

In essence, accountability in relationships is about being answerable to your partner for your past, present, and future behavior, recognizing that your actions have consequences, and being committed to personal growth and the health of the relationship.

COMMUNICATING OPENLY AND EFFECTIVELY

As we discussed in Chapter 16, effective communication is the cornerstone of healthy, thriving relationships. When we communicate openly and authentically with our partners, friends, and loved ones, we create an environment of trust, understanding, and emotional intimacy.

This involves not only clearly expressing our own thoughts, feelings, and needs, but also actively listening to the other person's perspective with empathy and an open mind.

Communicating effectively means being vulnerable enough to share our deepest hopes and fears, while also respecting boundaries and allowing the other person to do the same. It requires the courage to have difficult conversations, to apologize sincerely, and to work through conflicts in a constructive manner. By honing our communication skills, we can learn to navigate relationship challenges with greater skill, resolve misunderstandings, and deepen our connections. Ultimately, open and effective communication is the lifeblood of any healthy relationship, fostering stronger bonds, greater mutual support, and a profound sense of being truly seen and heard..

One of the most impactful strategies for open and effective communication is the ability to shift from a reactive mindset to one of genuine understanding. It's all too easy to get caught up in the heat of the moment, formulating our next response before the other person has even finished speaking. However, when we make a conscious effort to truly listen and seek to understand the other person's perspective, it can transform the dynamic. By suspending our own agenda and biases, and instead focusing on empathizing with how the other person feels, we create an environment of trust and mutual respect.

This shift allows us to have more meaningful, productive dialogues where both parties feel heard and validated. Rather than simply reacting defensively or trying to "win" the argument, we can respond with compassion and a genuine desire to find common ground. Over time, this approach helps to resolve conflicts, deepen intimacy, and foster stronger, more resilient relationships built on a foundation of mutual understanding.

CULTIVATING A GROWTH-ORIENTED MINDSET

Adopting and nurturing a growth-oriented mindset is a powerful strategy for improving relationships over the long-term. In terms of relationships, this mindset is characterized by a belief that challenges, conflicts, and even failures within a relationship are opportunities for learning and positive change, rather than insurmountable obstacles. When we approach our relationships with a spirit of curiosity and a willingness to evolve, it allows us to navigate difficulties with greater resilience and adaptability.

Rather than becoming defensive or rigid when problems arise, a growth-oriented person will seek to understand the root causes, take accountability for their part, and collaborate on constructive solutions. This openness to feedback and commitment to personal growth demonstrates maturity and a genuine investment in the relationship. It also inspires the other person to adopt a similar mindset, creating an upward spiral of mutual understanding, compromise, and a shared desire to strengthen the bond between you.

Ultimately, cultivating a growth-oriented perspective enables us to see challenges not as threats, but as opportunities to deepen intimacy, build trust, and develop the skills necessary for maintaining healthy, fulfilling relationships over time. By embracing this mindset, we unlock our potential to weather any storm and emerge from it with an even stronger, more meaningful connection.

BELIEFS ABOUT RELATIONSHIPS

Our beliefs about relationships, the thoughts we let govern our interactions with loved ones, and our behavior around others all go back to the quantum realm of mindset. Part of the quantum work we are accountable for (especially in regard to our relationships with others) is to understand where those beliefs come from so that we can identify why we relate to others the way we do, and how to make changes at a quantum level that will positively impact our relationships in the present.

As we have discussed, we cannot see the voices in our heads—the intra-communication of what we say to ourselves inside occurs on a quantum level—but those internal conversations impact how we choose to interact in relationships. For many of us, the thoughts, beliefs, and attitudes that we formed about relationships were fed to us before we were able to consciously choose what to feed our minds. Belief systems about what constitutes a healthy, desirable relationship were formed when we were young, before we could process that information from a state of true accountability.

Now that we are adults, it is our responsibility to examine these beliefs and determine whether they serve us, align with reality, and produce the results in our relationships that we want. So many factors can influence a child's outlook on relationships. Were they raised in a big family versus a small family? Were their parents married? How long had they been married by the time a given child came along? How did the family (and the parents specifically) deal with relationship challenges? How did they communicate? How did they stick it out through tough times? Or did they call it quits? Maybe even call it quits several times? All of these experiences at a young age can leave a lasting impression on a growing mind of what is deemed valuable in relationships and how to approach them.

Once we recognize the power of these quantum beliefs regarding relationships that was instilled in us as children, we can take accountability for them. And then we can work to change what does not serve us. We can intentionally capitalize on the positive beliefs that we grew up with while also working to change the negative ones. Thus, Quantum Accountability in our relationships means being more intentional and conscious of how the quantum factors of our lives impact the things that we value in relationships and how we engage in them, and then actively working to address those issues to improve our relationships.

COMMUNICATION IN RELATIONSHIPS

Intentions, Expectations, Time

In the previous chapter, we discussed communication and listening skills to a greater extent, but we cannot emphasize enough the importance of effective communication in relationships. We can all improve our communication. The most important thing we can do is to spend a little time and a small amount of effort at the quantum level to achieve this improvement. Organize your thoughts and think about your expectations before you begin to communicate.

If your goal is to cook a magnificent meal, you gather the best ingredients and kitchen tools and then follow a recipe. You follow in the success of a cooking expert who has experimented and tested certain combinations of ingredients and cooking times. The recipe is the blueprint for success in the kitchen.

Success in communication when dealing with any relationship can be viewed the same way. It's just like a recipe. You set yourself up for success by taking some time before the conversation. This system can be used with any communication and with any relationship. For simplicity's sake, let's use the example of a personal relationship as it can be the most difficult to navigate.

The first step is to recognize intentions. It is ideal that both parties are viewed as having only the best intentions. Remember that your relationship is more important than any topic of discussion. Next, think about what you are wanting out of the conversation as far as expectations. Are you wanting advice, validation, or just a chance to vent? Are you open to another viewpoint that may be different from your own? Disagreements and hurt feelings can be the result if this expectation isn't identified. Next, define your parameters as far as time. Is this a good time to have this discussion? Are both parties in a good energy state? Is one party exhausted and unable to listen effectively? Would it be better to schedule a time in the near future? Remember, communication either brings us closer or pushes us further apart. Don't continue in conversations when you or both of you feel that the communication is pushing you farther apart.

When both of you keep the simple concepts of Best Intentions, Define Expectations, and Ideal Time (BIDEIT) at the forefront of your minds, then your communication, and therefore your overall relationship, will get better and better. This ideology can also be used in professional conversations.

OUR NEED FOR COMMUNITY

Our thoughts, beliefs, and feelings at the quantum level may be so deeply rooted that we have yet to unravel and understand them. Even so, those thoughts and beliefs impact who we value spending time with. Conversely, who we choose to spend time with can also influence what we think, believe, and feel. We frequently teach the importance of who we choose as mentors and coaches. And it is just as important to understand the value of who we choose as peers. These groups are what are referred to as your chosen community.

Ultimately, the relationships you choose have a huge impact on where you end up in life. Nowhere is this more apparent than in your need for community. How you relate to people and how you actually connect with others contributes to your sense of community. And the community of people you have around you affects every aspect of your life. This idea underscores the profound impact that social environments and networks have on individuals.

This influence can be observed in various aspects of life, including your Emotional Well-being. The support, empathy, and companionship provided by a community contribute significantly to emotional health. Positive social interactions can boost mood, reduce stress, and mitigate feelings of loneliness. They can also influence your behavior and habits. In fact, people often adopt behaviors and habits prevalent within their community. This can include lifestyle choices, such as diet and exercise, as well as habits related to work, leisure, and social norms.

Your chosen community can also affect your opportunities and growth. Communities can open doors to opportunities for personal and professional growth. Networking within a community can lead to job opportunities, educational resources, and personal development experiences.

Furthermore, the virtues and beliefs prevalent in one's community can shape individual perspectives and ideologies. Communities often play a crucial role in the development of moral and ethical standards. They also provide resilience and support. In times of hardship or crisis, the community acts as a support system that provides emotional comfort, practical assistance, and resources to navigate challenges.

And finally, community can influence health outcomes. Research has shown that social connections and community support can have

273

tangible effects on physical health, including longevity, cardiovascular health, and immune function.

In essence, the community of people around an individual plays a critical role in shaping their experiences, opportunities, and overall quality of life. Engaging with a supportive and positive community can enhance well-being, foster personal growth, and provide a sense of belonging and purpose.

We have all been in certain circumstances where our need for community has been starkly apparent. Having the right people in our lives in these times can make all the difference in our healing, growth, and abundance. These people can change the way we think, how we see the world, and the priorities we set in our lives on a daily basis.

We all need a sense of community. Whether it's a church or a pickleball league or your coworkers, find that group of people that you look forward to spending time with and with whom you have meaningful relationships. Your relationship with your primary partner in life, your relationship with your kids, and your relationship with friends and peers, these are all matters of great worth. Relationships are lasting elements of abundance.

The Iroquois nation is credited with the belief in the concept of seven generation stewardship. This concept urges the current generation to consider the impact of their actions on seven generations into the future. This principle is believed to have originated in the Great Law of the Iroquois and inspires us to live and work for the benefit of our descendants. Similarly, the Japanese have developed a culture that looks to the sustainability, longevity, and intergenerational continuity of their endeavors, often developing 100 or even 200-year plans for their businesses, lives, etc.

In America, we're often taught to forge our own path, pursue our own goals, work for much of our life, and then retire to enjoy the rewards of our hard work. That's all fine and good, but that mindset may be too narrow and internally focused. It's not lasting. It is only as we bring other people and our relationships with them into the equation that there is anything lasting in what we pursue.

We talk to our kids about the concept of a family legacy. It is this idea that we can build something that lasts beyond us. Whether that's 100 or 200 years down the road, if we all pitch in together because we understand that we're here together for a reason, we can build something that can have a meaningful, lasting impact on the world. That is the power of community. That is the power of connection. And that is the power of relationships and their lasting impact on our lives and the legacy we leave behind.

BUILDING RELATIONSHIPS AND COMMUNITY AT WORK

Because of the power of relationships, creating exceptional relationships in your business can benefit you as a person and the organization as a whole. Creating a positive work environment increases collaboration and teamwork, improves communication, and boosts job satisfaction, which impacts your bottom line. When your team feels supported and valued and connects with their colleagues, they collaborate, cooperate, and take fewer sick days.

When your team members get together, you can introduce personal growth and learning into the organization and improve your professional development as a group. When your team has solid relationships with you and each other, your company provides a more fulfilling and enjoyable work experience. Team members who feel satisfaction in their careers stay with you. We don't want to give good team members a reason to leave. I've read many Napoleon Hill books because he inspires me to create exceptional relationships as part of my path to personal and business success. The strength and quality of our personal and professional relationships is tied directly to our personal and professional success.

In our business, when we look to hire someone, we look for someone with a solid work ethic and technical skills who will be a positive addition to the dental team. We can always teach the technical skills they need, but teaching work ethic and positivity toward others is difficult.

Knowing what works for our team and what we need is part of communicating that position to the public so that the right person comes in for the job. When you are clear on your expectations and know what makes your team tick, the right candidate stands out, making hiring significantly easier.

CULTIVATING MEANINGFUL CONNECTIONS FOR A FULFILLING LIFE

In this world of over 8 billion people, it is said that the typical person knows about 150 people well. Research has shown that if you have close, meaningful relationships, you will not only live longer but you will also be less lonely and much happier. You don't have to have a ton of good relationships to reap the benefits, either. Sometimes, it's just one quality relationship that makes the difference.

As humans, we are relation-driven beings. How we relate to others is an essential component to our overall physical and mental health and longevity. As we explore the final chapters of this book, we will examine the skills and beliefs we are responsible for in our relationships with others. How we lead within our businesses and families, how we sense and respond to our own needs and those of others, how we communicate, how we deal with conflict, and how we grow in a sense of oneness with those around us… these are the ingredients of relational accountability that will enrich our lives with the relationships that we will be able to build, nurture, and watch flourish into abundance.

ACCOUNTABILITY ANCHORS:

1. Relationships are integral in amplifying our happiness and mitigating our hardships.

2. Strategies for improving relationships include: Self-Awareness, Taking Accountability and Understanding Your Triggers, Communicating Openly and Effectively, and Cultivating a Growth-Oriented Mindset

3. Define your intentions, outline your expectations, and determine an appropriate time before communicating.

4. We as humans have a need for community.

CHAPTER 18

THE FREEDOM OF FORGIVENESS, UNLOCKING PEACE AND RECONCILIATION IN YOUR HEART

"Forgiveness is not an occasional act; it is a permanent attitude."

— MARTIN LUTHER KING JR.

Holding on to negative feelings like anger and resentment is like swimming with an anchor tied to your leg. As long as it's attached, you're limited in your movement, unable to appreciate the beauty in the world around you. Forgiveness is untying that anchor. It isn't about giving in and saying that what was done to you is okay, it's about putting you first. It's unburdening yourself so you can swim freely. The freedom from forgiveness is a gift you give yourself. It's the gift of letting go of the anchors you've been carrying, and thereby unlocking peace and reconciliation in your heart.

In the biblical tale of Joseph and his brothers found in the Hebrew Bible and recounted in Genesis chapters 37-45, Joseph frees himself from the anchor. This narrative is also recognized in Christianity's Old Testament and is similarly recounted in Islam's Quran. Joseph, the favored son of Jacob, incurs the jealousy of his brothers due to the special treatment he receives from their father and his own dreams that suggest he will one day rule over them. In their envy, the brothers conspire against Joseph, initially planning to kill him but ultimately deciding to sell him into slavery. Joseph is taken to Egypt where, through a series of events, he rises to become the Pharaoh's trusted advisor.

Years later, a famine strikes the region and Joseph's brothers come to Egypt seeking food, not realizing that the brother they betrayed is now in a position of power over them. Joseph recognizes his brothers but does not reveal his identity immediately. After testing their character and seeing their change of heart, Joseph eventually makes himself known to them. Despite the opportunity for retribution, Joseph forgives his brothers for their past actions, providing for them and their families, and inviting them to live in Egypt.

This story of Joseph is a powerful example of forgiveness and reconciliation. It shows that forgiveness can transcend even the deepest betrayals and lead to healing and unity. Joseph's ability to forgive his brothers, despite their grave mistreatment of him, highlights the transformative power of forgiveness and its importance in human relationships.

OUR QUANTUM LIMITATIONS OF FORGIVENESS

Let's face it, every one of us has a grudge or a resentment we can't seem to let go of sitting next to the skeleton in our closet. It's human nature. We are very much like Joseph's brothers. When someone holds on to something and can't forgive, it is often referred to as harboring a grudge or resentment. Holding a grudge implies a persistent feeling of ill will or resentment resulting from a past insult or injury that one is unable or unwilling to forgive. Resentment is a similar concept, where negative feelings are retained against someone for perceived wrongs, and forgiveness is not granted. These feelings can be detrimental to one's emotional well-being and interpersonal relationships. Letting go allows you to swim in any direction, at any pace you want.

Resentment and grudges often operate on the quantum level, subtly influencing behaviors and feelings without full awareness. These feelings we harbor can originate from various psychological and emotional factors. Holding onto grudges may serve as a protective mechanism, where we use resentment as a shield against future harm, minimizing vulnerability. Additionally, a desire for justice can drive us to maintain grudges; we seek fairness and accountability for perceived wrongs, using resentment as a means to ensure offenders face consequences for their actions.

We could also have an underlying fear of vulnerability. Forgiving can sometimes be seen as a sign of weakness or as opening oneself up to the possibility of being hurt again. Holding on to resentment can then feel like a way to maintain control and strength. As time goes on, this grudge or resentment turns to victimhood. For some, the grudge becomes a part of their identity. Letting go of it would mean redefining who they are without that anger and resentment, which can be a challenging and uncomfortable process.

Difficulty forgiving could also be because of a lack of closure. Without a sincere apology or acknowledgment of the wrongdoing from the other party, individuals might find it hard to move on, leading to prolonged feelings of resentment. Or maybe you fail to forgive because of the deep emotional pain caused by the initial hurt or betrayal. Holding onto a grudge can be a way of not fully confronting or processing these painful emotions.

Understanding these underlying reasons can be the first step towards addressing and overcoming the inability to forgive. It requires assessing your quantum level thoughts, feelings, and emotions to determine what is holding you back. Rest assured, forgiveness is worth its weight in gold.

FORGIVENESS IS A SKILL

The ability to forgive is a powerful tool for healing and personal development. Like your physical muscles, it is a skill that needs to be exercised to grow. Each time you forgive, you build that muscle and strengthen it for use in the future. Forgiveness leads to a range of psychological benefits that enhance your quality of life, including reduced negative emotions, decreased stress and anxiety, improved mental health, enhanced self-esteem, better relationships, greater life satisfaction, improved physical health, and enhanced personal growth.

Forgiveness is crucial in any professional setting, including running and managing a business office. While it might seem odd to connect the concept of forgiveness with business, the day-to-day operations of your workplace are as much about human relations and effective communication as clinical procedures are in a dental office.

Accountability and forgiveness are connected because they relate to how we deal with mistakes or wrongdoings, whether our own or someone else's. Accountability means taking responsibility for what we've done.

It's saying, "I did this, and I accept it was my fault." When we're accountable, we admit our actions, try to make amends if necessary, and work on not repeating the same mistake.

Forgiveness is when we let go of our anger, hurt, or blame toward someone who has done something wrong. It's saying, "I acknowledge that you made a mistake, but I'm not going to hold it against you forever." Or "I know this happened, but I am going to let it go so I don't feel bad about it any longer." Forgiveness is not about forgetting or condoning past events or behaviors but rather about letting go of negative emotions and finding peace within yourself. Forgiveness is about overcoming the hurt and giving someone a chance to make things right or start over. It's also about letting yourself off the hook for feeling bad. When someone is accountable for their actions, it becomes easier for others to forgive them. If someone admits they made a mistake and genuinely tries to improve things, it can help heal the hurt and rebuild trust.

Clients might miss appointments, fail to follow your instructions, or sometimes need to be more cooperative in their interactions with you. Instead of becoming confrontational or dismissive, understanding and forgiving these actions (while educating and setting boundaries) can lead to a better relationship and continued loyalty from the people you serve.

In a business office, teamwork is essential. Misunderstandings, mistakes, or disagreements among team members can hinder the office's functioning. By fostering an environment of forgiveness, team members can move past disputes more quickly and focus on providing excellent guest care.

Forgiveness in a professional setting also involves cultivating a culture where mistakes are viewed as opportunities for learning rather than reasons for punishment. This perspective encourages employees to take risks and innovate, knowing that their efforts are supported even when outcomes aren't as expected. By prioritizing forgiveness, leaders can inspire a more dynamic and resilient workforce. Employees who feel safe from harsh judgment are more likely to engage fully, share ideas, and commit to their roles wholeheartedly. This not only boosts morale but also enhances productivity and creativity across the organization.

Moreover, implementing a systematic approach to forgiveness can help in resolving conflicts more amicably and maintaining a peaceful work environment. When team members are encouraged to express their grievances and seek resolution through understanding and mutual forgiveness, it reduces tensions and builds stronger, more cohesive teams. This approach ensures that conflicts are not just superficially resolved but are addressed deeply, promoting lasting peace and cooperation. Such an environment not only improves employee satisfaction and retention but also sets a strong foundation for collective success, aligning individual goals with organizational objectives.

Holding on to resentment or anger can be mentally and emotionally draining. For business leaders and their teams, letting go of past mistakes—whether made by others or the leader themself—can lead to a healthier work environment and personal well-being.

Everyone makes mistakes. When those mistakes are met with forgiveness, it creates an atmosphere in which team members are more likely to admit to and learn from their errors. This results in continuous professional development and fewer repeated mistakes.

A forgiving attitude can lead to second chances. Guests who feel judged or dismissed due to a mistake (like missing a payment) are less likely to return. However, a forgiving approach and clear communication can mend the relationship and retain the guest.

Forgiveness is also a key component of healthy personal relationships, contributing to mutual respect, understanding, and a supportive emotional climate. Forgiveness heals emotional wounds by allowing us to heal from emotional pain and move past conflicts or hurtful events. It also strengthens bonds. By forgiving, we can rebuild trust, leading to more resilient and enduring relationships. Forgiveness also reduces toxicity. Holding onto anger and resentment creates a toxic environment. Forgiveness helps to alleviate negative emotions and promotes a more positive and supportive relationship dynamic.

Incorporating forgiveness doesn't mean avoiding accountability or overlooking repeated errors. It means recognizing human fallibility, allowing for growth, and moving forward constructively. It's about balancing understanding with the need to maintain professional standards.

Addressing problems and conflicts directly and respectfully while practicing forgiveness and compassion is essential. By balancing forgiveness and accountability, we can create an environment that fosters growth, success, and positive relationships.

Personal relationships can grow and mature when forgiveness is practiced. It allows both parties to learn from their mistakes and develop greater empathy and compassion. It also enhances physical health. The stress associated with holding grudges can have negative health effects. Forgiveness can lead to lower stress levels and better physical health for both parties. And last, but not least, the act of forgiving models an ideal positive behavior. Demonstrating forgiveness in relationships can set a positive example for others, such as children or siblings, about how to manage conflicts and maintain healthy relationships.

FORGIVING NEGATIVE ONLINE REVIEWS

In the digital era of business, online reviews significantly influence a business' reputation. Handling negative reviews with understanding and a willingness to rectify the situation can demonstrate a forgiving and guest-focused attitude, attracting more guests to your business in the long run. A forgiving and understanding approach can lead to a more loyal guest base, a cohesive team, and a positive reputation—all essential components for the sustained success of any business.

Responding to negative reviews with a forgiving attitude not only mitigates the immediate damage but also showcases your business's commitment to customer satisfaction and continuous improvement. When a business acknowledges a negative review promptly and empathetically, it communicates to both the reviewer and potential customers that their feedback is valued and taken seriously. This approach can transform a potentially harmful situation into a demonstration of your business's reliability and dedication to its customers. By offering to discuss the issue as well as solutions by inviting the customer to discuss their concerns in more detail offline, a business can effectively turn a critic into a supporter, enhancing its reputation in the process.

Moreover, a strategy of embracing and learning from negative feedback can lead to significant improvements in products and services, which ultimately benefits the business. Negative reviews often contain valuable insights that can highlight areas for improvement that might not have been previously considered. Acknowledge the problem as it is, without understating or overstating its significance. By analyzing the issues brought to light with the reviews and implementing changes based on this feedback, businesses can enhance their offerings and prevent future complaints.

This proactive approach not only improves the quality of the customer experience but also strengthens the business's market position by demonstrating adaptability and a genuine commitment to meeting customer needs. In this way, forgiving and learning from negative reviews not only salvages potentially lost customer relationships but also propels the business towards greater innovation and success.

IDENTIFYING AREAS NEEDING FORGIVENESS

Identifying points where you may need to work on forgiveness can be a deeply personal and reflective process. How do you start the identification process? You can begin by paying attention to your feelings and notice if there are any recurring negative feelings, such as anger, resentment, bitterness, or sadness that may be associated with past events or relationships. These feelings may indicate unresolved issues that require forgiveness work.

Reflect on your past and present relationships and consider whether any strained or damaged ones may require forgiveness. Are there any conflicts, grudges, or unresolved issues with family members, friends, colleagues, or others that may impact your well-being and happiness?

Remember the quantum element of accountability and listen to your internal running dialogue and language when discussing past events or relationships. Are you harboring negative self-talk, self-blame, or self-condemnation related to past events or actions? Harboring or ruminating may indicate a need for self-forgiveness. Are there situations or people consistently triggering negative feelings or reactions in you? These patterns or triggers may indicate unresolved issues that require forgiveness. Remember, you are accountable for your triggers.

Reflect on how holding onto grudges, resentment, or unresolved issues may impact your physical, emotional, and mental well-being. Are these negative emotions and unresolved issues affecting your overall quality of life, relationships, and personal growth?

Consider seeking input from trusted friends, family members, or a coach who can provide an outside perspective on whether forgiveness may be needed in some regions of your life. They can offer insights and suggestions for areas where forgiveness may be beneficial.

WHAT DOES IT MEAN TO FORGIVE YOURSELF?

Forgiving yourself means acknowledging and accepting your past mistakes, shortcomings, and regrets and releasing self-blame, self-condemnation, and negative self-talk. Give yourself grace and recognize that everyone makes mistakes and that your past actions do not define you.

Practice self-compassion and treat yourself with kindness, understanding, and forgiveness, just as your friends would. You must take responsibility for your actions, make amends if necessary, and commit to learning from your mistakes and growing.

One of our favorite sayings is that what matters more than the mistake is what you do after you make it. Thinking of errors as an opportunity to learn and grow helps you move from shame or regret to a positive action faster after making mistakes.

FORGIVENESS EXERCISE

When discussing forgiveness, either in a business setting or with your family, exercises can be conducted to grow understanding, empathy, and open communication. Consider introducing a system that allows team and or family members to address mistakes without fear and create an environment where everyone can learn and grow together. Here is a team-building session that I used that takes about 60 minutes and requires only a notepad and pen for each participant, a comfortable space, and a small, soft object to be passed around (like a plush toy or a beanbag).

Share a personal story about when you made a mistake and someone forgave you, explaining its impact on you. Discuss the benefits of forgiveness, such as reducing stress, preventing conflicts, and fostering a more positive work atmosphere, and introduce this quick two-minute focus meditation.

Ask everyone to sit comfortably, close their eyes, and take deep breaths. Guide them to recall when they made a mistake and felt regret. Reassure everyone that we all make mistakes. Ask them to imagine the feeling of being forgiven, the weight lifting off their shoulders, and the warmth of understanding from someone else. Have everyone slowly open their eyes, bring their attention back to the room, and introduce the sharing circle.

Explain that everyone will have a chance to share a mistake they made in the past and what they learned from it. This is not about judgment; it's about understanding and growth. Pass the soft object to the first person. Whoever holds the object has the floor to speak. After sharing, the speaker can ask for feedback or pass the object to the next person. Encourage listening without judgment and giving constructive feedback.

Once the last person speaks, hand out notepads and pens. Ask each person to write down one commitment they'll make to foster forgiveness in the workplace or at home, whether it's being more patient, communicating more openly, or something else. If comfortable, participants can share their commitments with the group.

Wrap up the session by emphasizing that mistakes are a part of growth and happen whenever we stretch beyond our knowledge and limits. By creating an environment of forgiveness, our office or our family can operate more harmoniously. Encourage everyone to keep their written commitments somewhere they can see them daily as a reminder.

Always emphasize that this exercise is voluntary. Some may not be comfortable sharing, and that's okay. The aim is to create an atmosphere of understanding and support. We must remember that not everyone is in the same lane as us or going the same speed and might suffer from significant discomfort confronting themselves. When we hold these sharing exercises, it's for the benefit, not harm.

THE ROLE OF KARMA AND LIFE LESSONS

Forgiveness has a unique connection to the eastern spiritual belief of Karma. While karma and forgiveness operate within different conceptual frameworks, they both play important roles in shaping our experiences, relationships, and spiritual journeys. Understanding the interplay between them can lead to greater insight into the nature of cause and effect, personal growth, and the pursuit of abundance.

Karma originated from Hinduism, Buddhism, and other spiritual traditions, and it generally refers to the idea of cause and effect, when the consequences of your actions can affect your present or future experiences.

Karma teaches that our actions have effects, and the choices we make in life can impact our future experiences. If we make positive choices and take positive steps, we may create good Karma, resulting in positive outcomes or life lessons that align with our growth and development. If we make bad choices or do something wrong, we may create bad Karma, which can result in challenging or complex life lessons meant to help us learn from our mistakes and grow.

When we experience the consequences of our positive or negative actions, we can reflect on our choices and behaviors and learn from them. Positive results can reinforce positive behaviors and preferences, while harmful consequences can highlight areas where we need to improve or change our thoughts, beliefs, or actions.

Karma also emphasizes the interconnectedness of all beings and the interplay of actions and reactions in the universe. The recognition of interconnectedness can foster a sense of responsibility, compassion, and mindfulness as we become more aware of the potential ripple effects of our choices and behaviors. It helps us to think about the greater good in our decisions and actions.

Understanding the role of Karma in learning life lessons can also inspire us to cultivate positive Karma by making conscious choices and taking positive actions, which may involve practicing virtues such as kindness, compassion, generosity, and forgiveness and aligning our efforts with our values and principles. By cultivating positive Karma, we create a foundation for positive life lessons and experiences that contribute to our personal growth, fulfillment, and happiness.

Karma can have different interpretations and meanings in various spiritual or philosophical traditions, and our beliefs about Karma may vary. Some may view Karma as a literal law of cause and effect, while others may see it as a metaphorical or symbolic concept. It's always advisable to approach the topic of Karma with an open mind and respect for diverse perspectives.

THE INTERSECTION OF KARMA AND FORGIVENESS

The intersection of karma and forgiveness lies in their mutual emphasis on personal responsibility and transformation. Karma encourages individuals to be mindful of their actions and their impacts on others and themselves. Similarly, forgiveness is an act of consciously choosing to release negative feelings and thoughts related to past actions—either one's own or those of others.

From a karmic perspective, practicing forgiveness can be seen as a positive action that generates good karma and breaks negative karmic cycles. By forgiving, individuals not only free themselves from the burden of negative emotions but also contribute to a cycle of positive energy and outcomes. Forgiveness can halt the cycle of retaliation and negativity, creating space for healing and positive growth. By cultivating forgiveness, individuals may transcend the cycle of karmic retribution and move closer to the abundance of enlightenment or liberation.

In essence, both karma and forgiveness highlight the power of individual actions in shaping one's life and relationships. They encourage individuals to live with awareness, compassion, and a commitment to personal growth, leading to a more harmonious and fulfilling existence.

SHORT KARMIC MEDITATION:

Meditation is a great way to explore the concept of Karma internally.

Find a quiet space where you won't be disturbed. Sit or lie down comfortably, ensuring your spine is straight. Close your eyes and take a deep breath. Allow any tensions or concerns of the day to melt away.

Take another deep breath through your nose and exhale slowly through your mouth. Feel the weight of your body as it settles into your chosen position. Each breath grounds you deeper into the present moment. Imagine a vast, still lake. This lake represents the universe and the law of Karma.

Every action, every thought, every word we speak is like a pebble thrown into the water. See the ripples created by these pebbles, moving outward in rings, affecting the whole lake. Each ripple is the consequence of our actions. Some ripples are immediate, while others take time to expand.

Think of a recent action or decision you made. Imagine it as a pebble you're holding in your hand. Gently toss it into the lake. Watch the ripples. Without judgment, observe how actions have consequences, some seen and some unseen.

As you watch the ripples, breathe in the understanding that you have the power to choose your actions. With each breath, set the intention to create positive ripples in the universe. Bring your focus back to your breath, taking deeper breaths now. Feel gratitude for this moment of reflection and understanding. When you're ready, come back and open your eyes.

OUR ACCOUNTABILITY FOR KARMIC FORGIVENESS

Karma reminds us of the interconnectedness of all things. It is often understood as the principle that our past actions, both positive and negative, shape our present circumstances and future experiences. However, this view of karma as a cosmic "scorecard" is an oversimplification. Rather, karma is more accurately seen as the natural consequences that arise from our thoughts, words, and behaviors. It is the flow of cause and effect that governs our lives.

Forgiveness plays a crucial role in interrupting negative karmic cycles. By forgiving others who have wronged us, as well as ourselves for our own mistakes, we release the emotional burdens and resentments that can perpetuate harmful patterns. Forgiveness is an act of accountability, because we take responsibility for our role in relationships and choose to move forward with compassion rather than retaliation. This aligns with a deeper understanding of karma as not a system of rewards and punishments, but a reflection of our own consciousness and the degree to which we are identified with the ego versus our higher, more expansive sense of self.

Ultimately, the interplay of karma, forgiveness, and accountability points to the power we have to shape our lives through self-awareness, humility, and the willingness to grow beyond our past limitations.

ACCOUNTABILITY ANCHORS:

1. Freedom from forgiveness is a gift you give yourself.
2. The ability to forgive is a powerful tool for healing and personal development.
3. Karma teaches that our actions have effects, and the choices we make in life can impact our future experiences.
4. When we forgive, we allow ourselves and others to transcend karmic retribution and move closer to the abundance of enlightenment.

CHAPTER 19

GUIDING THE WAY, THE ESSENTIAL QUALITIES OF IMPACTFUL LEADERSHIP

A leader is one who knows the way, goes the way, and shows the way."

– JOHN C. MAXWELL

True leadership is not about titles or positions of authority; it emanates from within, shaping the course of lives through the power of influence. At its core, impactful leadership is the ability to inspire others to embrace a shared vision, to challenge the status quo, and to unlock their full potential. It requires a delicate balance of courage, humility, and an unwavering commitment to personal growth. Whether you find yourself at the helm of a multinational corporation or simply navigating the intricate web of relationships in your daily life, the principles of impactful leadership can serve as a guiding light, empowering you to leave an indelible mark on the world around you. This chapter will explore the essential qualities that distinguish truly great leaders, providing a roadmap for cultivating the mindset, skills, and authentic presence necessary to motivate and uplift those around you.

When you think of a great leader, who comes to your mind? Here are some examples of great leaders from various fields and historical periods, along with a brief description of their contributions:

1. **Mahatma Gandhi** - Known for leading India's independence movement against British rule through non-violent civil disobedience, Gandhi's philosophy of peace and resistance has inspired movements for civil rights and freedom across the world.

2. **Nelson Mandela** - Mandela was a key figure in the fight against apartheid in South Africa. After spending 27 years in prison, he emerged to become the country's first democratically elected president, focusing on reconciliation and unity.

3. **Martin Luther King Jr.** - A leader in the American civil rights movement, King advocated for nonviolent resistance to racial segregation and inequality, most famously in his "I Have a Dream" speech.

4. **Abraham Lincoln** - The 16th President of the United States, Lincoln led the country through its Civil War and made the Emancipation Proclamation, which began the process of freedom for America's slaves.

5. **George Washington** - The first President of the United States and a Founding Father, Washington's leadership during the American Revolutionary War and his presidency set many key precedents for the new nation.

6. **Napoleon Bonaparte** - A French general and Emperor, Napoleon is known for his military tactics. He was instrumental in shaping the future of Europe with his reforms such as the Napoleonic Code.

7. **Marcus Aurelius** - A Roman Emperor who was an adopted son, he reigned during a time of military conflict. He is known for his Stoic Philosophy, as represented in his work "Meditations".

8. **Benjamin Franklin** - One of the Founding Fathers of the United States, he had a lifelong commitment to self improvement. Franklin was an inventor, innovator, and a key figure in the formation of the United States of America.

9. **Dalai Lama (Tenzin Gyatso)** - The 14th Dalai Lama is known for his teachings on compassion, nonviolence, and peace. A Nobel Peace Prize laureate, he advocates for the rights and autonomy of the Tibetan people.

Did any of these people make it on your list? Even if your list was different, one thing for sure is that effective leaders lead by example. Have you ever heard of this example of leadership?

One of the most inspiring leadership stories is that of Malala Yousafzai, a Pakistani activist for female education and the youngest Nobel Peace Prize laureate. Malala's story begins in her hometown in Northern Pakistan, where the Taliban had often banned girls from attending school. Despite the dangers, Malala became a vocal supporter of female education, leading a local activist movement focused on women's rights and empowerment.

Her advocacy, however, made her a target. In 2012, a Taliban gunman shot her three times in the head in an assassination attempt as she was returning home from school. The attack provoked worldwide outrage, and in Pakistan, it led to the ratification of the Right to Education Bill. Malala survived the shooting after spending time in a critical care unit in the United Kingdom. While she was in the hospital, the United Nations launched a petition in her name demanding better access to education for girls worldwide.

After her recovery, Malala continued to lead the movement for female education, extending her message from her local, early activism days in Pakistan to a global stage. She addressed the United Nations, met with world leaders, and founded the non-profit Malala Fund to support her cause. In 2014, at the age of 17, she became the youngest person to receive the Nobel Peace Prize for her struggle against the suppression of children and young people and for the right of all children to education.

Malala Yousafzai's story is a powerful example of leadership through adversity. Her courage, resilience, and unwavering commitment to her cause, even in the face of life-threatening danger, have inspired millions around the world. Her leadership has not only advanced the cause of female education but has also shown the impact one individual can have on the world by standing up for what they believe in.

When business leaders demonstrate accountability in their actions and decisions, they set a standard for their team members to follow. Effective leaders have similar identifiable traits as those we've mentioned, from Gandhi to Malala Yousafzai. Here is a list of characteristics that effective leaders consistently demonstrate:

1. **Energy:** Many great leaders have been known for their almost boundless energy and work ethic, often being workaholics who are deeply committed to their roles.

2. **Ability to Plan and Adapt:** Successful leaders are meticulous planners but also possess the flexibility to adapt their plans

based on changing circumstances, demonstrating both strategic foresight and agility.

3. **Empathy:** Understanding and sharing the feelings of others is crucial. Leaders who can empathize can connect deeply with people from all walks of life, regardless of their own backgrounds.

4. **Awareness:** A keen sense of timing, observation, and the ability to seize opportunities are essential for navigating complex landscapes and achieving objectives.

5. **Communication Skills:** Effective leaders are often excellent communicators, able to articulate their vision and inspire others to follow them.

6. **Courage and Determination:** The willingness to take risks and persist in the face of challenges is a hallmark of many historical leaders.

7. **Humility:** The ability to admit mistakes and learn from them, without letting ego get in the way of progress.

8. **Decisiveness:** The ability to make quick, firm decisions, even in the absence of complete information, and to act confidently on those decisions.

9. **Persistence:** Successful leaders often exhibit a remarkable ability to persevere through setbacks and failures, maintaining their focus on their ultimate goals.

These are some of the traits that have enabled leaders throughout history to inspire and lead their followers toward achieving remarkable feats, demonstrating that effective leadership is a complex interplay of personal qualities, skills, and the ability to connect with and motivate others.

Strong leadership skills enable business owners to motivate, guide, and support their teams effectively. The principles of Quantum Accountability throughout this book are some of the same characteristics of good leadership. When your mindset, thoughts, beliefs, feelings, virtues, and attitudes are aligned with your Quantum Purpose, your growth and abundance will expand exponentially. Developing leadership characteristics fosters self-accountability.

In essence, effective leadership skills not only enhance one's ability to lead others but also significantly improve personal accountability. These skills enable you to set clear goals, make informed decisions, manage your time and feelings effectively, communicate clearly, learn continuously, and face challenges with resilience. As you become more accountable to yourself, driving personal growth and achievement, you become more reliable to others, and hence a better leader.

As you can see, the first step is for you to become accountable to yourself, then to lead others to this level of accountability. Whether it is your team, your family, or any other group, effective leadership enables you to expand the quantum growth you have experienced and increase its power in all areas of your life by sharing the abundance of accountable living.

HOW WE INFLUENCE OTHERS

When I was 14, I asked my mentor, my father, what book I should read next. He handed me the 1936 classic by Dale Carnegie, How to Win Friends and Influence People. Carnegie provides guidelines for communication and interpersonal skills. Examples are 'give honest and sincere appreciation', and 'arouse in the person an eager want'. One of my personal favorites is 'smile'. These attributes on aligning with others can lay the foundation for effective leadership.

In the book, Power vs. Force by Dr. David R. Hawkins, he teaches that there are two primary ways to influence and motivate people: power and force. Our influence is greatest when we act from a place of power by connecting with others meaningfully and making positive changes in the world.

Power, especially in the context of accountability, involves motivating people through inspiration, shared virtues, and a sense of purpose. Power in business leadership relies on intrinsic motivation, where team members feel a genuine connection to the goals and virtues of the business. When the team shares a common vision and understands the importance of their roles in providing excellent customer service, they are more likely to hold themselves accountable for their actions. This approach creates a positive and collaborative work environment where accountability arises naturally.

On the other hand, using force to influence and motivate, involves external pressure, coercion, or punishment to make people comply with specific rules or expectations. Using force to enforce accountability might result in strict rules, closely monitoring employees, and applying penalties for non-compliance or mistakes. While this approach can yield short-term results, it often leads to resistance, resentment, and an ineffective work environment. Your team might also get nervous or anxious and make mistakes because they focus on avoiding punishment rather than completing the task correctly.

By creating a culture of shared virtues, teamwork, and intrinsic motivation, team members are more likely to take responsibility for their actions. Business cultures like these lead to a happier, more engaged team.

LEADERSHIP STYLES

A leadership style refers to a leader's characteristic approach to providing direction, implementing plans, and motivating people. It encompasses the behaviors, attitudes, and methods a leader uses to interact with their team and drive the organization towards its goals. Different leadership styles can be employed depending on the leader's personality, the team's dynamics, the organizational culture, and the specific situation at hand.

John C. Maxwell, in The Five Levels of Leadership, developed a model for growth as a leader. Where you are in your journey and the size of your organization will determine your leadership style. Like personal growth, leadership is something you cultivate and grow during your lifetime. Here are some common leadership styles. These could be considered a progression where the early styles are more primitive and less effective than the later styles.

1. **Autocratic Leadership:** This style is characterized by individual control over all decisions with little input from team members. Autocratic leaders typically make choices based on their judgments and ideas and rarely accept advice from followers. This is the "What I say goes" way of leading. This style might be necessary in a small company with one ideator and a lot of workers. However, if you plan to scale and grow your organization, you must grow your people, and thus transition out of this style of leadership. Even in large companies, we will see examples of this when innovators are treading on an uncharted path—for example, when Elon Musk says he is going to build a rocket to mars, or Steve Jobs says we are going to build a touch screen iPhone and put our iPod out of business. Sometimes, an innovator must trust their gut, take the risk, and

not listen to others' input to be transformational. They can see what others do not.

2. **Transactional Leadership:** This style is based on a system of rewards and punishments. It relies on cause and effect circumstances. Transactional leaders are focused on routine and regimented activities and are often more concerned with maintaining a normal flow of operations. This is often referred to as the 'carrot and the stick' approach to leadership. It has been argued that, though it may motivate in the short term, it is not the best style to implement lasting change.

3. **Democratic Leadership:** Also known as participative leadership, this style involves the leader including one or more employees in the decision-making process. However, the ultimate decision-making authority remains with the leader.

4. **Laissez-Faire Leadership:** A laissez-faire leader is hands-off and allows group members to make the decisions. This style can be effective in situations in which team members are highly skilled and motivated. This style can also be detrimental in situations where team members are not highly skilled and/or motivated. This is achievable if you have a vision of creating a self-managed company, but you must make sure you have the right people on board to effectively hand over the reins. A founder/CEO that scales a company and eventually hands over the duties to a more effective CEO and steps into a Chairman of the Board seat would be a successful example.

5. **Servant Leadership:** Servant leaders put the needs of their team first and help people develop and perform. Instead of focusing on their own advancement, servant leaders aim to nurture their team members. Servant leaders prioritize the

needs of the team and community above their own. They prioritize active listening, valuing the perspectives and inputs of their team members, and strive to understand and empathize with the needs and concerns of others. They take responsibility for the roles and resources within the business and act with a sense of community and commitment. Servant leaders focus on their team members' personal and professional development, recognizing that growth benefits both the individual and the community. They strive to foster community within their teams and organizations, ensuring everyone feels connected and part of a larger purpose.

There is a sixth leadership style known as "transformational leadership" that was originally coined by James V. Downton in his 1973 book *Rebel Leadership: Commitment and Charisma in the Revolutionary Process*:

6. **Transformational Leadership:** Transformational leaders inspire their team through effective communication and by creating an environment of intellectual stimulation. They are focused on initiating change by motivating and transforming individuals to improve the organization. In transformational leadership, leaders inspire and motivate their team members to achieve exceptional outcomes and, in the process, help them develop their leadership potential. This leadership style encourages a shared vision, fosters creativity, and challenges the status quo. Leaders in this category are motivational. They encourage creativity and innovation within their team. They challenge team members to think critically and encourage them to solve problems in novel ways. Transformational leaders prefer one-on-one mentoring and coaching. They pay attention to the developmental needs of each team member and support their personal and professional growth. They act as role

models, leading by example. Their integrity, determination, and dedication inspire trust and admiration among followers.

Each of these leadership styles has its own set of advantages and disadvantages. And each style is dependent upon the mindset of the leader. Which type of leadership style appeals to you?

THE LEADERSHIP JOURNEY

Once you have identified the type of leader you are naturally, the next step is improving your skills, which often requires change. Stephen M. R. Covey's book Trust and Inspire, is a wonderful resource to learn about a more modern form of leadership. Rather than the traditional leadership carrot-and-stick approach to incentivizing and disciplining your workforce, you inspire your team and trust they will do the job.

Before reading the book, I developed the core principles of our leadership company, Kremer Leadership Institute (KLI). KLI oversees and manages our portfolio of dental practices and counsels and mentors non-owned dental practices. You can go to www.kremerleadership.com to learn more.

I created the core principles of Kremer Leadership Institute to align with the KLI: Knowing, Leading, and Inspiring. I was pleased to find Stephen M. R. Covey has a model in his book of three circles connecting: Modeling, Trusting (how you lead), and Inspiring. It was apparent we are strongly aligned on our leadership models, which gave me confirmation that I was onto something meaningful.

I have realized there is so much to learn on a leadership journey. There are always opportunities to grow and improve. What was once a focus on how to incentivize or bonus my team to achieve results has shifted. Though incentives are acceptable, I have changed my approach as servant leadership has grown to have a primary question, "How can I help you?"

If your people know their job (description), what is expected of them (how do they win at their job), feel they are in the right seat and desire to achieve their success, then get out of their way and check in to make sure they are feeling supported in their role. Be there to help them.

ACCOUNTABILITY ANCHORS:

1. Leadership is the ability to inspire others to embrace a shared vision, to challenge the status quo, and to unlock their full potential.

2. There are characteristics of effective leaders.

3. There are several leadership styles including: Autocratic, Transactional, Democratic, Laissez-Faire, Servant and Transformational.

SECTION 4

A
JOURNEY
WITH
PURPOSE

Embarking on a journey with purpose is an enriching quest that calls each of us to dive deep into the essence of our being. We are to uncover the unique mission we are meant to fulfill on this Earth. It is a voyage that invites us to unveil our life's purpose, a beacon that guides our choices and illuminates our path towards fulfillment and meaning. Along this journey, we are called to embrace the infinite, to connect with the boundless potential and interconnectedness of all existence, recognizing that our individual purpose is part of a grander, universal tapestry.

This understanding empowers us to create a life of excellence, where every thought, choice, and relationship are infused with intentionality and aligned with our virtues. By being accountable to this purpose-driven life, we not only elevate our own existence but also contribute to the collective flourishing of humanity, leaving a legacy of impact and inspiration.

CHAPTER 20

THE QUEST FOR MEANING, UNVEILING YOUR LIFE'S TRUE PURPOSE

"The two most important days in life are the day you are born and the day you discover the reason why."

– MARK TWAIN

Within each of us lies an innate longing, a profound yearning to discover our life's true purpose—that singular guiding force that imbues our existence with meaning and significance. This quest, though deeply personal, is a universal human experience that transcends boundaries of culture, creed, or circumstance. For some, it manifests as a burning desire to uncover their unique gifts and leverage them in service of a greater cause. For others, it presents itself as an insatiable curiosity, a relentless pursuit of knowledge and understanding that extends beyond the material world. Regardless of how it reveals itself, this search for meaning is an integral part of our journey of self-discovery, propelling us to explore the depths of our being and to peel back the layers that obscure our authentic selves.

At the heart of this journey lies the process of self-reflection and heightened self-awareness—a crucial step towards taking responsibility for one's thoughts, feelings, and behaviors. Finding one's life purpose is about aligning one's life with core values and beliefs, requiring the courage to live authentically and make choices that are true to oneself, rather than succumbing to external pressures or expectations. This often involves identifying and challenging limiting beliefs that may be holding an individual back, taking accountability for these beliefs and actively working to shift them as part of the ongoing process of personal growth and evolution. Maintaining a growth mindset and a sense of accountability to something greater than oneself is a hallmark of a life of meaning and purpose, as individuals who live in alignment with their true calling are more likely to have a positive impact on the world around them.

Ultimately, the quest for meaning and life purpose is fundamentally grounded in the principles of Quantum Accountability, which serve as the foundation upon which a life of fulfillment and contribution can be built. In this chapter, we embark on a transformative odyssey, one that will illuminate the path to unearthing your life's true purpose and harnessing its power to create a life of profound fulfillment and lasting impact.

THE PURPOSE FORMULA

Agne grew up in a privileged family, where hard work was seen as the pathway to success. This formula, deeply ingrained from childhood, led her to pursue a successful corporate career, believing that climbing the corporate ladder was her purpose in life. However, despite her achievements, Agne felt something was amiss. This feeling prompted her to take a bold step back from her corporate life and embark on a volunteering assignment working with women in rural Uganda. This drastic change of environment from a corporate, money-driven world to volunteering work was Agne's attempt to find a more meaningful purpose.

However, the journey to discovering your purpose is rarely straightforward. Agne learned that expecting one job or activity to fulfill all her needs and desires was unrealistic. Instead, she discovered that her purpose was multifaceted. She loved her corporate career but also yearned to contribute more meaningfully to others' lives. This led her to engage in activities that supported causes she cared about, such as empowering women in Uganda and sharing her knowledge and experiences with her home country, Lithuania.

Agne's story underscores the realization that purpose is not a singular, fixed formula or destination but a dynamic and evolving journey. It highlights the importance of awareness, self-discovery, and the courage to step out of your comfort zone. Understanding that purpose can encompass multiple passions and contributions is a concept that we can all embrace. Through her narrative, Agne illustrates that living your life's purpose involves balancing various aspects of your life.

As we discussed in Chapter 9 "Harmonizing the Many Roles We Play in Life", fulfillment is found in not just what you do but also in your mindset. Agne's story is a testament to the idea that purpose is about creating a life that is rich in meaning and impact, reflecting a deep engagement with the world around you. Agne Nainyte's "The story of a girl who realized that purpose isn't just ONE thing" offers us a narrative on the importance of living our life's purpose.

THE CIRCLE OF ABUNDANCE

As Agne discovered, your true purpose extends beyond your job and paycheck. Satisfaction in life comes from balance. A balanced life creates harmony amongst the components of our existence, such as spirituality, career, time, self, finances, and relationships. Striking a healthy balance helps prevent the stress that comes from neglecting any one area. This balance is what we refer to as the Circle of Abundance. Stress results when one area of the circle is shorter than the others, it can throw the whole circle off balance, symbolizing how neglect in one area can affect overall life satisfaction.

This exercise encourages you to take a "helicopter" view of your life, providing a visual representation of where you are excelling and where there is room for improvement. By identifying the gaps between your current state and where you want to be, you can create a map for designing your life, thereby increasing your life satisfaction. The Circle of Abundance is a circle divided into the following six segments:

- **Spirituality**: includes your spiritual or religious beliefs, practices, connection to your higher self, and your sense of purpose
- **Career/Work**: encompasses your professional life, including your job, career aspirations, work-life balance, and job satisfaction.
- **Time:** consists of planning, time management skills, and control of energy

- **Self**: includes your physical, mental, and emotional well-being, including exercise, nutrition, self-care, and overall health and wellness habits.
- **Finance**: encompass your financial well-being, including budgeting, saving, investing, debt management, and financial goals.
- **Relationships**: includes your relationships with family members, such as spouse/partner, children, parents, siblings, and other significant relationships. It also consists of your social life and friendships.

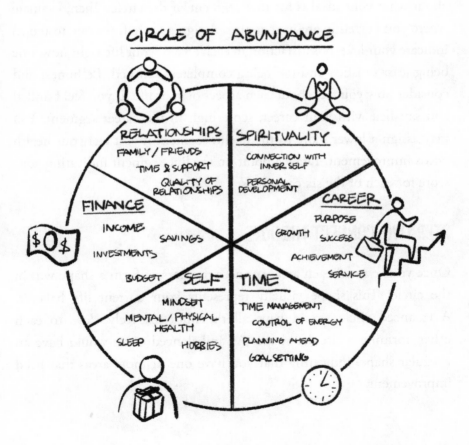

CREATE YOUR CIRCLE OF ABUNDANCE

Creating and evaluating your Circle of Abundance can be a helpful exercise to assess various areas of your life and determine areas that may need improvement. Go to KevinKremer.com/resources to download your customizable circle.

STEP ONE: SCORE YOURSELF

Start by evaluating each segment on the Circle of Abundance. Think about what your ideal is for that segment of the circle. Then, evaluate where you currently are in that area. Assign a score from one to ten to indicate your level of satisfaction in each area of your life right now, one being least satisfied and ten being completely satisfied. Be honest and consider how you feel about each aspect of your life. If you feel fulfilled and satisfied with your career, score high in the career segment. You may assign a lower score to the health segment if you feel your health needs improvement. Draw a point on the line segment indicating your score for each of the six categories.

STEP TWO: CONNECT THE DOTS

Once you've rated each area, connect the dots to form a shape within the circle. This shape visually represents your current life balance. A balanced circle would have all the lines relatively close to each other, forming a circular shape. An imbalanced circle would have an irregular shape, indicating that you have one or more areas that need improvement.

STEP THREE: EVALUATE YOUR RESULTS

The goal is to work towards a more balanced circle, but remember, balance doesn't necessarily mean having high scores in all areas. It's about achieving satisfaction in areas most important to you. Based on your self-assigned scores, the gaps in the Circle of Abundance are where you feel less satisfied or fulfilled than others. If your health segment received a low score, it may indicate that you need to make an effort for your physical well-being and make changes to improve your health. If your relationships segment received a low score, maybe you need to spend more time and effort building and maintaining meaningful relationships. Take a close look at your results and identify the areas that scored lower or that need improvement. Choose one area to start with, or if you feel like it, tackle multiple areas.

STEP FOUR: BRAINSTORM YOUR DEFICIENCIES

Now that you see where you are as opposed to the ideal circle, it's time to make progress. Below the title on the blank lines, brainstorm ideas, actions, or concepts that would get you from where you are in that segment to your definition of ideal of the circle. This is an opportunity to dream up all of the things that you could that are missing between where you are and your ideal.

STEP FIVE: DEVELOP AN ACTION PLAN

Pick one of the ideas in the segment that would have a significant impact. List the action steps you could take to get you from where you are to where you would like to be. The steps should be small, simple, achievable items you can accomplish in one week. Action steps are the stepping stones along your journey. If you get stuck, remember, you do not have to know how to do everything. Sometimes, a step is finding the right 'who' or person that can perform the step for you. Write the steps down on a piece of paper. What are you willing to commit to doing today or tomorrow? Decide the one, simple next step to gain momentum, the Most Important Action (MIA). Commit to writing it down on a To-Do list, with a 'by when' date.

STEP SIX: REVIEW AND ADJUST

Regularly review your Circle of Life and the progress you are making towards your goals. A quarterly or annual review is a good cadence to monitor your life's progress towards your ideal self. This review is a great way to maintain accountability to your pursuit of abundance. Life is dynamic, so your wheel will change over time. Adjust your scores and action steps as needed to reflect your current priorities and circumstances.

Remember, the Circle of Life is a personal and subjective tool. It's meant to help you gain insights into your life balance and motivate you towards personal growth. Use it as a guide to help you live a more balanced and fulfilling life.

UNVEILING YOUR LIFE'S PURPOSE

Once you have completed your Circle of Abundance, you can take the steps to unveil your life's purpose. Acting as a compass, your purpose steers your decisions, shapes your actions, sets your goals, and fills your journey with meaning. For some, this sense of purpose is discovered in their profession, where work becomes not just a duty but a source of deep satisfaction and joy. Others find their calling in the bonds of family, the camaraderie of friends, the pursuit of spiritual enlightenment, or the devotion to religious beliefs. It's important to recognize that our life's purpose is often a rich tapestry of several elements, intricately woven and uniquely customized for each of us. As we navigate through life, our purpose is ever-evolving, shaped by our experiences, aspirations, and personal growth. It's this dynamic, ever-changing nature of purpose that adds color and vibrancy to the tapestry of our lives, making each day an opportunity to live more fully, passionately, and meaningfully. Unveiling your life's purpose is a deeply personal process that involves introspection and self-discovery.

Your life's purpose is the heartbeat of your existence, the very spark that ignites your will to greet each new day. Yet, what eludes many of us is the realization that our quest is fundamentally a chase after a certain feeling—a profound longing for fulfillment that resonates deep within. This elusive feeling is what we truly seek. What feeling do you seek? Fulfillment, Joy, Gratitude, Confidence, Peace, Motivation, Connectedness, Hope, Significance, Love?

Now that you have identified the feeling(s), take action. Here are some possible action steps to consider to guide you in determining your life's purpose:

1. **Reflect on Your Passions:** Consider what activities make you feel those feelings that you seek. Your passions often point towards areas of life that hold deep meaning for you. To gain clarity on your life purpose, envision a scenario where you have limitless options, such as winning $100 million. Contemplate how you would spend your days and how your life would transform. This thought experiment can help shape your understanding of your true desires and aspirations. With a renewed grasp on your values, passions, and the life you envision.

2. **Identify Your Talents and Strengths:** Recognize your natural abilities and where you excel. Your unique talents can offer clues to your purpose.

3. **Consider Your Virtues:** Determine what values are most important to you. Your life's purpose is likely aligned with these core principles. Revisit them to assess whether they have evolved. Do they still resonate with your life's vision, passions, and interests?

4. **Contemplate How You Can Serve Others:** Reflect on how you can contribute to the well-being of others. A sense of purpose often involves making a positive impact on the lives of others.

5. **Look for Patterns:** Review your past experiences and look for recurring themes or patterns that might indicate your purpose. Take time to reflect upon your experiences and the whispers of your heart. Reflect back on what you wanted to be when you were young. What did you foresee feeling by being this?

6. **Seek Feedback:** Talk to friends, family, or mentors who know you well and can provide insights into your purpose. Sometimes, others close to you can offer clues that we may overlook. No one is meant to walk this path alone.

7. **Experiment and Explore:** Try new experiences that align with potential purposes to see how they resonate with you. It is often the unexpected journeys that bring the greatest insights that can lead us to discover our true selves. Frequently, it is in the moments of greatest challenge that one's purpose becomes clear. Courage is not the absence of fear but the decision to act in spite of it.

8. **Be Open to Change:** Understand that your life's purpose may evolve over time as you grow and have new experiences.

Defining your life's purpose is a continuous process, not a one-time task.

EMBRACE THE JOURNEY

Remember, it's the journey itself that shapes you, and the quest that matters the most. Rather than frantically searching for your purpose as if it were a hidden treasure, allow it to reveal itself organically through your experiences. You may find glimpses of it in the quantum, in the unseen moments and subtle shifts that are not always perceivable to your senses. Every path you take, every choice you make, has the potential to lead you closer to your life's purpose. Ultimately, you will realize you've unveiled your life's purpose when you experience that sought-after feeling of deep fulfillment, purpose, and alignment with your authentic self.

ACCOUNTABILITY ANCHORS:

1. Your life's true purpose is that singular guiding force that imbues your existence with meaning and significance.
2. A balanced life creates harmony amongst the components of our existence, such as: spirituality, career, time, self, finances, and relationships.
3. The Circle of Abundance Worksheet aides in discovering your balance.

CHAPTER 21

EMBRACING THE INFINITE, GOING BEYOND THE SELF TO DISCOVER UNIVERSAL CONNECTION

"You are not a drop in the ocean. You are the entire ocean in a drop"

– RUMI

Each of us, while seemingly small and individual like a single drop of water, contains within ourselves the essence and vastness of the entire ocean. This concept speaks to the interconnectedness of all things and the idea that within each of us lies a small part of a greater whole. Rumi's words encourage a recognition of the depth and potential within every person. It's an invitation to look beyond the surface and realize that we are not isolated or insignificant but are, instead, integral parts of a larger, more complex system. It is a call to understand our own worth and the profound impact we can have on the world. It's an expression of the belief that the universe is reflected within each of us, and we, in turn, reflect the universe.

Embracing the infinite and going beyond the self to discover universal connection is deeply intertwined with the concept of taking accountability. At the heart of this journey lies the process of expanding one's self-awareness, a crucial step towards taking responsibility for one's thoughts, feelings, and behaviors. By letting go of the ego and the attachments that define the limited sense of self, individuals unlock the flexibility and adaptability required to navigate the constant change and impermanence inherent in the infinite.

This expanded perspective fosters a profound recognition of our fundamental interconnectedness with all of life, which in turn encourages a greater sense of responsibility and accountability towards the greater whole. No longer bound by the constraints of the false self, people are empowered to engage in authentic self-expression, living in alignment with their core values and purpose. This level of accountability to one's authentic self is a hallmark of a life of meaning and fulfillment.

Ultimately, the quest to embrace the infinite and transcend the boundaries of the individual self is inextricably linked to the principle of taking accountability. It is through this expansive worldview that individuals cultivate the self-awareness, adaptability, and commitment to their deepest truth required to forge a life of purpose, growth, and positive impact on the world around them.

Jim Carrey, a well-known actor and comedian, experienced a moment when he went beyond himself and discovered a universal connection. This is his story of a spiritual awakening. During a heartfelt talk in 2009, Carrey described the first time he recognized that his sense of self was something beyond his mind, body, or thoughts. He recounted an experience where he suddenly understood how thought was merely an illusory aspect of the human experience, responsible for much of the suffering people endure. This realization led him to a perspective where he observed his thoughts from an external viewpoint, prompting a profound feeling of freedom from his problems. Carrey described this moment as being thrown into an expansive, amazing feeling of freedom, where he felt a deep sense of connection. He no longer saw himself as a fragment of the universe but as the universe itself. This experience brought him a sense of being larger than his actions, his body, and indeed, everything around him, marking a significant spiritual awakening in his life.

Carrey's story is a powerful example of how individuals can encounter moments of deep spiritual connection, leading to a sense of unity with the universe and a profound understanding of their place within it. Jim Carrey embraced the infinite and went beyond the self to discover a universal connection.

EMBRACING THE INFINITE

If you haven't already, take a step out of your comfort zone and consider introducing the concept of embracing the infinite into your belief system. For some of you, this may be a small step, and for others a gigantic one. Imagine no past, future, or time—just eternal peace, harmony, equality, and unconditional love without fear. This is oneness. It's not so far-fetched because we've all had experiences which we couldn't explain and these were in fact, embracing the infinite.

When you embrace the infinite, you experience a profound sense of unity with all that exists. It is a state or moment where the boundaries between the self and the external world dissolve, leading to a deep realization that everything in the universe is interconnected and interdependent.

This experience transcends the usual perception of separateness between individuals, objects, and the environment, fostering a feeling of being part of a larger, cohesive whole. Embracing the infinite experiences are often described as transformative, offering new perspectives on life, existence, and the interconnectedness of all things. They can challenge and expand one's understanding of the self and the universe, leading to personal growth, increased mindfulness, and a more harmonious way of living.

Experiences of embracing the infinite can manifest in various contexts, including deep meditation, moments of awe in nature, during spiritual practices, or even spontaneously in deep relationships with others. Individuals may feel a profound sense of peace, love, and understanding, as well as a diminished sense of ego or self-importance. This can lead to greater empathy, compassion, and a sense of responsibility towards others and the environment.

The concept of embracing the infinite, also called Oneness, transcends our usual perceptions of time, space, and reality. This profound connection underscores the idea that our actions and choices send ripples through the vast interconnected network of existence. Understanding that we are integral threads in this universal tapestry instills a deep sense of accountability for the effects of our behaviors on others and the environment. When we acknowledge our role in the collective whole, we are inspired to make more deliberate and responsible choices, reflecting our commitment to the greater web of life.

SPIRITUAL BEINGS LIVING IN A PHYSICAL BODY

This concept that "we are spiritual beings living in a physical body here on Earth" is a philosophical and spiritual viewpoint suggesting that our essence or true nature transcends our physical existence. This perspective is rooted in various religious, spiritual, and philosophical traditions, each offering its own nuances to the idea. Here's a breakdown of the core elements of this concept:

This concept posits that humans have a dual nature: a temporary, physical aspect (the body) and an eternal, non-physical aspect (the spirit or soul). The physical body is seen as a vessel or vehicle for the spirit during its journey on Earth, subject to the laws of nature and the physical world. In contrast, the spirit or soul is considered the true essence of a person, eternal and not bound by physical constraints.

From this viewpoint, life on Earth is an opportunity for spiritual growth and learning. The physical world, with its challenges and experiences, serves as a school for the soul. Life's trials and tribulations are seen as lessons designed to foster spiritual development, enhance understanding, and ultimately lead to enlightenment or a higher state of consciousness.

The concept often includes the belief that spiritual beings are connected to a higher power or divine source, this is what we refer to as embracing the infinite. This connection is intrinsic and eternal, transcending the physical realm. Life on Earth is an opportunity to deepen this connection through acts of love, compassion, and self-discovery, aligning one's actions with higher spiritual principles.

The idea also embraces the notion of life after death or the continuity of the spirit beyond physical existence. Death is not seen as an end but a transition to another state of being or another phase of the soul's journey. The experiences and growth achieved during the physical life have implications for the soul's journey beyond.

Embracing the belief that we are spiritual beings in a physical body can influence how individuals approach life, ethics, and personal development. It encourages living with a sense of purpose, striving for personal growth, valuing connections with others, and acting with kindness and integrity. It also fosters a sense of peace and acceptance in the face of life's uncertainties, with the understanding that physical experiences, both good and bad, contribute to the soul's evolution.

THE LIFE ON EARTH DECISION

Envision your essence as a spirit in a celestial domain, in harmony with those you hold dear. From this vantage point, life on Earth appears as a captivating ride at Disneyland, beckoning you to join in its thrilling escapade. Drawn by its allure, you elect to journey to Earth, take on a physical body, and dive into the rich tapestry of human existence. Your presence here, suggests a decision made in a realm beyond memory— the enigmatic quantum domain. Reflect on the possibilities: Could you have made other pre-life choices? Might you have selected your family, your birthplace, or the socioeconomic status into which you were born?

Being a spiritual being on Earth implies existing within the physical realm while maintaining a connection to a higher, more enlightened state of being. This means our consciousness resonates with the spiritual or divine facets of existence. In terms of accountability, it involves living in harmony with our authentic selves and determining our purpose.

Building on this premise, we can ponder what aspects of Earthly life were so enticing that we chose to embark on this life journey. As we explored in Chapter 2, the allure may be intrinsically tied to the concept of a growth mindset. The essence of why our spirit opted for an Earthly experience is encapsulated in the pursuit of growth—to evolve, transform, and enhance our being.

To honor (and be accountable for) our commitment to self and the elevated spiritual facet of our consciousness, we must uphold the choice our souls have made—to embrace growth and utilize our Earthly journey to accrue wisdom and evolve into our best selves. Embracing our Quantum Purpose means committing to this growth. To delve deeper into this idea, let's examine the notion of Earth as a school for the soul.

The concept compares our human journey to an educational experience, like a school here on Earth, where life's trials and triumphs serve as lessons for our soul's growth and spiritual maturation. We are here to learn, develop, and ascend, both individually and as a collective, through the myriad of experiences life throws our way.

Acknowledging and taking accountability for your actions signifies your active engagement in life's curriculum, owning up to your personal development. Life's hurdles, from personal conflicts to profound losses, are not just obstacles but catalysts for introspection, growth, and enlightenment. While often perceived as negative, these experiences are the crucibles in which we forge our resilience and wisdom.

Our souls are on an evolutionary quest, with Earthly experiences enriching this spiritual voyage. Being accountable means accepting your choices and their outcomes, learning from missteps, and applying this insight to future decisions.

This model resonates with universal laws like cause and effect, Karma, and the law of attraction. By enhancing our consciousness, practicing mindfulness, and deepening self-knowledge, we advance spiritually and embrace accountability. The lesson you learn here is your Quantum Purpose—the overarching reason for your Earthly sojourn. Yet, we also possess individual life purposes that demand recognition and accountability as we discussed in the previous chapter. Thus, our journey on Earth is not just about navigating the physical realm but about embracing the profound spiritual growth that comes from understanding and fulfilling our Quantum Purpose as well as our individual life purpose. In taking accountability, we align ourselves with the cosmic flow, contributing to our own evolution and the collective elevation of consciousness.

ACCOUNTABILITY ANCHORS:

1. Interconnectedness is the idea that within each of us lies a small part of a greater whole.
2. When you embrace the infinite, you experience a profound sense of unity with all that exists.

CHAPTER 22

ATTAINING EXCELLENCE, ELEVATING BEYOND THE SELF TO FORGE A UNIVERSAL BOND

"There is no passion to be found in playing small, in settling for a life that is less than the one you are capable of living".

– NELSON MANDELA

Complacency is the enemy of the soul; to truly live, one must relentlessly pursue greatness, shattering the shackles of a mediocre existence that threatens to confine our boundless potential. In the quote above, Mandela is advocating for the pursuit of one's highest potential and not settling for anything less. The essence of the quote lies in the belief that true passion and fulfillment come from challenging oneself, taking risks, and aiming for the highest possible achievements in life. It's a call to action to live boldly and with purpose, to not shy away from the possibilities of greatness that lie within each individual. This perspective encourages individuals to break free from self-imposed limitations and societal constraints, to explore their capabilities fully, and to live a life filled with passion and purpose, a life of excellence.

The pursuit of excellence and the quest to forge a universal bond are intrinsically linked to the principle of taking accountability. At the heart of this endeavor lies a deep commitment to personal growth and development, where individuals are willing to take responsibility for their actions, beliefs, and behaviors, and continuously work to improve and expand their capabilities.

This commitment to self-improvement is rooted in a willingness to embrace adaptability and change, recognizing that growth often requires shedding old patterns and perspectives. By expanding beyond the confines of the ego, individuals are able to cultivate a deeper sense of empathy and compassion, fostering a profound understanding of our fundamental interconnectedness. This, in turn, instills a sense of accountability towards the greater good and a desire to positively impact the world around us.

Aligning one's actions with a deeper sense of purpose and core values is essential for achieving fulfillment and making a meaningful contribution. Taking accountability for living in accordance with these guiding principles empowers individuals to transcend the limitations of the ego and connect with the infinite. Ultimately, this journey requires a willingness to be vulnerable and to express one's authentic self, as it is through this level of accountability to one's true nature that genuine connections are forged and the collective growth of humanity is advanced.

THE GREEK GODDESS ARETE

In Greek mythology, Arete is personified as a minor goddess, embodying the concept of virtue and excellence. She is depicted as the daughter of Praxidike, the goddess of judicial punishment and exactor of vengeance, and Soter, a daimon associated with safety and preservation. Arete is a term that, in its most basic sense, refers to "excellence" of any kind, particularly the full realization of potential or inherent function. This concept was central to Greek culture and philosophy, and it was personified in the form of a Arete, who, along with her sister Homonoia, formed the Praxidikai, or "Exacters of Justice."

The idea of Arete is deeply embedded in Greek mythology and philosophy, where it is often associated with the fulfillment of purpose or function: living up to one's potential. A person of Arete is someone who uses all their faculties—strength, bravery, and wit—to achieve real results. In the Homeric world, the virtue of Arete involves all of the abilities and potentialities available to humans, and it is frequently associated with bravery, but more often with effectiveness. In some contexts, Arete is explicitly linked with human knowledge, suggesting that the highest human potential is knowledge, and all other human abilities derive from this central capacity.

Arete is exemplified in the stories of Greek heroes and heroines. For instance, in Homer's "Iliad" and "Odyssey," characters like Achilles and Odysseus are described as having Arete due to their exceptional qualities as a warrior and a strategist, respectively. Achilles' prowess in battle and Odysseus' cunning and intelligence in overcoming obstacles on his journey home from the Trojan War are seen as the embodiment of Arete, the pursuit of excellence and the realization of their full potential.

The story of Arete is not just about individual excellence but also about the broader implications of living a life that strives for the highest virtues and fulfillment. It is a story that encourages individuals to seek out their unique capabilities and to live a life that is true to their nature and abilities. The pursuit of Arete, therefore, is closely tied to the pursuit of knowledge and the development of one's intellectual and moral virtues. Arete's story is a powerful narrative about the importance of determining one's purpose and striving for excellence.

YOUR PURSUIT OF EXCELLENCE

Excellence in anything increases your potential in everything. Pursuing excellence is an endless journey, a continuous endeavor that requires constant learning, dedication, and hard work. For professionals who have chosen the life of an entrepreneur and business owner, the path to success is far from linear.

Crafting a life of excellence is a comprehensive endeavor that requires a blend of critical elements, all aimed at nurturing personal growth, achievement, and a sense of fulfillment. At the heart of this pursuit are several key components:

- **Accountability:** The foundation of personal excellence is built on a deep understanding of oneself. After becoming aware, the next step is holding yourself accountable. This includes accountability to your thoughts, examining your beliefs, discerning your feelings, living in alignment with your virtues, and recognizing attitudes.
- **Mindset:** The way you perceive the world shapes your reality. It's about pushing beyond your comfort zones and choosing to adopt effective mindsets geared towards continual improvement and abundance. This is crucial for

transforming challenges into opportunities and failures into lessons.

- **Personal Mental Skills:** To live a life of excellence, developing key mental skills is essential. Examining your choices, awareness of the roles you play, effective time management, paying attention to your focus, being aware of your financial perceptions, harnessing effective energy management, and avoiding digital overload are all vital in leading a life of excellence.

- **Embracing Accountability to Others:** By improving areas of your life such as your emotional intelligence, communication skills, relationships, forgiveness, and leadership abilities, you are taking accountability for your reality. William Johnsen said, 'If it is to be, it is up to me.' This underscores the individual's role and responsibility in achieving desired outcomes. Through personal effort, you acknowledge that while success may depend on more than one person, it begins with individual initiative.

- **Action:** Success is achieved by setting Specific, Measurable, Achievable, Relevant, and Time-bound (SMART) goals, and then taking action on them. This strategic approach applies to all areas of life. In addition, discipline, defined as negotiating daily with your brain to sacrifice immediate rewards to receive greater satisfaction in the future, is imminent for success. Creating habits, making course corrections, and maintaining self-control are all important elements, as well. Action will be the focus in the second book in this series.

- **Connection with Your Higher Self:** Aligning with your higher self fosters a deeper sense of purpose and direction, guiding you towards actions that resonate with your virtues and aspirations that will lead you to the Abundant Life.

By diligently integrating these components into your life, you embark on a path of personal excellence. Embrace the challenges and rejoice in the triumphs. There will be days when the journey feels uphill, but remember, every step you take toward improvement is a step toward excellence.

Life can be viewed as a magnificent playground where we embark on a profound journey of learning, growth, and spiritual evolution. In this vast playground, the experiences we encounter—both joyous and challenging—serve as our teachers, imparting wisdom and insight.

To truly thrive in this playground, we should not take ourselves too seriously. The pursuit of excellence should be accompanied by a light-heartedness that reminds us of the beauty in laughter, spontaneity, and embracing imperfections. Extend forgiveness to yourself and others, understanding that we are all travelers on this unique journey, bound to stumble and rise time and again.

Love becomes the vibrant thread weaving through this journey. Love for oneself, with all one's flaws and aspirations, and love for others, recognizing their shared humanity. Through love, we find connection, empathy, and the courage to traverse life's terrain with open hearts.

Pursuing excellence is not a destination but a perpetual odyssey. It's the continuous refinement of our character, the unending quest for self-improvement, and the commitment to leave the world a better place than we found it.

Enjoy the ride.
Embrace the adventure.
Savor every moment.

Life is a gift.
The journey is the destination itself.

ACCOUNTABILITY ANCHORS:

1. Complacency is the enemy of the soul; to truly live, one must relentlessly pursue greatness, shattering the shackles of a mediocre existence that threatens to confine our boundless potential.

2. Excellence in anything increases your potential in everything.

3. Pursuing excellence is not a destination but a perpetual odyssey.

4. The journey is the destination itself.

RECOMMENDED READING LIST

Please check out www.KevinKremer.com/resources for additional information.

Albom, Mitch. *Tuesdays with Morrie: An Old Man, a Young Man, and Life's Greatest Lesson*. Doubleday, 1997.

Allen, David. *Getting Things Done: The Art of Stress-Free Productivity*. New York: Penguin Books, 2015.

Barks, Coleman (translator). *The Essential Rumi*. HarperOne, 1995.

Braden, Gregg. *The Divine Matrix: Bridging Time, Space, Miracles, and Belief*. Hay House, 2007.

Branson, Richard. *Business Stripped Bare: Adventures of a Global Entrepreneur*. Virgin Books, 2008.

Campbell, Joseph and Bill Moyers. *The Power of Myth*. Doubleday, 1988.

Carnegie, Andrew. *The Gospel of Wealth*. Signet Classics, 1962.

Carnegie, Dale. *How to Win Friends and Influence People*. Simon and Schuster, 1936.

Chernow, Ron. *Titan: The Life of John D. Rockefeller, Sr.* Random House, 1998.

Cialdini, Robert B. *Influence: The Psychology of Persuasion.* Harper Business, 1984.

Collins, Jim. *Good to Great: Why Some Companies Make the Leap... and Others Don't.* Harper Business, 2001.

Covey, Stephen R. *The 8th Habit: From Effectiveness to Greatness.* Free Press, 2004.

Dispenza, Joe. *Becoming Supernatural: How Common People Are Doing the Uncommon.* Hay House, 2017.

Durkheim, Émile. *The Elementary Forms of Religious Life.* Free Press, 1915.

Dweck, Carol S. *Mindset: The New Psychology of Success.* Ballantine Books, 2006.

Dyer, Wayne. *The Power of Intention: Learning to Co-create Your World Your Way.* Hay House, 2004.

Dyer, Wayne. *There's a Spiritual Solution to Every Problem.* HarperOne, 2001.

Easwaran, Eknath (translator). *The Bhagavad Gita.* Nilgiri Press, 1985.

Easwaran, Eknath (translator). *The Upanishads.* Nilgiri Press, 1987.

Ferriss, Timothy. *The 4-Hour Workweek: Escape 9-5, Live Anywhere, and Join the New Rich.* Crown Publishing Group, 2007.

Franklin, Benjamin. *The Autobiography of Benjamin Franklin.* New York: Dover Publications, 1986.

Gibran, Kahlil. *The Prophet*. Alfred A. Knopf, 1923.

Gordon, Richard. *Quantum Touch: The Power to Heal*. North Atlantic Books, 2002.

Harnish, Verne. *Scaling Up: How a Few Companies Make It...and Why the Rest Don't*. Gazelles, 2014.

Hawkins, David R. *Power vs. Force: The Hidden Determinants of Human Behavior*. Hay House, 2002.

Hay, Louise L. *You Can Heal Your Life*. Hay House, 1984.

Hicks, Esther and Jerry Hicks. *Ask and It Is Given: Learning to Manifest Your Desires*. Hay House, 2004.

Hicks, Esther. *The Law of Attraction: The Basics of the Teachings of Abraham*. Hay House, 2006.

Hill, Napoleon. *Think and Grow Rich*. The Ralston Society, 1937.

Hill, Napoleon. *The Master Key to Riches*. TarcherPerigee, 2009.

Kabat-Zion, Jon. *Wherever You Go, There You Are: Mindfulness Meditation in Everyday Life*. Hyperion, 1994.

Keller, Gary, and Jay Papasan. *The ONE Thing: The Surprisingly Simple Truth Behind Extraordinary Results*. Bard Press, 2013.

Lencioni, Patrick. *Death by Meeting: A Leadership Fable...About Solving the Most Painful Problem in Business,* Jossey-Bass. 2004.

Lencioni, Patrick. *The Ideal Team Player: How to Recognize and Cultivate the Three Essential Virtues*. Jossey-Bass, 2016.

Lipton, Bruce H. *The Biology of Belief: Unleashing the Power of Consciousness, Matter & Miracles*. Hay House, 2005.

Lowndes, Leil. *How to Talk to Anyone: 92 Little Tricks for Big Success in Relationships*. McGraw-Hill Education, 2003.

Maltz, Maxwell. *Psycho-Cybernetics*. Simon & Schuster, 1960.

Marshall, Perry. *80/20 Sales and Marketing: The Definitive Guide to Working Less and Making More*. Entrepreneur Press, 2013.

Maxwell, John C. *The 21 Irrefutable Laws of Leadership: Follow Them and People Will Follow You*. Thomas Nelson, 2007.

Maxwell, John C. *The 5 Levels of Leadership: Proven Steps to Maximize Your Potential*. Center Street, 2011.

Meacham, Jon. *Thomas Jefferson: The Art of Power*. Random House, 2012.

Millman, Dan. *Way of the Peaceful Warrior: A Book That Changes Lives*. HJ Kramer/New World Library, 1980.

Nasaw, David. *The Chief: The Life of William Randolph Hearst*. Houghton Mifflin Harcourt, 2000.

Pickens, T. Boone. *The First Billion Is the Hardest: Reflections on a Life of Comebacks and America's Energy Future*. Crown Business, 2008.

Renard, Gary. *Love Has Forgotten No One: The Answer to Life*. Hay House, 2013.

Renard, Gary. *The Disappearance of the Universe*. Hay House, 2004.

Renard, Gary. *The Immortal Reality: A Course in Miracles*. Fearless Books, 2006.

Robbins, Tony. *Awaken the Giant Within: How to Take Immediate Control of Your Mental, Emotional, Physical and Financial Destiny!* Free Press, 1992.

Robbins, Tony. *MONEY Master the Game: 7 Simple Steps to Financial Freedom*. Simon & Schuster, 2014.

Ruiz, Don Miguel. T*he Four Agreements: A Practical Guide to Personal Freedom*. Amber-Allen Publishing, 1997.

Rumi. *The Essential Rumi*. Translated by Coleman Barks, HarperOne, 2004.

Scheinfeld, R. *Busting Loose From the Money Game: Mind-blowing strategies for changing the rules of a game you can't win*.

Wiley, 2006.Schroeder, Alice. *The Snowball: Warren Buffett and the Business of Life*. Bantam Books, 2008.

Schucman, Helen. *A Course in Miracles*. Foundation for Inner Peace, 1975.

Sinek, Simon Et al. *Find Your Why: A Practical Guide for Discovering Purpose for You and Your Team*, Portfolio *2017*.

Sinek, Simon. *Start with Why: How Great Leaders Inspire Everyone to Take Action*. Portfolio, 2009.

Singer, Michael A. T*he Untethered Soul: The Journey Beyond Yourself*. New Harbinger Publications, 2007.

Stack, Jack, and Bo Burlingham. *The Great Game of Business: The Only Sensible Way to Run a Company*. Currency, 1992.

Stone, W. Clement. *The Success System That Never Fails*. Prentice-Hall, 1962.

Sullivan, Dan. *10x is Easier than 2x: How World-Class Entrepreneurs Achieve More by Doing Less*. Hay House, 2023.

Sullivan, Dan. *Who Not How: The Formula to Achieve Bigger Goals Through Accelerating Teamwork*, Hay House 2020.

The Bible. King James Version.

Turner, Ted, and Bill Burke. *Call Me Ted*. Grand Central Publishing, 2008.

Vitale, Joe. *The Attractor Factor: 5 Easy Steps for Creating Wealth (or Anything Else) from the Inside Out*

Vitale, Joe. *The Key: The Missing Secret for Attracting Anything You Want*. Wiley, 2007.

Willink, Jocko, and Leif Babin. *Extreme Ownership: How U.S. Navy SEALs Lead and Win*. St. Martin's Press, 2015.

Yogananda, P. *Autobiography of a Yogi*. Self-Realization Fellowship, 1946.

PRE-READ ANALYSIS QUESTIONNAIRE

The purpose of this pre-read questionnaire is to establish a baseline understanding of your self-awareness, accountability, beliefs, attitudes, emotional intelligence, and openness to personal growth. This will help you to contextualize your experience and learning as you engage with the contents of this book.

1. How would you rate your current self-awareness on a scale of 1-10? To what degree do you feel you understand your own thoughts, feelings, behaviors, and their underlying drivers?

2. On a scale of 1-10, how would you describe your level of personal accountability? To what extent do you take responsibility for the outcomes in your life?

3. What are some of the key beliefs, both empowering and limiting, that you feel currently shape your decisions and actions on a daily basis?

4. How would you characterize your general attitude towards personal growth and self-improvement? Is this an area of focus for you, or something you tend to deprioritize?

5. When faced with challenging situations, how effectively are you able to manage your emotional responses? Do you have specific strategies or techniques you rely on?

6. How conscious are you of the potential consequences, both short-term and long-term, when making important decisions in your life?

7. Which virtues or principles do you strive to embody in your interactions with others and in your approach to life?

8. What are some of the primary fears or anxieties
    that you feel may be holding you back
    from achieving your full potential?
9. How would you assess your current level of emotional
    intelligence and communication skills? Where do you feel
    you excel, and where is there room for improvement?
10. On a scale of 1-10, how open are you to critically
    examining and potentially shifting your current mindsets,
    if you determine they are not serving you effectively?

POST-READ ASSESSMENT QUESTIONNAIRE

The purpose of this post-read questionnaire is to determine the change in your self-awareness, accountability, beliefs, attitudes, emotional intelligence, and openness to personal growth. This will help you to determine how you have contextualized your learning as you engaged with the contents of Quantum Accountability.

Mindset:

1. How would you describe your current mindsets?
2. How would you go about determining the effectiveness of your current mindset and change it, if desired?

Accountability:

3. How do you hold yourself accountable for your actions and decisions?
4. How do you take responsibility for
the outcomes in your life?

Thoughts:

5. How often do you engage in positive self-talk?
6. Are you aware of any recurring negative thought patterns that impact your well-being?

Feelings:

7. How do you manage your emotions during challenging situations?
8. Are you aware of your emotional responses to stressful events in your life?

Attitudes:

9. What is your general attitude towards personal growth and self-improvement?
10. How do you maintain a positive attitude in the face of adversity?

Beliefs:

11. What beliefs shape your decisions and actions?
12. Are there any limiting beliefs that hinder your personal growth?

Choices:

13. How do you make decisions that align with your long-term goals?
14. Are you always aware of the consequences of your choices? If not, how do you become aware?

Virtues:

15. Which virtues do you prioritize in your daily life?

16. How do these virtues guide your interactions with others and when things don't go your way?

Fear:

17. What are your primary fears or anxieties that impact your personal growth?
18. How do you confront and overcome these fears in order to progress?

Emotional Intelligence and Communication:

19. What are some of your triggers? Circumstances that cause you to overreact?
20. What skills do you use to communicate effectively?

A COLLABORATIVE EFFORT

This book is the culmination of a deeply personal and collaborative journey undertaken by Dr. Kevin Kremer, a respected dentist and entrepreneur, and his wife, Kelley Kremer, M.Ed., a multi-book author, educator, and life coach.

The original concept and much of the foundational work was the creation of Dr. Kremer, who drew on his decades of clinical and business experience, as well as his immense love for self-improvement, to craft a comprehensive guide to cultivating meaningful, fulfilling connections in all areas of life. However, as the project progressed, Dr. Kremer recognized the immense value that his wife's expertise could bring to the endeavor.

Kelley Kremer's profound understanding of human psychology and interpersonal dynamics, coupled with her unique perspective and writing prowess, have been instrumental in shaping this work into the cohesive, impactful resource it has become. Through countless hours of discussion, debate, and joint writing, Dr. Kremer and Kelley have poured their hearts and minds into this book, blending their complementary knowledge and experiences to provide readers with an unparalleled exploration of the skills, mindsets, and practices essential for cultivating meaningful, lasting relationships.

It is through the voice of Dr. Kremer that this collaborative effort is presented. It is our sincere hope that the insights and strategies contained within these pages will empower you to strengthen the bonds that enrich your life, whether in your personal or professional spheres. This book is a testament to the power of partnership and the transformative potential that emerges when we are willing to open ourselves to the wisdom and support of others.

ACKNOWLEDGMENT

We would like to express our heartfelt gratitude to the many individuals who have supported us throughout the creation of this book.

First and foremost, we are deeply thankful to our four children - Kara, Kevin, Jake, and Luke - whose boundless energy, unwavering support, and inspiring accomplishments have been a constant source of motivation and joy. Watching you grow into such remarkable young adults has been the greatest privilege of our lives. You bring so much joy to life, whether it be your successes in sports like achieving MVP status of your high school basketball teams and winning state and national championships, or the deep spiritual conversations around the dinner table; meditating and breathing together, witnessing the invention of Iron Man suits in the garage, or seeing you embark on similar paths in healthcare, business leadership,engineering and psychology. We have been immensely impressed with your thoughtfulness, caring, and maturity. This book is a testament to the lessons you have taught us. You are our motivation to strive for greatness, to build a better future, and to cultivate a mindset of abundance.

To our extended family and dear friends, thank you for your encouragement, your willingness to lend an ear, and your invaluable insights that have helped shape this work. Your presence in our lives is a true blessing.

We are also immensely grateful to our professional networks and communities - the colleagues, mentors, and collaborators who have generously shared their expertise, challenged our thinking, and believed in the power of this project. Your contributions have been instrumental in refining and strengthening the ideas presented here.

Finally, we wish to acknowledge the countless individuals whose stories, struggles, and triumphs have informed and enriched this book. Your experiences have taught us invaluable lessons about the human condition, and we are honored to have the opportunity to share them with the world.

To the many authors and speakers who have inspired and influenced us, your words have been our roadmap, shaping our thoughts and directing our path. Your work is an ongoing source of inspiration, providing the building blocks of the ideas expressed within these pages. This book represents a mosaic of all these influences and support systems. We hope to have done justice to your shared wisdom, teachings, and experiences.

To our readers, it is our hope that this book will inspire you as these incredible individuals have inspired us.

This book is a testament to the transformative power of connection, accountability, and abundance. It has been a formidable labor of love that pushed us, outside our comfort zones - for it is there that all true growth lies. We are humbled and honored to have played a role in its creation, pouring our hearts, minds, and decades of collective experience into these pages. It is our sincere hope that this work will inspire readers to embark on their own journeys of self-discovery and relational fulfillment, empowering them to cultivate the meaningful connections and personal accountability needed to live lives of profound purpose and impact. This book represents a new chapter in our own growth as authors, partners, and catalysts for positive change. We are grateful beyond measure for the opportunity to share these transformative insights with the world.

Sincerely,
Kevin and Kelley Kremer

ABOUT THE AUTHORS

Dr. Kevin Kremer has a passion for helping others. He is a thought leader and entrepreneur. Beginning his career as a dentist, after being elected into the national dental honor society, Omicron Kappa Upsilon, he has dedicated over twenty five years to providing exceptional dental care, specializing in Full Mouth Cosmetic and Implant Dentistry.

Dr. Kremer's commitment to excellence is exemplified by a multitude of continuing education certifications, including Diplomat status in the International Dental Implant Association and Fellowship status in the ICOI, placing him among the top two percent of dentists nationwide. As an entrepreneurial second-generation dentist, Dr. Kremer has successfully completed eight Mergers and Acquisitions.

Driven by his passion for leadership and impact, Dr. Kremer takes pride in his thought leadership. He is a speaker, advisor, and mentor. Through his collaboration groups and coaching, he has assisted thousands of people on their way to greater levels of success. Kremer Leadership Institute provides Knowledge, Leadership, and Inspiration to help people on their journey to new levels of exceptional and excellence.

Kelley Kremer, M.Ed. is a multi-book author, educator, and life coach with a profound understanding of human psychology and interpersonal dynamics. Kelley's educational background includes a Bachelor's degree in Psychology and a Master's Degree in Education, providing her with a strong foundation in the study of the human mind and behavior.

Combining her natural empathy and keen observational skills, Kelley has enabled clients to achieve personal growth and fulfillment. As a life coach, her approach blends cognitive-behavioral techniques with mindfulness practices, helping her clients cultivate the self-awareness, emotional intelligence, and relational skills needed to thrive.

In addition to her coaching work, Kelley is the author of several acclaimed books, including the well-received *How to Be An Effective Teacher* and *Life Should Feel Good*. Her writing is praised for its accessibility, warmth, and practical applicability, as Kelley demonstrates a unique ability to translate complex psychological concepts into actionable strategies. This has made her a trusted voice in the personal development space, as she continues to inspire others to unlock their full potential and forge deeper, more meaningful connections in all areas of their lives.

Connect with Dr. K

Follow him on your favorite social media platforms today

    f

Connect with Kelley Kremer

Follow her on your favorite social media platforms today

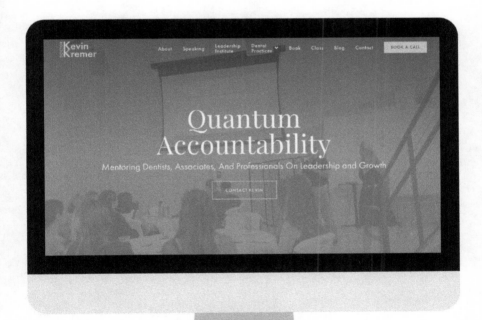